Take Back Your Power

You Becoming YOU

By Sherry Anshara

QuantumPathic Press®

Printed in the U.S.A.
Published by QuantumPathic Press®,
6701 E. Clinton Street, Scottsdale, Arizona 85254 U.S.A.

You can contact the author at www.SherryAnshara.com.

First Edition: September 2018

Library of Congress Control Number: 2018940351

ISBN: 978-0-9742144-3-6

Book Cover Design by Dru Patrick DeLong
www.phixbrand.com

ACKNOWLEDGMENTS

In gratitude, gratefulness and thankfulness, I acknowledge all of the individuals who have come into my life from the moment I came into this lifetime. Everyone has contributed to my journeys along my paths throughout all the moments of my experiences. For all of them, I am so blessed, no matter who, how, what, where, or why they showed up in my life. Everything happened as it is "contracted" to happen between me, them, the time, and the place. Everything happened according to the "contracts". These moments provided me with the most amazing experiences which I crafted and created to experience in this timeline of my life! Thank you all for the experiences we experienced together. And now, as an Involved Conscious Evolutionary Revolutionary, I only make "agreeable agreements", which are so much more fun, more productive, more viable, and the most deeply connected. Wahoo!!

Great thanks and respect to Wind Ohmoto, who so clearly assisted me in editing this book. She is a reminder every day of the exquisite synergy we have as friends from this and many lifetimes.

Also, great gratitude to Dru Patrick DeLong of PHIX Brand Development for his brilliant design of this book cover. You can feel the resonance of the Power of You.

With admiration, I thank Wind Ohmoto, Cindie Hubiak, Bob Wyndelts, Phyllis Masunaka, Myrna Solano, and so many amazing individuals for being in my life.

From my Heartness, I am eternally grateful for my many Multi-Dimensional mentors who have supported me, guided me, and taught me about being my Multi-Dimensional Self... Bashebar Metaphista, Norla, Risa, Akido Secal, my "Original Peeps" including Lyrical, and my favorite 12 Wise Guys who I met during the 3rd of my 4 Near-Death Experiences... and the many more who have taught me so much about my Self, about being Human, and about all my contracts throughout my continuum to this very moment of time in my life. They unconditionally accepted me and loved me in this "limited" Human form. They "showed" me that as Humans we do not have to be limited. They "showed" me the Essence of being Human. To become the Real Human Race is the Ascension of Consciousness in this Human Body. It is not in our deaths that we ascend; it is in being alive that we ascend. The word "gratitude" cannot even explain how or what I feel for these Beings.

> **They taught me that searching outside of my Self for a Master is not the Truth. Your Master is within you, in your Conscious Non-Duality Human Body. You are REAL, no longer a follower. You are a Leader of your Self.**

In thankfulness to all of these incredible individuals who have shared valuable information which has expanded my own personal insight to embrace and value all Life and Soul forms on Earth, the Universe, and the Multi-verse...and to honor the connections amongst us.

I am so grateful to share this message as we progressively process from limitation into Allness as unique individuals, minus the labels of sameness and separation, into the Multi-versal collective connections of life to everyone and everything. We are ALLNESS!

TABLE OF CONTENTS

Illustrations

PREFACE

Born too early according to the doctors, I arrived in Highland Park, Michigan, a fourth child, 12, 11, and 9 years younger than my three siblings. To me, they seemed to come as a "pod", and I showed up by my Self. Funny, I always called my Self the younger "only child".

Seldom does anyone know what is about to happen when you pop out of the womb. Do you simply forget your "contracts"? At the core of my being, I knew! What the heck was I thinking?! So, the Truth of it is, all of you do know! The limitations of Duality, life, and sometimes the contracts and Belief Systems (B.S.) just get in your way.

Well, for sure, I would live out the "scripted parts" of my contracts and interact with everyone who participated in my script and I in theirs. I would "do" the Duality Programs (the good and bad, high and low, right and wrong) to get through the agendas of my script, going in and out of scenes in my ages and stages, some of which were brilliant times and some not so brilliant. All perfect!

Yet I cannot judge any of the scenes or anyone who participated with me. We did all that "stuff" together. What did we learn? Does it really matter? We were just living out scenes to see what is really important and what is not. If we are too physically and emotionally attached to the past – the places, the people, and the things (even past lives) – perhaps we can't *see*, *hear*, or *learn*. Perhaps this is the main point of Duality and the "do-overs" in our lives and in our lifetimes…to see how long it takes to get conscious.

In 1991, I had my 3rd Near-Death Experience (out of my 4 Near-Death Experiences). I discovered my Self in a stranger's car at the bottom of the Connecticut River. I had a severe head injury and a broken neck in 2 places. And eventually I found out that 3 of the vertebrae in my back were cracked.

I had no clear idea what would be in store for me from that pivotal moment! In this present moment, I can say dying is a "trip" like no other.

As I was beginning this Multi-Dimensional journey, lives began to change...especially mine. Without any measurements from the perceptions of Duality, I totally comprehend that my perspectives of the facts are that the Multi-Faceted, Multi-Dimensional benefits far outweigh the physical and emotional trauma of this so-called "accident". As I have benefited, so have thousands of clients, students, friends, and even strangers who connected with me throughout these years also benefited, as well as their families, friends, and businesses.

Did it happen immediately? Absolutely not! Cutting my physical and emotional ties to the past was and is a progressive progress of learning about my Self. The information I began to receive in 1991 unfolded one day at a time, though in terms of the Multi-verse, it is a millisecond of time from 1991 to 2018 (27 Earth years). It's not even a blink of an eyelash in the Universe or the Multi-verse.

From 1991, it took me 12 years to publish *The Age of Inheritance: The Activation of the 13 Chakras*. At that time, no one to whom I submitted the manuscript understood any of this information. They had no category for Consciousness. It was determined that it was not self-help, metaphysical, science or whatever categories they did have; this book simply didn't fit. Finally, in 2003, I self-published this book through QuantumPathic Press®.

The Age of Inheritance: The Activation of the 13 Chakras has transformed thousands of lives, including mine. I live every day through these tools which were shared with me by my mentor, Bashebar Metaphista, and all of these "enlightened" Beings who so readily shared with me their wisdom, their knowledge, their total acceptance, and their unconditional love.

It is 2018, the perfect time to expand the resonance of this book. The time has come to give a new title with expanded practical information and tools to comprehend your own Self. Together we can now begin to transcend in our own unique ways beyond this dualistic Third Dimensional World and dualistic Universe.

It is time to BE Multi-Dimensional, to stand in your own personal Power, and become the Master from within you of your own Life and your own Creativity.

TAKE BACK YOUR POWER....

Enjoy your journey…
Enjoy becoming YOU…

In Heartness, Allness, and Connectedness,

Sherry Anshara

Chapter 1

YOUR INHERITANCE

This is the Age of Your Inheritance. You *becoming* your Real Self happens here and now with your willingness. This is the perfect moment for you to take a stand for *your* personal Truth.

My teaching has consciously evolved over the past 27 years into what we now know as the Anshara Method of Accelerated Healing & Abundance. Rather than "reinvent the wheel" to introduce the Anshara Method to you, this chapter is an excerpt from my recent book, *The Intelligence Code*. For further clarity, I have also included a glossary of terms at the end of this book.

Enjoy this excerpt from *The Intelligence Code:*

The Intelligent Reasons for this Book

The minute the sperm hits the egg, you are in! You are a conscious being absorbing all the feelings and emotions of your parents. You experience from your mother's womb the outside world through your mother's and even your father's points of view from their experiences and Belief Systems. In this world we all experience a dimension known as Duality.

The difference in how you experience life is the difference between the resonances of clear feelings *and* dysfunctional emotions. Feelings come from the Heart. The Heart has a resonance that is at least 500 times more expanded than your brain. Emotions and the resultant dysfunctional repeatable patterns come from the left brain.

The left brain, which is connected to the right Male *manifesting* side of your body, has a very low resonance. The repeated results are the repeated patterns of behaviors. The left brain and the right Male side of your body run the Duality do-over programs. The left brain is the culprit of your repeated relationships, repeated patterns of dysfunctional behaviors, and the repetition of your emotional challenges.

The right brain, your creative brain which connects to the Female left side of your body, appears most of the time to be dormant, while the left brain is repeatedly dominant. Since we are not taught or shown the difference, feelings and emotions are categorized as one and the same. They are not. The differences between feelings and emotions are significant in how your computer/brain affects how you create your life.

The experiences you experience from your very inception are directly linked to how you create your illnesses, diseases, and relationship trauma dramas that occur as a result of your emotional body. Your experiences from a clear Heart support you to be very powerful and healthy. Your emotional body "supports" you to experience life through the trauma dramas, always seeking validation outside of your Self regardless of what you have accomplished in your idea or not.

Your emotional re-actions are the results of Duality. Your Heart-based feelings are your intuitive guidelines. In your emotional computer/brain, life is always challenging. Emotionality is the ups and downs that drive you crazy. In your clear Heart, your life flows as though your particles are soaring on a wave of Consciousness.

What is Duality? Duality is the good and the bad, the high and the low, the "this" and the "that" of life. Duality is all the judgments of each other and especially of your Self. Never being good enough! Never really validated! Never, never, never something or other. From the beginning, without judging your parents or family, Duality is a constricting resonance that keeps you confined and limited and always waiting to be happy. Is happiness a temporary figment of Duality's reality?

Whatever Belief Systems your parents and/or grandparents have about ideas, perceptions, or limitations, you are taught to experience your life from what they know and don't know. They have their agendas about what you are to be or to do. You are to be the next generation of their version of Duality's family line.

When there is strife, fighting, or abuse in the family, the next generation usually perpetuates what happened before. More times than not, your parents followed in your grandparents' footsteps with perhaps the same ideas, the same limitations, the same Belief Systems, the same behaviors, and the same old same old. In the case of adoptions, abandonment, or kicked out of the family, you still carry their programs from the minute the sperm hits the egg and you are in. You will still process their "stuff". The interesting thing is that their "stuff" may not show up for years, but eventually it does.

Duality's teaching for you is to belong to the "perfect" group: politics, religions, social-economic, ethnic, academic, right side, wrong side of the tracks, etc. You are taught from the beginning that you have to "belong" in order to be validated or accepted. You have to fit in!

How funny when one of the most challenging emotional issues is the one of not being validated. Years along the timeline of your life are spent trying to fit in, trying to be accepted. Yet one of the greatest emotional hang-ups is just that…not being validated outside of your Self.

You are programmed to fit in, which brings about many emotional issues of not fitting in. You are not supposed to be different. Yet many of you reading this book may experience the emotionality of not fitting in your own biological or even adopted family. How many of you are the "black sheep" of the family? Or the different one? Or are you bluntly asked, "Where did you come from?!!"

Without judgment or blame, this is the "because" factor or the "Why's" of how your parents influenced and affected your life from the beginning. They just did the best and worst they could with what they knew and didn't know. Mostly it was what they didn't know. They were following some Belief System so they could fit in, and then you, as their offspring, could fit in too. The Truth is…who really fits in?

"Fitting-in" is a Duality Belief System. "Fitting-in" is a delusional illusion. Look back, as the Non-Emotional Observer (NEO), to the times in your past when you did fit in and then for some reason you didn't fit in anymore. Was it "them" that cast you out? Or did you cast your Self out and you didn't realize you created being cast out? Is the result of you being cast out an opportunity for you to change, shift, or expand your Self? Or were you too emotional to *see* the value of being cast out and you did not recognize the opportunity to grow beyond the Belief System of "not fitting-in"?

The emotional issue is that you "thinky-thinky" from your computer/brain that it was all about "them". You did not recognize that it was all about you! Remember, this is not a judgment. This is the way it is in Duality. If you are a good child, they are good parents. If you are a bad child, they ask,

"Where did you come from?" The results of your life are directly connected to those formative years of what you were taught about your Self. Get it? What you were taught about your Self.

Rarely, if ever, were you asked about what was going on inside of you or about what thoughts you had regarding how you were processing your life. In life's process of Duality, the inner turmoil is the inner fight that is to be expected when you follow someone else's idea of you instead of supporting your Self to progressively process your own inner Self as you journey along your path.

Your results in any given situation along your path are processed through the Duality Programs that are imprinted in you. They are in direct relationship to what you were programmed through the Belief System that influenced your ideas, thoughts, interactions, relationships, marriage(s), careers—virtually every aspect of your life at all your ages and stages. What others imprinted in you, if you were not able to discern for your Self at your young age, you then just had to accept what was said to you about you.

From the beginning, you are imprinted with information. It's how you process the information, *in-form-at-ion*, which means how you are formed at your ion or Cellular Level of your beingness. The information imprinted in you and your cells is how you have learned or have been programmed to experience your life from the beginning. Your body records every experience, every event, every situation, and everything you have said or has been said to you. These recordings are called Cellular Memory.

Your computer/brain doesn't remember all of your experiences. Your body does. Accessing your Cellular Memory as the Non-Emotional Observer (NEO) is an important step to sorting out your past from a clear, objective, non-emotional viewpoint to heal. Without addressing the emotionality of your experiences, you become sick. Billions are spent on ways to heal. Yet people are getting sicker.

The first place to begin healing emotionally, physically, spiritually, mentally, and financially is to connect to your past experiences as the Non-Emotional Observer (NEO). Now *listen* to what your body has to say. Your body will provide you with your answers when you are not attached to the emotionality of your past experiences. When you do this, you are connected to your Heart; your computer/brain can no longer control you, judge you, and make you sick.

Knowing at my deepest knowing I cannot change the past. What I can do is release the past from the Cellular Level of my Consciousness where it no longer serves me. As the Non-Emotional Observer, I can *see* everyone's part in my life, especially my own.

This is where the Contracts become evident. In the past, no one mentioned to me about any Contract? What? The Truth is you did choose your parents, your placement in your biological family or adopted family or no family, and your path. You can call it destiny or fate. They are the same. They are two words, two descriptives, yet the same Duality Program. Guess what? You can change everything…if you choose! All Contracts can be changed, deleted, and completed as you become more involved in your Conscious Evolution.

So, as you become more of an Involved Conscious Evolutionary Revolutionary for your Self, destiny and fate are not relevant. Why? Because you are choosing how you create, implement, manifest, and actualize your life. You are in charge of your path!

The problem with Duality is you are supposed to be stuck in one or all of the Karma, Lessons and Re-Incarnation Programs. You don't have to do it. Actually, all three of these are exactly the same programming; just different words that describe the same limiting, repeatable Belief Systems, the B.S. Programs.

You did not come here to live someone else's idea of your life. You didn't come here to be "born" to die, to suffer, to sacrifice, to be less-than, to take a back seat to anyone. These are programs. You have the ability, regardless of your circumstances, to rise above the resonance of Third Dimension's Duality Programs by taking charge of your life. To be controlled by Duality's limitations is to be stifled and blocked. Free your Self from the boxed-in walls of Duality. You can truly break the ingrained habits of limitation.

"What you say makes your day.

**You can either make or break your day or life
or someone else's day or life
by the words, language, and vocabulary you speak."**

-Sherryism

Everything is about your resonance. How you resonate to life, relationships, experiences, and your Self depends upon whether you are fear-based *or* in the process of becoming consciously clear of who you are. The more you detach from the Duality Programs of Fear, regardless of when the imprinting began, the more powerful you become.

As a society of humans, we have not been taught that fetuses are absorbing the details of their parents' experiences. This could be a very scary realization! Or not! Perhaps by reading this book, the realizations or the "realize" with "real eyes" will be the wake-up call that can change the dynamics of the future of this world for every human being. This is a paradigm shift.

This could be The Shift that has been alluded to for many years, if not decades. This is the paradigm shift of Involved Conscious Evolution. Whatever your age or stage of life, you begin in the moment of clarity in which you choose that you have had enough of limitation, enough of Duality's boxes of confinement preventing you from being in your own Power. You now have the opportunity to choose to express your creativity as an Involved Conscious Evolutionary Being. You definitely deserve to have the life you desire and require to have.

Clarity, detachment, and willingness are keys to the Involved Conscious Evolution. Become involved in your own life. Stop looking outside of your Self for the answers. Outside of you are only the Duality Programs which encourage you to deny and question your innate natural abilities to be the God Self within your human Self. You were never meant to be less or live in physical and emotional pain. Duality itself is a program.

How does the Shift begin for you? Your Consciousness paradigm shift happens when you begin to question everything. Question without judgment EVERYTHING! Question with the focus that you already have your Truth inside of you!

Without judgment or the fear of not fitting in, you do not have to accept the "trues" which you were taught or were programmed into you. You are conditioned to think that what you think are your own thoughts. Until you question, how do you know for sure that what you were taught is really what you are feeling? Even when you knew that these limited Belief Systems did not *feel* correct to you deep inside, you were programmed to accept these limitations as a reality for you. When you are limited, you are very controllable and easily led away from your Self. Remember, from the minute the sperm hits the egg, you are in. You are being conditioned to be controlled and manipulated. You are taught to not be you.

Begin by examining all your Belief Systems. How do you do this? In quantum physics, in order to witness a change, you must become the observer. As the Non-Emotional Observer (NEO), you are not trying to force a change or re-experience the past. As an example, PTSD, Post-Traumatic Stress Syndrome, is the re-experiencing of the trauma emotionally and physically. As the observer, you allow your Self to detach by recognizing the facts of the circumstances. Without the tremendous fears in these experiences, you begin to release and eventually eliminate the emotional attachment to the traumatic events that kept you bound to the past.

Physical and emotional experiences are physical because you are physical. In Candace Pert's book, *Molecules of Emotions*, she describes how neuronets in your brain are established. As an example, you could have been abused as a child or praised as a child. The neuronet in your computer/brain is based upon your experience or experiences. If you are victimized, your neuronet says you are a victim. If you are praised, the neuronet says you are praised. When an experience happens to you, let's say at six years old, you have established a pathway of communication in your brain. Someone says to you at six years old you are "stupid". You experience the imprinting of being stupid in your brain and your body has to go along with this limited Belief System.

Now let's say you are working at your first job at age sixteen. Your supervisor says to you that you did something stupid, maybe not because you did but maybe he or she was having a bad day. You don't know the facts. You can only re-act, re-experience you being stupid by someone else's limitations or restricted ideas. In that moment, regardless of your actual age, you are emotionally six years old. As you go through life, any time you are called stupid, again regardless of age, stage, education, or credentials, emotionally you are always six years old.

Any person who calls a six-year-old stupid is coming from his or her own judgment from his or her past of being called stupid. The neuronet in your brain recognizes an attack. Your brain does not know what time it is. In this moment, you are emotionally six forever.

Let's say you make it to the boardroom of a corporation. You are the CFO, Chief Financial Officer, and the CEO, Chief Executive Officer, says your report is stupid. How old are you? What happens is your dormant neuronet re-fires and you are six again. Your brain has no clue how old you really are.

Without judging your past, your parents, the groups in which you participated, and especially your Self, by sticking to the facts, instead of the emotional attachments triggered by your neuronets, you realize with "real eyes" you are not stupid. Perhaps you "bought" the stupid program, but now as an Involved Conscious Evolutionary Revolutionary you can delete this particular "stupid program". You can take charge of your life. You can imprint in your own neuronets whatever makes sense to you.

As an Involved Conscious Evolutionary, examine all the words, sentences, and vocabulary that trigger upsets in you. As soon as you recognize that you are in an unnatural state of emotional upset, take this as an opportunity to connect to your body and your computer/brain. Your body has all the answers. It knows why you are upset. It knows the time and circumstances that upset you. Your computer/brain is the trigger for your upsets.

As you stay the Non-Emotional Observer (NEO), you will get your answers clearly. With the answers and all the information imprinted in you, you can now begin clearing the non-productive, non-functional, emotional, and repeatable neuronets in your computer/brain. You do not unconsciously have to be stuck in your dysfunctional past continuing to be re-triggered over and over again. Clearing those disabling neuronets frees you to create fun, functional, and productive neuronets for your Self.

FREE YOUR NEURONETS!

Chapter 2

YOU BECOMING YOU

The Programming of the Duality Belief Systems

"Helix Double, not meant this trouble
Helix Double, soon to burst the bubble,
Man Transforms."

-Wei Chen
Ancient Chinese Poet

Only YOU can make the choice to empower your Self. Only YOU can step out of the box and transcend above Third Dimensional Duality.

You have a lot of Self-Sabotage Programs running throughout the physicality of your body. You also have a clear core in your Cellular Memory where your Truth is buried underneath all the rubble and rubbish of dogmas and limited Belief Systems. WITHIN YOU is your ability to rise to the occasion with courage and bravery to Take Back Your Power.

Look around! The old Belief Systems are breaking down rapidly. The instability around the world is evident, personally and collectively. It's affecting and influencing business, governments, religions, and relationships.

From the confusion in the Belief Systems globally, your life is being influenced by the impact of society's inability to cope with the situations. The core Belief System of "grow up, get married, have children and live happily ever after" is not working. The Truth is it never did. It was a wonderful unconscious delusion. The time for illusion and delusion is over.

You project the world inside of you to your world outside of you. The question is: what do you do about it? You **Take Back Your Power**. This book gives you the tools to do it.

This is not a self-help book for dummies. You are a not a dummy. You have been programmed to NOT believe in your Self. You have been insidiously conditioned to "think" the outside authority figures had *your* answers. YOU have *your* answers. You, however, were not shown, taught, or even expected to have your own answers. These are limited and limiting Belief Systems. And they begin in the womb.

This book is a tool to show you the way to your answers. The key is in comprehending how to ask the questions. You are programmed to answer the question, "What is wrong with me?" And then you have to search outside of you for the answers. The correct question to ask is "Why do my Belief Systems prevent me from Believing in my Self?"

"To thine own Self be true" is an oxymoron. To thine own Self be Truth. True is the programming. **Truth is you.**

Your life begins the minute the sperm hits the egg and you are "in". You are a fully Conscious Being. However, in the Belief Systems of Duality, you were not included in the equation of who you are naturally. Your parents, the authority figures, had no idea who you are because they had no idea who they are. They are simply a composite of the same limited Belief Systems.

It does not matter what the religious, social, ethnic, political, or whatever background you were born in was, you were embedded and programmed to follow the programs of your predecessors. Your past, present, and future are the same repeats of the embedded programming of limitations.

As an example, the "Not Good Enough" program is instilled in you from the beginning. You are "Set-Up" to fail. You are Set-Up to constantly repeat dysfunctional programming. Here's a not so great one: "Everything is going so well, it can't last." So the "going so well" doesn't last. "Your parents had *it*, so you will get *it*." "Who do you think you are?" "Successes happen to other people, not you." "You don't have what it takes." "If you do have what it takes, you don't have the support, because you don't have the resources." The list can go on and on and on.

Abandonment, addiction, illness, failure, and all the fear-related programs which Take Away Your Power begin from conception and continue throughout your life. You are *expected* to have problems. You are *expected* to get sick. You are *expected* to have dysfunctional relationships. You are *expected* to *not* live a fully participatory creative life. On and on the Duality Programs of Fear run your life.

Being in charge of You and Your Life is a first step in Taking Back Your Power. Get off the gerbil wheel. You are not a gerbil. Just like Truman in The Truman Show movie, who, at last in Taking Back his Power, completely comprehended he was living an illusional life created for him by the outside programming, the controlling and manipulating authority figures who don't give a rat's ass about you, only that you are compliant and follow the programs like Truman did initially.

He became completely conscious. He let go of the illusion, the fears, and the dysfunctional relationships and walked through the door of Consciousness. Why? Because he was brave, courageous, and determined to be his Authentic Self. Metaphorically and physically, he faced the death of the illusion. He chooses his life. He chooses to be in charge of creating his own world. He chooses to Take Back his Power.q2

Through the reading of this book, you will comprehend how the limiting dysfunctional programs of Third Dimensional Duality and the Fear Programs have controlled you over and over again. Whether the over and over again is in this lifetime or if you believe in other lifetimes, the times are the same. You don't have to do it anymore. You have the capacity and the Clear Consciousness to be your own Tru-Man or Tru-Woman.

These limited programs of Third Dimensional Duality require to be dissolved. You are the one who has the Power to dissolve the illusion. You are the one who has the Power to be the Conscious Creator of Your Life.

Considering this from a Judeo-Christian Belief System, if you are made in the image of God, then why settle for less? You are the More. Jesus said, "You shall do as I do and more." Let's get to the More. Less never worked, did it? It was always the ups and downs, have it and have it taken away. This is Duality. How is Duality working for you? Not so much…for anyone!

Be willing to let go of the past, your experiences of the past, and your emotional attachments to the past however you define them. Whether defined as guilt, shame, blame, remorse, or the wishing and wanting that things should have been different, the fact is when you are emotional, you cannot be whole. When you are emotional, you are only a product of these limited Duality Belief Systems.

You are *not* a product. You are a human being who was not allowed to be a "being". You were programmed to be a definition of someone else's idea or interpretation. Giving your Power Away from the time you were conceived and throughout your life did not allow you to allow your Self to be you.

The Truth is things weren't the way it appeared anyway. It was just easier to buy into the delusion. The fact is buying into the delusions is no longer working. The wave of change is rippling across the face of this planet from within you and each individual, radiating from the deepest levels of human Consciousness. An Involved Conscious Evolution Revolution is at hand. When you become clear about who you are and you Take Back Your Power, your life becomes clear and intentional with the purpose of living your purposes.

You may have been told that you have Free Will. What does that mean? In Third Dimensional Duality, there is no Free Will...the concept of Free Will is a lie. You have been programmed to fear your own Power. When you are afraid of your Self and your own Power, you drop down to your knees. The Will of the collective authority figures, whoever they are in religion, politics, governments, etc., bend your Will to theirs and they take away your Power. So, Take Back Your Power! Free Your Will!

Through all the experiences in my life, I became me. I found my Self, my Power, and my purposes. The tools in this book work for me, and they continue to work for me. I make conscious choices every day and I choose to participate fully no matter what. No one takes away my Power. I am the Power.

Consciousness is the Key to living life fully and truthfully. Consciousness and life begin at the Cellular Level. This is the place which is clean, clear, and has all the answers.

The limited Belief Systems take up room in your cells. They are viscous, snotty, and gelatinous. They only collect more sediment, weighing you down and making you sick.

When someone asks me, "Is your glass half empty or half full?", my response is "What is it half full of?" If it is the same old B.S., then give me the empty glass and I will fill it up with life. Don't accept what isn't you. Accept you as you. What a great place to begin becoming conscious!

So, what exactly are the Fear Programs which have denied you your creativity and your life? Fear is certainly NOT False Evidence Appearing Real. That is an emotional conjecture that creates yet another disempowering Duality Belief System.

Fear is simply LACK OF INFORMATION. When you have all the information, you have the facts. You are not emotionally stuck in the past. When you stick to the facts, you can make a clear conscious choice of how you choose to participate or not. When you are stuck in the emotions, you are giving away your Power.

Third Dimensional Duality relationships are predicated on you and everyone giving away their Power to each other. A perfect example includes divorce rate statistics. Whether it is a divorce of marriage, business, partnerships, or families, the programming says someone is *right* and someone is *wrong*.

There is no solution in *right* or *wrong*. There is a resolution when you and everyone involved can *see* his and her own part of the relationship without the blame (be-lame) game. Don't cripple your Self! Get to the facts. A resolution brings solution. The emotional push-me-pull-ums of the Divorce Game never have a resolution. Therefore, a solution is never reachable. Consider this. hmmmm…

The same Profiles happen. The repeated patterns perpetuate. How many times did you say or hear someone say "I met this new person" or "I have this new partner", whether business or personal? And how did it happen that they turned out to be the same Profile as the one or ones before?

The emotional attachment to the Profile is the cause of the repeated patterns and behaviors of being stuck in the past or pasts. Without addressing the facts, the Profiles repeat. Divorce, again whether personal or professional, is the result of the emotional attachments to the past and the Blame Game, without viewing the facts or recognizing your part in the equation of the relationship. That's how Duality works you!

You have been taught, conditioned, programmed, and molded with a Belief System that your brain is your intelligence. Not so much. Your brain functions like a computer. The concept is that you use 10% of your brain. If you are only using the left brain, which is connected to the right Male side of your body (the Male manifesting side), and you are only using 10%, what is the other 90% of your brain doing? Is it out to lunch, in another dimension, or just hanging out?

The Truth is…**your intelligence and intellect are in your body.** Your Cellular Memory, which is the composite of all your experiences in this lifetime and throughout your continuum, is stored in your cells. You have access to *every* experience.

For instance, if you have a Belief System that this lifetime of yours is so awful, you have a resource that can provide you with incredible practical information that can guide you out of the "awful" experiences you think you have. Your Cellular Memory is the encyclopedia of you, your historical records. You have a plethora of experiences to utilize so you can change the awful to great.

Everything is resonance. You are resonance. If you are embodying the resonance of "negativity", then all you can remember are the "negative" experiences. So, what happened to the good experiences you had? They are hidden in your Cellular Memory, overridden by the "negative" Cellular Memorization.

Your Soul and Spirit function at a more expanded resonance. They are housed in your physical Earth body. In the limited Third Dimensional Duality Belief Systems, you are taught or programmed that each aspect is separate from the whole of you. This is definitely not the Truth.

Every aspect of you…your physical body, your Soul, your Spirit, your Divine Mind, the energy field emanating from your physical body, all dimensions of your Consciousness, and every experience in your time continuum…is YOU! What separates you from your Self are the limited Third Dimensional Duality Belief Systems. You are whole as you are!

It is very difficult to Take Back Your Power when you are stuck in the trauma-drama of the negative experiences. Allow your Self to "remember" all the great things you did create. This can be a challenge due to the Belief System that your life is influenced and created outside of you. However, this is not the Truth.

You created everything…every situation, every experience, and every relationship. This does not mean you are bad, wrong, stupid, or whatever. This is how you are supposed to act in the Third Dimension. You are supposed to be the Victim of circumstances. The Victim Program reigns on this planet Earth!

Rejoice! Commend your Self on some of the experiences, relationships, and situations you created so wondrously

UN-consciously. These moments are your experiences to *see* the difference between Truth and True. True is the limitations, True is the victimization, and True is all the negative stuff. The Truth is you have all the answers to draw upon from your Cellular Memory. Get the facts, get the Truth, and move forward in your Power.

This book is about letting go of Duality, honoring the journeys, acknowledging your *Truman Show,* and walking out of Third Dimensional Duality with a huge smile on your face. Free at last! My Free Will reigns!

Both collectively as an individual and collectively as an individual who is part of the collective, the time is perfect to ascend and transcend beyond the Third Dimensional Duality Fear Programs. These fear-based programs have held everyone, individually and collectively, in a paradigm of opposition, first to their Selves and then to each other.

This is the perfect control and manipulation of individuals, people, and society at large. Be afraid of your own Power and you will be afraid of everyone else. These long-playing programs are reaching an end in this re-cycle bin of pretend evolution.

Over and over again, these Third Dimensional Duality Programs have interfaced in every relationship on this planet Earth. Individuals, groups, cultures, and civilizations are continually being manipulated and controlled by this limited, fear-based programming. The Duality Belief Systems maintain order through the dis-order of the oppositional rules governing religions, governments, groups and then, of course, individuals.

3D Duality is *Fear.* Judgment or judgmental behavior insists upon a *right* and a *wrong* point of view. This view must include good and evil in the paradigm. Without the judgmental standards from the standpoint of good and evil, the control and manipulation of individuals and groups cannot exist. There is always the proverbial "good guys" and "bad guys" scenario. How interesting that the good guys can become the bad guys so quickly and vice versa. Who can really tell "who is on first"? "First" changes all the time!

The idea of good and evil allows for the space on this planet Earth to hold and maintain the resonance to control you, a group, a region, a nation, a continent, and an individual place to be held hostage by the 3D Duality Fear. How many must continue to die for the "right" of something when they are the "good guys" who die?

Remember the ridiculous statement, "the good die young"? So if you live, you are already assigned the label of "bad" because you live. Living is bad and dying is good. What a perfect 3D Duality message of control and manipulation! Not only is your life controlled and manipulated, so are the circumstances of your death.

Over the course of his-tory and her-story too, the he-said, she-said, and the rules of authority have changed many times and in many places. The rules of engagement, however, have never changed. The rules of engagement are scripted. The winner takes all…temporarily. To the individual, the winner is *right* and the loser is *wrong* until the tables are turned in the 3D Duality illusional reality. The "reality" is the winning group has and had more force over another group. However, in this reality, the winner always wins because the invoked "God" was or is on his or her side.

Because Earth is fixed in a linear time of minutes, hours, days, weeks, years, centuries, and eons, the evolutionary process of Consciousness takes "time". In this slow process of linear time, the 3D Duality Consciousness of this Earth is finally evolving. The change is coming from within you and each individual who wrote in their script, like you, to be here at this time.

What is required now is your Involved Conscious Evolution. The key is that you have to be involved. No one can evolve you or your Consciousness. You must do it.

Don't wait for someone else to take the first step to lead you. You take the first step and lead your Self. Be the leader you are. You don't have to wait for someone else to do it first. Stop being a follower. If you're waiting for someone else, you're still on the bench, still in a holding pattern. When you get off the bench, you Take Back Your Power and begin to be involved in the evolution of your Consciousness.

In a sense, time is accelerating because your Consciousness is speeding up and expanding at a more progressive rate. You are asking more questions instead of just accepting what the programs say for you to be and to do. You are your own personal paradigm shifter. You are the Shift and you are creating the Shift within your Self. The "not acceptable" is not being accepted. The unasked questions are being asked out loud. The challenge of keeping your mouth shut is no longer viable when it comes to speaking your Truth. The evolution is occurring within the Double Helix of your DNA.

DNA is deoxyribonucleic acid, which gives the instructions for the development and functions of all living things. The idea of "so above so below" is shifting to "so inside so outside". By being the Becoming of your Self, by becoming clearly conscious, you are changing the coding of your Self. You are creating a new formula and a new format for your Self.

The old structure is based on Duality's old, fear-based programming, such as getting old and sick and losing your vitality. The Double Helix, your DNA, is the matrix of Duality. The Truth now is that DNA can be removed from the cell and the cell continues to live without the template of Duality. So, the Double Helix, the 3D Duality Fear Programs of Judgment, Lack, and Take-Away, is what drains you of your Power and makes you sick.

To maintain the outside control and manipulation of you is to continue to be without your Power. If you do have periods of *feeling* powerful, they are temporary because the "force" of the Duality Programs forces you back into servitude and victimhood.

Every individual, including you, is unique. It's the Duality Programs that are the same. You create your life, whether you are aware of it or not, in your own unique way. The 3D Duality Programs are designed for you to fit in the boxes of control and manipulation. If you are round, you cannot fit into a square hole, so you cannot be whole. You are shaped by the Duality Fear Programs to fit in, whether you like it or not. The fact is being in the resonance of your Involved Conscious Evolution, you cannot resonate to Duality anymore. You are freeing your Self.

Looking at limited Belief Systems from a historical point of view provides so many clues that smack you in the face. Regardless of the his-tory or her-story, the governments, the religious orders, or whoever was in charge at the time demanded their followers to follow without question. This makes it very easy to manipulate and control you as well as the group members. It is also easy to pit one group against another group, while the "leaders" get their points across to each other. Regardless of the consequences of the followers, the leaders make their statements even at the cost of lives. They have to be *right*, even if the conflict is *wrong* for you. You have to obey.

To get validated, you have to go along or you won't fit in. The Validation Program knows no limits or boundaries for controlling you or others. The desperation to be validated is the important factor in keeping you in line. In Truth, validation of your Self is up to you. The outside-of-you validation issue is the delusion.

The peculiarity of the Validation Program is that you could "wrong" your Self to get the outside validation. Of course, the "outside" world will definitely support you to invalidate your Self. To be *right*, you validate that you are *wrong*. Is this the perfect 3D Duality world of control and manipulation?

The change, occurring at your DNA level, is affecting your entire physical body at your Cellular Level of Consciousness. You are in a fabulous time to evaluate and assess in newness what serves you and your life, and what does not serve you. From a perspective of non-judgment, begin to evaluate your life, your relationships, your purposes, and your values. You have this right. This is a right not based on *right* or *wrong*. This is your right to be your own inheritance now. Take advantage of *this* lifetime. At whatever age or stage you are, ask your Self, "Is what I am being and doing the best for me?"

You have access to more information than ever in the history of this 3D Duality World and the Duality Universe. The rise in Consciousness, Ascension, Transcension, call it what you will, is happening. Once you begin to open your Self up to your Self, to your Truth, and to becoming clearly conscious, there is no turning back. The 3D Duality World is not appealing anymore. This is the Shift. The Shift or expansion of Consciousness is accelerating at a very rapid rate.

This is why it *feels* like time is speeding up. This is analogous to someone illiterate who has learned to read or to someone who has learned a new language; the person wants to learn more and quickly. This is where you are now…anxious and excited to know more, to learn the facts, and to discern what serves you or not.

The fear-based 3D Duality Belief Systems are embedded in your DNA. This is the Double Helix. There is no accident that the number 2, which represents Duality, identifies the configuration of the double strand of DNA. Duality is programmed into your 2 strands of DNA. What is transpiring now is that the resonance Shift within your body is happening in your DNA as you become the Involved Conscious Evolution within your Self. Can science prove you have more than 2 strands of DNA at this moment? Perhaps not *yet*. But it is happening. A lot which science could not prove throughout history eventually has been proven. You are ahead of the curve.

Astronomer Mike Brown, who wrote *How I Killed Pluto and Why It Had It Coming*, states, "Science isn't a set of facts or beliefs about the world but a process of continually challenging and expanding our understanding. Every answer in science is provisional, never final."

For those who have a difficult time with the changes, they will leave the planet, whether through death, accident, disease, or denial. It could be either an actual death or existing as an out-of-body zombie.

The emotional and physical pain they may experience is their own resistance to their Selves. They may be terrified to discover all their Belief Systems may not be their Truth. It may be much too painful for those who are not willing to expand their personal and professional worlds.

> "A mind that is not free is simply
> a self-referential belief machine
> that continuously spins off useless and
> unprofitable thought energy.
>
> Belief and fear are the only ties that bind a mind,
> while unconditional love and
> open minded skepticism set it free...
>
> In substantive matters of long-term significance,
> there is no good belief."
>
> *- Thomas Campbell, Physicist*
> Author of *My Big TOE, Theory of Everything*

Having to admit that one's Belief System may not match or connect to their deep core can be a very difficult challenge. For some it is too difficult. They will either choose to move on to another dimension or think they will have to suffer the consequences.

The consequences are what they will unconsciously choose as a punishment for going against the grain of the Belief System. The punishment could be an illness, a disease, or a disaster in their lives. Very sad, indeed, to stay closed and fear-filled because of the 3D Duality Programs. Death is not a release, just an interruption until the next time. What is not cleared in this lifetime, like all lifetimes, is a re-cycled pattern brought forth in the individual's time continuum. Nothing ventured, nothing gained...how Truth is this!

As the resonances within your body change, the Earth shifts its resonances. This is the happening for you and for everyone participating in this Involved Conscious Evolutionary change. This is a co-participation event. Again, for those who choose not to participate, they won't. For those who choose, the resonance changes occur from the inside out.

Yes, it is time to let go of limiting, fear-based Belief Systems which are out of sync with your Involved Conscious Evolution. You simply are not resonating with Duality. You are free to create your life as you choose it each and every moment of *your* each and every moment.

In 3D Duality, to fit in, you have to override your own personal resonance and Truth. When you go against your own Truth, you give up your Power. This may give you false approval, so you do it willingly to be accepted. However, is it worth your life and your creative abilities to give up your Power by lowering your Self to fit in?

If you give up your Power to an individual because of the 3D Duality Programming, you will find your Self in a very dysfunctional relationship. Again, you may do this to fit in, and not because it resonates with you.

With the divorce rate at over 60% in the United States, do you "think" there is a tremendous amount of Power being given away and a tremendous amount of Power being taken away? Not a great scenario for a reliable relationship for sure! This is the way of 3D Duality. It's the duel of opposing forces. Some even call this love?!

The sticky bands of glue holding everyone stuck in their versions of the 3D Duality Programs is coming unglued. Even the expression of not wanty-needying to be stuck in a relationship, a job, or in a place is being expressed all over the planet. There is discord in the illusional resonance of 3D Duality. This is not harmony.

Many are simply not resonating with the Fear Programs anymore. A change is happening, whether you believe it or not. The happening of this change is from your inside at your deep core level of your Cellular Consciousness. You are waking up from the delusional Fairy Tale Nightmare, "the happily ever after story" which omits the question, "after what?"

You are not resonating to the 3D Duality Fear Programs anymore. The confusion is what do you do about it? The wavelength of Consciousness is expanding and broadening from deep inside your clear core. Embrace your Truth at your inner core. Ask your Self questions, instead of asking questions outside of your Self. The outside is just a reference point for you; it does not have your answers or your questions.

This is why you are reading this book...to look for a pathway to the inside of your Self which is practical. And you can apply this practicality to your life, especially during this change of his-tory and her-story.

The Awakening is the "wake" of energy which is beginning to flow through you from a clearer Consciousness from deep within you. Your entire body of Consciousness, the physicality of your cells, particles, and molecules to the sub-atomic level of you, and every dimension of you is beginning to wake up so you can connect with all those aspects of your Self you were told were not Real and did not exist. You were taught that all that you were and are is in this 3D Duality world. Duality and your interaction in Duality are the many limited realities.

The question you must ask your Self is, "What is Real?" Duality is realities...realities involving race, color, creed, religion, politics, professions, etc. The Truth is...You are Real. You are a Multi-Dimensional Being. And as you embrace your Truth, you become YOU.

The Universe is a 3D Duality resonance. The Universe is a part, an aspect, of the Multi-verse. This is the same for you. You can "decide" to stay in Duality, or you can consciously evolve by choice to be Multi-Dimensional in every aspect of your life.

Allness is Multi-versal. There is only one verse in the Duality Uni-verse. You are many voices and verses of experiences throughout your continuum, not just here on this Earth plane. Allness is a unifying field of resonances coming together in unity and connectedness as you resonate beyond Duality's limitations. The separation of your Body, Soul, Spirit, and your Expanded Consciousness of Mind is no longer a viable option. Being separated from your Self on any dimension or realm of your Self is too limiting, too controlling, and too manipulating *for you* anymore.

3D Duality does not have the place or space of Consciousness to hold or maintain the resonance of Allness. As your field expands in cohesiveness, your progressive process of Transcension, Ascension, and Expansion begins.

Transcending, rising above, and shifting out of 3D Duality and its dogma of opposition to your Self and to others is about YOU becoming clearly conscious that you are in your Power. This progressive process of your Multi-Dimensional Self is your Involved Conscious Evolution out of 3D Duality – *of* "it", Inner Truth, not *in* "it", Duality, anymore.

The Seven Chakra System is Duality. It has seen its time. The Thirteen Chakras are the clear steps out of the box, out of the control and manipulations. Will it be easy? It's totally up to you. How much do you require to Take Back Your Power? How much do you require for your Self to live a healthy and prosperous life? Only you can make the determination. The choice is up to you to make. Clear Realness *or* a single delusional reality of the same old same old stuff?

You may feel extremely emotional at this time. You may be experiencing outrageous fears. You may feel more sensitive to your external environment than ever before. This is okay. Go with it. Don't be afraid of your Self.

Your intelligence and intellect are in your body; it is not in your computer/brain. Get out of your head and get into your Heart. This book is a guide for you to do this. Your computer/brain is a tool to organize the information you are sorting through. Keep what serves you and dump the rest. Your body is the experiencer of all your experiences. What *feels* correct to your Heart, keep it. What does not *feel* correct, dump it out of your body.

The old 3D Duality paradigm was to hold it all in, stuff it down, keep your mouth shut, and take what life gives you. This is the old paradigm. The new paradigm is Trust Your Heart, use your computer/brain as a tool to organize information, Take Back Your Power, and Live Your Life to the fullest, Multi-Dimensionally. In the journey through this book, the guidance is for you to step up and Take Back Your Power *now*.

Remember, all the 3D Duality Programs are counting on you to be fear-filled. You are very controllable this way because you do NOT trust your Heart, you are NOT *listening* to your intuition, and you are NOT being your Self. After all the seconds, minutes, hours, days, weeks, months, years, centuries, and eons, isn't it about time to let go and discover *more* of who you are instead of existing in the *less* of who you are?

Just to be clear here, money has nothing to do with *more* or *less*. Money is energy. Money is a tool.

If money is really the objective, whether rich or poor, did it make your life rich and fulfilling? Could it? Sure, it could, when money is the by-product and is used as a tool.

Money is a by-product of energy. Whether you are hoarding money or making money, the measurement of your prosperity, abundance, and affluence does not make you measure up to your Self. It is only a measure of how you think the outside sees you.

What do you *see* inside your Self? Again, having money is neither *right* nor *wrong*. What you do with the tool of money is what makes the difference in the happiness and joy of your life. You have to choose whether money is more important than you are <u>or</u> is money the tool to be put to great use to support you and to assist others to be powerful? The choice is yours.

The delusion is that if you are a part of a group, you have your Power. This is only an illusionary source of Power and it is always temporary. What if you fall into disregard with the group? You will either have to find another group in which to fit in, or you will exist as the ostracized victim who fell out of favor with the group. What occurs is that you become their victimized victim with a sad tale to tell. The repeated story you tell only further victimizes you and you become the victimizer of your Self-victimization. What a fabulous program to keep you from your own Power!

You will have to find a way to validate your Self in some other way. Whether it's a government, a corporation, a company, a religious order, or a social or business group, the group dynamics will only support you as long as you fit into their Belief Systems. If you don't, you are out! If you are out, the illusion is you have no Power. The reality is that being a part of a group dynamics neither makes you powerful nor weak. Your Belief System about how you fit in or don't fit in is how you draw the illusional validation to validate your Self through the group dynamics. In Truth, only you can validate your Self by Believing in Your Self. A Belief System of outside validation for you or anyone is not empowering.

Every 3D Duality Fear Program is designed to immobilize you and to keep you controlled and manipulated. The illusion is that you appear to be in control of your own life. The Truth is you are not in control. Control is an extremely dysfunctional behavioral pattern which affects your life, your relationships, and your view of life. You cannot control anything. Through this book, you will *see* that the benefit to your Self is Being In Charge of Your Life. The progressive process is a Self-generated, hands-on, practical approach to life.

The controlling programs keep you powerless and under control, while making you "think" you know all the ins and outs of life as you are going in and out of emotional turmoil. As long as you are emotional, you cannot stand permanently in your Truth. This is the up and down emotional cycle keeping you off balance and swinging back and forth on the pendulum seeking balance. In this book, there is a further discussion of balance which will explain with clarity what balance is. For now, balance is not standing still and doing nothing. Balance is moving forward in life productively, pro-actively, and on purpose with purpose.

In the 3D Duality Programs, balance is impossible. Conflict in any and all of its forms (judgment, prejudice, bigotry) can never achieve balance or harmony with the Truth of nature. 3D Duality, by definition, means the conflict between opposing forces.

There is no Power in force. Force is controlling and manipulating. Self-Power is balance. You cannot be, metaphorically or physically, knocked off your feet by a force less than your Power. Only in the delusional illusions of 3D Duality is this dynamic the illusion of reality.

3D Duality is the game of war: war with your Self, war with others, wars of groups, wars of corporations, wars of countries and nations. War games, war games, and more war games. Always playing war games. All of them are based upon survival. There is no living in survival. It's not a very creative space in which to go through life!

The measure of war is not measured by the size, but the measure of control and manipulation. The persona of the controller is also not measured by size, but by the influence maintained over the manipulated. Whether the controlled is a battered wife, husband, or child, or a group, or a nation, fear allows the manipulation.

War comes in all forms. When you war with your Self, you will create and manifest the participants of your conflict to war with you. This is the perfect scenario for the Victim/Victimizer Roles. Sometimes, it is difficult to *see* which Role you are playing. Many times, the victim is the victimizer and the victimizer is the victim. Both are caught up in the same war.

3D Duality continues the game of rulers and subjects, masters and slaves, victimizers and victims, abusers and abused, haves and have-nots, good and evil, right and wrong. These old worn-out programs have painfully been playing long enough.

The Dr. Jekyll and Mr. Hyde Syndrome is a perfect example of the 3D Duality inner turmoil, representing the perception of good and evil, right and wrong, and the inner heaven and inner hell going on inside of you. This reality is the expression of how you use your energy based upon your Consciousness. You are either wrapped up in the programming or you can choose to move beyond 3D Duality. As you stay wrapped up in 3D Duality, the external manifestation of your life, however it is expressed, is judged as good or bad in 3D Duality terms. You have to be either *right* or *wrong*.

The illusion of good and evil is the expressive energy field which is determined by the resonance of Consciousness. Through the propulsion of energy is how the intention of Consciousness is manifested into behavior. What does this mean? What and how you create and manifest your life are absolutely determined by your Consciousness. If you are fear-based, your life is full of fear.

Your internal conflict through the limiting programs is externalized by conflicts outside of you in your external life. The conflict of the Male and Female aspects of your Self also resides within you. This conflict has nothing to do with gender, sexual preference, or sex. Your inner conflict has to do with your Belief Systems and emotional perceptions, not perspectives, of what is masculine and what is feminine from the standpoint of 3D Duality.

In 3D Duality, it is difficult to conceptualize a unity of the Male and Female aspects within you without thinking about gender. The Allness of Consciousness is not relevant to gender or to 3D Duality. Your energy in the Allness of your Consciousness is not fragmented or separated within you by opposition. Opposition is irrelevant.

As long as you are conflicted with your Self, you will have conflict outside of your Self. You will search out and find the person or people to engage in conflict. You may not be consciously aware you are doing this, nonetheless you are.

Everything in the Universe and the Multi-verse is comprised of energy. Energy is the vibration and frequency of Consciousness. All frequencies and vibrations of energy are in the Universal and the Multi-versal Consciousnesses. Yes, plural Consciousnesses, meaning Multi-Dimensional.

Matter vibrates at a lower frequency, making everything appear solid. When you use your physical eyes and yardsticks to measure physical realities, your physical bodies appear solid in your perception. What is *unseen* by physical eyes and physical measurements still exists. Often the unseen remains undetected when only using 3D Duality physical means to provide confirmation.

Each particle, molecule, and cell of you, from the macro to the micro of you, is physical, no matter whether it is seen or unseen. Each aspect of you has a frequency, a vibration, and a resonance. When they are in harmony within you, you are Centered in Self and are powerful, power-filled, and fearless.

You are a series of frequencies and vibrations and resonances like the octaves of music and sound. Your Soul, your Spirit, and your Body as a Human Being represent a continuum of the make-up of you. Your continuum includes time, Cellular Memories, Cellular Memorizations, and Cellular Sounds...all imprinted and connected to your experiences throughout your time frames.

Throughout history, each decade has a collective Belief System. This collective Belief System becomes imprinted in you through your parents and through the collective Belief Systems of the society at the time of your birth.

For example, the 1930's imprinted depression and lack. The 1940's imprinted war. The 1950's imprinted "if you don't talk about it, it doesn't exist", the Madison Avenue *pretend* factor. The 1960's went from War to rebellion. The 1970's imprinted "tune out and turn on". The 1980's was the "Me Generation". The 1990's Generation X and the confusion caused by Y2K; the world was going to end. The 2000's imprinted Confusion, and the "What's next?" as 2012 and the world was going to end *again*.

All these eras of resonances were influenced by the resonances to offset the collective Belief Systems. This is 3D Duality in action.

For instance, during the 1930's Great Depression, the songs were nonsensical ditties to offset the nonsensical depression and lack issues. The 1940's musical influence was love and loss during WWII. The flat-lined 1950's were offset by the invention of Rock 'n Roll, to shake up the flat vibration and frequency of denial. The 1960's expanded Rock 'n Roll music into protest songs to protest the Vietnam War. The 1970's music of free love and folk music fit the drug scene perfectly. The 1980's music perfected the "all about me" factors of big hair, big shoulders, and just big everything. The 1990's music seemed as confused as Y2K, the end of the world. By the year 2000, the world as everyone knew it did change. The age of terrorism hit everywhere.

The resonance of Consciousness has shifted. As you raise your awareness and get connected inside your Self, you do not have to be terrified of your Self or your Power. Power is not force and force is not Power.

It is time to rise above the low-based resonance of 3D Duality and look beyond limitations. What you see only with your physical eyes is not what you have to get in life. When you open your eyes and raise your resonance above the low resonance of this 3D Duality world, your world changes. You are the Power source and resource for your Self.

Be the one person in your life who makes a difference. Begin the journey to Take Back Your Power. Begin now.

Chapter 3

THE PROGRAMS

Judgment, Lack, and Take-Away:
The Programs of Fear

"The seed of man does not look like man.
But all the possibility of Man is contained in it.
History is like that."

-Paulos Mar Gregorios
Cosmic Man, the Divine Presence

From childhood, regardless of the times, you are constantly programmed to give away your Power. You are not even aware you are doing it. Through the Duality Process of being told who you are, what you are expected to be, what you are expected to do, what group you are supposed to be a member of, or what other criteria has been assigned to you that defines you, you are continually programmed to keep you separated from your Self and from others.

The Duality Process "sets you up" for internal conflict right from your beginning…the minute the sperm hits the egg, you are "in"! Without consciously being aware of the programming, little by little, step by step, you are committed to giving away your Power. You give it away willingly to become this false sense of identity, which is assigned to you no matter how deep in your core you like it or not.

Your behavior then is determined and "acted out" from and through your Duality Programming. For example, if you are prejudiced about someone or a group, this prejudice may have been embedded in you by the prejudice of your parents. You may have picked it up in the womb!

Some years ago, Jerry Springer had members of the Klu Klux Klan on his show. There were three pregnant women, screaming hate into the audience. What was going on in their wombs? Their babies were being infused with this hate. Completely unconscious, these mothers-to-be were harming their babies.

Their hate for others, which is simply their hate for their Selves, was being imprinted at the Cellular Level of Consciousness of their children. They were too unconscious to know what they were doing. Their illogical fears perpetuated this emotional hate into the foundation of their offspring.

Look around you. Does this not happen all the time? Maybe it is in a different part of the state, the country, or the world, but this re-manifestation is exactly the same. It doesn't have to be the Klu Klux Klan. It can be any hate-mongering group who pro-creates the next generation of hate. These babies had their Power and their free choice taken away without being able to say NO! They were being forced to give up their Power.

As your thoughts continue to be manipulated, you are caught in repeated cycles of behavior, compliments of the Duality process. You "think" you are thinking for your Self, but you are, in fact, acting out the behaviors of the conditioning. For millennia, these Programs of Fear ruled and continue to rule the world…your world! They have ruled your life and your lifetimes.

Why do you think the Karma, Lessons, and Re-incarnation Programs, the do-it-over-and-over-again programs, were invented? On planet Earth, the Duality Programs present a scheme called "Karma". How many times have you repeated a program? If this was not the Truth, then why are so many individuals throughout the world having past-life regressions to understand why they are repeating issues? These individuals are searching for the reasons, the answers, the resolutions, and the solutions to their Karma.

Consider letting go of the concept of Karma as neither good nor bad. Now look at Karma from a Consciousness perspective. How many lifetimes, including this one, are you willing to invest your energy, your time, and your life in repeatedly "learning" the same lessons? Is this learning? NO! It's a non-productive pattern and a waste of your valuable time and creativity.

Giving away your Power to a concept of Karma and repeated lessons with no *real* outcome of learning is just repeating the same experiences over and over again with different backgrounds and different costumes. However, these experiences are nonetheless the same. Is this Karma loop worth wasting your life?

> **Are you willing to continue to invest your energy into the same lesson?**

Why not find out where these Programs are embedded in your body of Consciousness and at what level of your unconsciousness by bringing them to your surface awareness, evaluate the information, and make a conscious, clear choice to let the Programs go? If you choose to do the lesson again, then by all means, repeat it. It is *your* choice to continue *or* to cancel your Karma.

Healing your emotional issues will not happen by being punished through your Karma. Healing can only occur by Taking Back Your Power through your conscious choice and by making the commitment to your Self to comprehend these Duality Programs and their repeated Self-Punishing Karmic lessons.

**Karma is an assigned label
for a victimization Belief System
which burdens and commits you
to repeated non-productive patterns
which demand you to give up your Power**

Everything, all the systems which have been previously accepted as real and historically correct, is being challenged. It's about time. It's about the future. And it's about NOW.

Have you had thoughts about what you have been told is the Truth? What do you *feel* is your *own* Truth? Do you feel conflicted? Is there a duel going on inside of you? Are your questions *feeling* more profound than usual? Are you becoming aware that these questions are coming from a deeper level within you? Are you *feeling* these questions are not superficial questions, but are emanating from a place you had not previously connected with in your body?

The connection is through *feeling*. This *feeling* germinates the questions from the deeper levels of your awareness previously unconscious to you. These questions are signaling changes at the core of your being, at the core of your Consciousness. Hidden underneath the Programs at your Cellular Level, a change is happening.

The questions are the triggers to accessing the information of memories, memorizations, and sounds of your experiences. All of your personal information throughout your continuum is buried deep inside of you. This information can reveal the Truth of Who You Are from all of the experiences, the people, and the situations you have encountered in every journey of your time continuum (past, present, and future).

In this time of your journey, your "Quest" for your personal holy grail is found within the "Quest"-ions (quest at your Cellular/ion Level), discovering your answers from the information stored at your Cellular Level of your Consciousness. Information means your in-form-at-ion (in form at your Cellular Level of Consciousness). In this questing, you are now discerning the difference between what your Truth is and what is the "true" of the Duality Programs which have taken away your Power without your awareness.

There are many layers of Consciousness throughout your body. In these layers, there are many versions and personalized adaptations of programming. The Duality Programs are all based on fear. No matter how you label the expressions of fear, whether it is anger, frustration, disappointment, worry, depression, or anxiety, they are simply symptoms which eventually lead to sickness. Whatever label you use to describe the fear, it is still a fear of something. All the behaviors and consequences of the fears are the results of your participation in these Duality Programs, whether you are conscious of them or not.

These Fear Programs are designed to teach the lessons of the personal and the group journey through the evolution of Consciousness. Each individual and each group of individuals, whether they are aware at the time or not, are creating the experiences to learn the lessons, comprehend them, and release them or not. The objective is to move beyond the fears pertaining to the specific Duality Programs. Without conscious awareness, the journey continues through repeated cycles of programs and lessons, regardless of the versions or lifetimes.

The programs and the fears upon which they are based are illusionary. Although they may appear real, they are only an experience of one of the dimensions of Consciousness within your physical body. Once the fear has been seen as the illusion, fear has no Power over you. Without the manipulating force of the Duality Programs forcing you against your Self, the emotional attachment to the programs disappears. You are now Taking Back Your Power.

All of these programs have a commonality in their process. The commonality is the Childish Adult Ego. Contrary to popular belief, your Childish Adult Ego, not God, is who judges you as right or wrong. In this Role, your Childish Adult Ego is your best teacher. Through the programming, your Childish Adult Ego teaches you how destructive the force of energy becomes when it is propelled by fear.

You can finally accept this when you are tired of being controlled by fear. Your lessons may have been long and hard in your time continuum, but it doesn't have to be this way. It's the continuation of the Belief Systems in this reality that keeps you stuck. You can get free beyond the Duality Programs and uncover your *own* Truth.

You must be willing to stop judging your Self

You must be willing to stop being afraid of your own Power

At some point in your continuum, when you willingly choose with clear intentions and commitment to your Self to override your Childish Adult Ego's fear-based programmed indoctrination of survival, you will evolve your Consciousness. By allowing and embracing the blending of your Soul, Spirit, and your expanded Consciousness within your physical body, you move beyond the programming.

As the Consciousness of your Childish Adult Ego grows up, your physical body of Consciousness integrates and evolves on all levels of your Consciousness. You no longer have to survive. You now can live. Isn't this why you came here? To live and create consciously! Being in the survival mode all the time is difficult and makes it almost impossible to enjoy your life. Survival doesn't have anything to do with money. Survival is the program of continued existence. When you are forced to survive, you are not living in your Power.

By embracing the activation and the integration/blending of the Multi-Dimensional levels of Consciousness within the human body, the planet itself begins to change. Through this **Involved Conscious Evolution** and the integration of Consciousness, not only does the energy of the body change, the energy of the Earth shifts into an expanded resonance field of Consciousness. As a result of this Shift in Consciousness within the human body and the Earth, the frequency and the energy of the Duality Programs begin to dissipate. Allness begins to happen naturally.

THE DUALITY PROGRAMS

The JUDGMENT Program

One of the most heinous manifestations of the Duality Program is Judgment. Judgment determines that someone else is less than you are or that you are less than someone else. The criteria for judgment are not important. What is significant is that judgment reinforces the everyone-is-separate-from-everyone-else Belief System.

Someone has to be the most significant one in a group, and most have to be the followers of the Grand Poobah, who is the most significant member. And in this equation, the scale of measurement of less and more is of the utmost importance. Whenever you or your group judges another individual or group as less, you are giving your Self permission to say you are better. The judging gives rise to mistreatment and separatism.

Separation also reinforces hierarchy and rank. This illusion of Power is really force. In this illusion, the energy of judgment instills a Belief System that this force is true. It is not the Truth. Hurtful and harmful actions result from the illusional force of judgment, which is mistaken for Power.

When the judgment is professed as good versus evil, then the questions must be asked from both sides of the professed good and evil perception. In Nazi Germany, wasn't it "good" if you are a good Nazi to kill Jews? If you are a Jew, it is not good at all. It is evil. So, the good and evil perception doesn't work for anyone's good or evil. All it does is use force and gives the forcing group carte blanche permission to perpetuate their forceful Belief System and cause harm. The question is, "Is killing someone because they don't follow your illusionary Belief System correct?"

The answer is NO!

When you are observing the dynamics of relationships, whether between individuals or groups, what can be witnessed are the pain and fear of the judged, as well as the pain and fear of those doing the judging.

Judgment is fear. **Fear is Lack of Information.** Fear is not having all the facts. Not having the all the factual information leads to judgment. Judgment is a cyclical energy reinforced by fear.

The information being presented here is not just from your Childish Adult Ego's point of view. This information is now being presented for all your levels of Consciousness, not just from the limited Belief System perceptions of

Duality. All of these levels of Consciousness have always been part of the journey of your Childish Adult Ego, your Soul, your Spirit, and every aspect of your Self in your physical body and bodies throughout your lifetimes.

However, because of the dense frequency of Duality in this Third Dimensional world, you did not have the ability to access these Multi-Dimensional aspects of your Consciousness. Now you have the ability to access these multiple dimensional levels and spaces of your Consciousness. You must be willing.

You must be willing to let go of your limited Belief Systems and examine them. The question is not "Are they wrong? Am I wrong?" The question to ask your Self is, "Do my limited Belief Systems prevent me from believing in my Self?" Now that's a question to ask your Self to begin to Take Back Your Power! Are your Belief Systems "good" for you? Or, are they keeping you in the darkness of limitations?

Now is the time for you to choose to have the possibilities and potentials to make the productive and positive changes in your life. Free your Self from the Duality Programs and the Self-inflicted results of the Fear Programs arising from the depths of your unconsciousness. Here in these layers, the programs take up space in your body, affecting your life and your creative abilities.

There is no wonder why your human body breaks down and gets sick. The intelligence in your body is in constant conflict with your computer/brain, which runs the programs. Your Childish Adult Ego, always in the perpetual Survival Program of Judgment, runs your computer/brain. Your Childish Adult Ego does the best and worst he or she can do to survive. Survival has absolutely nothing to do with money! Survival is the fear-filled Belief System of "not good enough" and "not enough" no matter how much or how little is in the bank. You can bank on this!

All of your information is at your Cellular Level of Consciousness, which is called Cellular Memory or Cellular Memorization. It is the location of the "big picture" of you. Here's the clue: is it storing your truthful Consciousness or your programmed unconsciousness in which your Childish Adult Ego is running your show?

As you go inside in your Shift of Consciousness, you discover that the Truth about Judgment is that you are really judging your Self, whether it is this lifetime or your other lifetimes. In the Karma Program, when you have judged others, you will create and manifest scenarios in particular time frames of your journey "to be judged" by others. Whatever aspects of the Judgment Program in which you have participated, whether it is judging and/or being judged, if you have not cleared or "got the lesson(s)", you simply repeat and drag the past forward into another lifetime.

Now ask your Self...

"Is it time to get off the Karma Duality Cycle?
or
Continue the powerless ride?"

The ongoing foundation of the Duality Programs is Fear. Fear supports Judgment. Whatever judgment issue is feared most and is not cleared will most certainly be re-lived repeatedly until the judgment issue is resolved. The judgment issue is Self-Judgment. It begins within you.

The debilitating energy of re-living any situation of the Judgment Program is not just an individual's repeated Karma, it also affects the dynamics of the Karma of the group in which you participate. The size of the group does not matter. It could be a group of two who gossips or a group of Nazis or Klu Klux Klan or a hate group of any kind. Somewhere along the continuum timeline, the group of individuals will re-group for the judgment lesson again. Whatever side of the program in which they participated, they will re-create the event in the time continuum. However, if you or anyone chooses anywhere along the time continuum to get conscious, you can revoke the Karma contractual agreement by Taking Back Your Power and remove your Self from the Judgment Program.

In Duality, there are always the two sides of the coin. As long as the fear of being judged resides in your body of unconsciousness, the fear of being judged continues to play you. You have to create the situations or conditions to keep you in this loop. You will either judge *or* find the perfect scenario for you to be judged. So, as long as you and the collective of this Earth are held in the limited Belief System of Judgment, there will be space here to support the energy of Judgment.

> ### *Judgment is oppositional Force, NOT Power or empowerment.*

Looking at the bigger picture, a space can be created for you as the observer to *see* the divineness of this Judgment Program. Divineness does *not* mean it has to be accepted and continued, because everything in the Duality Universe is in divine order, even when it is in disorder. This Earth and this Universe is Duality...good, bad, or indifferent. The divineness is the lessons learned.

> ### *A Lesson...Get it or perpetuate it!*

In this space of observation, you have the potential to release the illusional fears and the programming of limitation. By *seeing* the fears as illusions, you then have the choice to release the controlling energy of opposition and Duality on this planet and in the Universe. You do it from within your Self.

What a fabulous place to start! You, as the Non-Emotional Observer (NEO), detach from the fear and the issues without judgment. You get the lesson and don't have to repeat it. You don't have to waste your Consciousness, your energy, your time, and your creativity focusing on an outside source which is simply not in agreement with you.

YOU DO NOT HAVE TO PARTICIPATE. Those opposing you, from your Childish Adult Ego limited perception, are also on *their* journey. Don't judge someone else's journey. Otherwise, you have just emotionally "hooked" your Self into their trauma-dramas.

This is an individual-by-individual commitment to become conscious. By allowing your *feelings*, and NOT your Childish Adult Ego's judgment, to direct the energy of your Consciousness, your conscious *detachment* from the fear of judgment is achievable.

Consciously shifting your Consciousness is only possible through your clear commitment to remove your Self from the Resonance of Fear. When you no longer resonate to being fearful of being judged, you can move forward without carrying the burden of "what will other people think". Understand, *they* are thinking "what are other people thinking?" and this may or may not include you. So what!

To shift a group Consciousness, it starts with individuals such as *you*. Every individual who stops judging others begins to form a new collective Consciousness. As long as any group judges individuals or other groups, Duality rules!

The ramification of the Judgment Program is always the same: WAR! Whether it is "my god is better than your god" or "my way is better than your way" or "my group is so much better than your group", ask your Self, "Is this way of existing on this planet Earth worth the expense to destroy my Self, each other, and this planet?" Not only is the fear harming you, others, and the planet, it is hurting the Universe. Earth is a part of the Universe. What happens here affects the Universe.

To change your future,
the future of the Earth and the Universe,
the present time must be cleared of fear.

TAKE BACK YOUR FUTURE!

In a Shift of Consciousness, it appears more chaotic *inside* your Self as well as *outside* of your Self. There is order in the chaos. The energy of this Shift, directed consciously with an intentional commitment to change from *fear* to *clear* from the inside out, creates the change from *chaos* to *order* on the outside. Everything outside of you happens from the inside out. It is not the other way around as the Duality Programs force you to *belief system*.

This order changes the outside dynamics of the "thinking" behaviors. You are your actions. As each individual's Consciousness shifts from *chaos* to *order*, the collective Consciousness of humans changes also. As the dynamics of the collective Consciousness of the people change, the space of the planet's Consciousness changes, and so goes the universal Shift from Duality to Unlimitedness. A new dimension is birthed for you and for everyone who chooses to participate. A new dimension for this planet and this Universe begins to be created. It begins with one person at a time.

You are becoming the Power of the individual contributing to the empowerment of the collective. Force or being "forced" is no longer relevant when you are clearly conscious and in your Power!

The LACK Program

The Lack Program is one of Duality's most debilitating programs. Lack labels you as "missing something" or "not having enough of something". Lack separates you from your Self and from others. Through this Belief System, it is easy to become paralyzed and dysfunctional through the idea of not being enough, not having enough, and not being good enough. This Belief System sets you up to be a victim of circumstances, a group, a person, and first and foremost, your Self.

These paralyzing fears of the Lack Program create a false sense of competition and promote the survival mentality of jealousy, envy, distrust, and hatred. The fears within the Lack Program manipulate your thinking or thinky-thinky patterns. You simply re-create a cyclical pattern of behavior which reinforces this Lack paradigm. Because you feel unworthy and valueless, you create scenarios providing you with the dys-opportunity to **validate the invalidation of your Self**.

You set your Self up to confirm to your Self you lack whatever you determine with your Self that you lack. This is a perfect example of the victim aspect of the Lack Program. You either draw to you, in the Law of Distraction, a victimizer who supports you in being less, or, if you can't find the victimizer in this Lack Program, you will do something to your Self, unconsciously of course, to prove you don't have what it takes to have good health, get a promotion, be acknowledged, be successful, or be anything else except less. Whatever you have defined as your potentiality of Lack, you will make it your potential. Wow, what a debilitating program, lived by so many in the Duality Belief Systems of Third Dimension! Lack transcends time in your continuum. This is a heinous trap.

Supporting the Lack Program is the underlying "taking-away" aspect which states, if you have something good, somewhere along your line of life and your timeline, the "you do not deserve to have it" feature (what a feature!) of the Lack Program will raise its ugly head. Poof, you lost it! You give it away. You lost your Power. But, if by chance you did get "it" back, deep within your unconsciousness there is a conversation happening. Unaware to you at your programmed Cellular Level, this conversation, more times than not, allows your Childish Adult Ego to step up and persuade you to sabotage your Self. Sometimes you even know it, but you still allow the sabotage to happen. The Take-Away Program repeats itself.

The Lack Programs rear their ugly heads repeatedly in your continuum. Remember the "you really did not deserve it anyway" program? So, you wait for the ax to fall. Yes, for sure, the ax falls. You create the ax in whatever scenario it happens...boss fires you, the relationship doesn't work out, the family excommunicates you, or you could be abandoned by a religious group or some group confirming to you that you lack whatever it is to be a member of the group. Again, **validating the invalidation of your Self**, the Lack Program is the perfect resonance for you to become the victim. Sabotage is the forte for the victim in lack.

Different settings, different ages, different times, but nonetheless they are exactly the same situations within the Lack Program. The conscious or unconscious saboteur shows up. The sabotage aspect of the Lack Program is off and running your life!

A Self-fulfilling prophecy of loss is initiated by the behavioral patterns of the Lack Program which say you will fail. Just another step in giving your Power away! This is how the past is the future. The past is one second ago and the future is one second from now. In whatever resonance of the Duality Programs you are existing, the past is the future and the future is the past.

What you drag along from the past,
regardless of linear time,
is the future dragging you down!

What a drag!

The frequency of the Lack Program is very low-based, dense, and demanding. The challenge of this low, dense frequency is your inability to *see* your Self as deserving. With the "bad" programs (being born in original sin, wrong side of the tracks, not good enough, not, not, not!), who would not "see" their Selves as lacking something or other?

Lack does not provide a place to fit in. Lack generously provides you with a space of *less than* with little room even for you. Since you don't deserve much anyway, there is no room for you to grow. Stay confined, accept your lot in life, and keep quiet!

By continuing to give your Power away,
you accept the unacceptable...
the perfect place and space for you
in the past, present, and future
of the Duality Lack Program

Throughout history, as the ruling forces change, the governments change, the nations change, and the changes appear to change, the results of the Lack Program remain the same. Though different faces, different places, and different times, the dynamics always remain the same. No one ever seems to have enough no matter how rich or poor. Lack has nothing to do with economics or material acquisitions, including ownership of land. Lack is a Belief System in limitation. It's as simple as that!

In the energy field of this fear-based program, there is never enough to go around. Regardless of what it is that "has to go around", the only thing which can be shared in the Lack Program is *lack* itself. Lack provides the foundation for the *victim* conversations heard around the world. Language doesn't have anything to with the conversations. The conversations heard around the world are *full* of support to be a victim.

Whatever type of victim of circumstances, whether it's the weather, war, family, work, relationships, and so on, the Lack Program is the low-based frequency of the victim aspect of this Belief System. As long as you Belief System that you Lack something, you will never be enough for your inside world or your outside world. You will be the victim of lack. Why? It's simple. You unconsciously give your Power away. You accepted the Belief System that you are not enough to Be In Charge of Your Life.

**When you continually accept
that your answers are outside of you,
you are easily controlled and manipulated.**

You give your Power away.

Even the concept of abundance in the Lack Program is based on the measurement of lack. For example, when you do your intentions in the venue of the Law of Attraction, you will get an abundance of lack if your core Belief System says you are not deserving of *real* abundance. But when you are "deserving" of less, you create an abundance of lack. Don't you hate when that happens? How's that for a convoluted Belief System? It is not that you are not asking, intending, praying, or whatever for a better life. In the core of this limiting Belief System, you expect less.

If you are embedded with limiting Belief Systems undermining your intentions and prayers, you may get some version of what you are asking, but it is only temporary. The Duality Programs run deep, whether you are conscious of them or not. They influence and affect your life on a daily, moment-to-moment lifetime of experiences, and longer than that. After you get what you want, the programming rears its ugly head. Oops, it's gone again.

The Truth is this planet Earth provides more than enough for everyone. However, the Belief System of this Lack Program is so deeply ingrained in the physical body at the Cellular Level that it will take a conscious, focused commitment and clear intention to erase the fear from the collective Consciousness of you and the collective Consciousness of the human race.

By recognizing that the Lack mentality impacts everyone on this planet, you can choose to exchange this limiting Belief System for a Consciousness of abundance, prosperity, affluence, and influence in which everyone can participate in the *real* meaning of sharing the wealth. The wealth is your Clear Consciousness first. The wealth is your ability to create constructively with each other. The wealth is in your unlimited Spirit's ability to love unconditionally. The wealth on this planet is the human race that is conscious!

The wealth on this planet is seeing each other for who we are beyond the Duality Programs

Sharing abundance and prosperity is an expanded frequency of Consciousness in which lack cannot exist. In sharing from your Heart, without the fear of losing, there is abundance and prosperity for everyone. The Earth expresses the energy of your Consciousness. In the Belief System of Lack, deficiency is the rule. The time has come to change the rule of the Lack Program on this planet and in the Universe.

The hidden agendas embraced by the Lack Program are not just scarcity. They also include sacrifice and disappointment. The theory states that if you work hard enough and long enough and make sacrifices, you will get what you deserve. The issue here is the word "deserve". In the context of the Lack Program, most of the rewards are temporary. As interpreted by many religious Belief Systems, you might or might not get them in the afterlife. Of course, it depends on the Judgment Program.

If the reward is manifested by chance in the Belief System of Lack, there seems to be a restriction of time limitations to hold on to the reward. "Things are going so great...it can't last." And it doesn't!

Good things or rewards are difficult to maintain because of the non-deserving agendas infused into your Cellular Level from the low frequency of the Lack Program directive. This has nothing to do with the concept of being temporary or permanent. Evolution is supposed to create changes. The difference is, through the process of being processed through Duality's evolution, the changes are only different versions of the same thing.

Although it may appear you are evolving from lifetime to lifetime or through your various ages and stages in this lifetime, and your material possessions might appear bigger and better or not, the only thing that is really changing is your ability to re-create different versions of the Lack Program. The versions now just appear to be more sophisticated.

The current Lack Program has expanded and includes all the classes—the rich, the middle, and the poor. In fact, there is confusion as to who is rich, who is in the middle, and who is poor. Oops! Confusing? No, there is no confusion when it is *you* who is in the loss mode of the Lack Program.

The disappointments about the systems are affecting your core Belief Systems and everyone's core Belief Systems on so many levels. Something is happening. And that something is not looking very well. Confusing disappointment is rearing its ugly head. What is going on?

The Systems indeed are breaking down. Lack is affecting everyone in one way or another. The "haves" are being challenged. The ranks of the "have-nots" are increasing. They are coming from the middle "haves" class. This loss/lack is not expected. Was the middle class considered safe?

At the core of this disappointment is the emotional issue of depression. The depression in the United States and around the world is significant. To handle the depression, drugs are offered as the solution. This is not a solution; this is the numbing of your Consciousness and the collective Consciousness.

If you are numb, you are controllable. Another step in the Take-Away of your Power is the overuse of medications and drugs, legal and illegal. In a frequency of numbness, your Consciousness and energy are depressed and so is your ability to have Power.

At the turn of the millennium, Y2K, another variable of the Lack Program manifested. Scarcity showed up, and so did the great hoarding which happened in the United States.

This scarcity, as ridiculous as it can seem at this time, took over.

Hoarding rules, separatism reigns. No sharing in this resonance. People fearfully ran to the store, bought groceries, water, guns, everything they could get their hands on. What was going on in the minds of the hoarders? Survival. That's what was going on! Who cares what happens to the "other" person(s). Hoard! Get on board. Grab it while you can.

Scarcity is a driving force for the Lack Program. In this paradigm, scarcity is the wedge maintaining separation of individuals, groups, and nations. Globally, dysfunctions operate through scarcity. In this resonance, it is very easy to control and manipulate others through this overwhelming fear. The fear is "what if I don't get my share of the pie?" I will die so I will comply. The fear of not having enough supports the Belief System that some will be provided for and some will have no provisions. When there is this Belief System of scarcity, there is no room for the Consciousness of sharing the wealth.

The amazing aspect of humanity's creativity is how many versions of the Lack Program there are on this planet. Whether it is an individual issue or the group collective's issue, lack is lack no matter what the version.

There are always times of lack appearing in your life—lack of friends, lack of support, lack of knowledge, lack of a job, lack of money, lack of opportunities, lack of a relationship, lack of this and lack of that. Then there's lack of time, lack of Self-esteem, lack of Self, lack of abilities, lack of courage, lack of choices, lack of information, even lack of possibilities. Lack, lack, lack. Because you are ingrained with the Lack Program at your Cellular Level, what else can you create except lack?

**Lack is a measurement for the Duality Program
to be successful and keep you under control
without your own personal Power**

Lack is the insufficiency Belief System which has cycled not just through individuals, but through civilizations time and time again. This false sense of scarcity invented the survival competition. All versions of the Lack Program are founded upon Fear. The Duality Belief Systems keep the Lack going.

The TAKE-AWAY Program

In the false sense of survival, competition is dependent upon Duality's third step in the process, the Take-Away Program. The Take-Away Program expresses itself in the outward appearance of taking something away from another person, a group, a country, a business or a corporation, and doing it in a perceived, impersonal way. However, the Take-Away Program is infused with huge emotional attachments. Not only is the person, ruler, or group leader who is doing the Take-Away invested in the right or righteous viewpoint that it is okay to do it, the person or group who is experiencing the Take-Away Program becomes invested as the victim.

Hatred can abound on both sides of the Take-Away experience. Both sides have their version of the emotional attachments. This is the perfect scenario of the victim/victimizer, abuser/abused, and leader/follower in action. Both sides are emotionally vested.

The old paradigm of half-forgiveness works well here. In this half, your Childish Adult Ego will forgive but never forget. There will be a time for the emotional revenge to kick in somewhere along the time continuum. It has to happen. The Take-Away Program has no time limit.

Whether it is this lifetime or other lifetimes, past or future, you will revenge the deed done to you somewhere in your continuum. Now or later, states the programs of Karma, Lessons, and Re-incarnation. Power given away again!

The Take-Away Program also prompts you when you think you are not deserving or, in a convoluted way, think you deserve to be punished. In Duality, it happens all the time. You create it, whether it is Self-Punishment or you have someone outside of you do it for you. There is no god who has the time to punish you. When you unconsciously or even consciously agree to punish your Self because you deserve the punishment, you will figure out a way to make it happen. It could be the Take-Away of a relationship, a job, a promotion, a business, or whatever it is that *should* be taken away from you. You will create it and even agree you deserve it.

Now you can step up to the plate of the Take-Away Program and incorporate the Self-Sacrificing piece of it. This aspect doesn't look like you are Self-Punishing; it appears as the do-gooder, martyr/victim phase. It sounds like this: "Oh my, look how much I have done for you. I gave away my entire life to make you happy. I have always put you first, blah, blah, blah."

There is no validation for the martyr/victim Role except **validating the invalidation of Self**. Taking-Away your life for someone else or some group only causes resentment on both sides of the Duality Program. The measurement of the sacrifice is resented even more. Then it becomes an ongoing reminder. No one likes it! Relationships can be destroyed by this controlling and manipulating martyr/victim Role. This Role is very destructive to having a healthy life and healthy relationships. It almost makes it impossible for both sides of this Take-Away version. The fact is it is not functional for anyone involved.

This Self-Sacrificing programming, debilitating as it is, offers no value to anyone. Not for the person whose Power is being taken-away and not for the person who is taking the Power away. Both parties are so caught up in their Roles of being the victim and the victimizer. Half of the time, no one really knows what side of the Take-Away road they are on. The Power is being tossed back and forth like a bouncing ball. The victim *forces* the victimizer to victimize. The victimizer *forces* the victim to submit. Everyone loses their Power in this situation. It happens all the time. And in this scenario, more times than not, it is called love. Is this really love?

Both have lost their Power and continue to feed off of each other's weaknesses, draining each other's energy. Both swing back and forth until eventually someone becomes conscious and moves on. Or, in the worst-case scenario of the Take-Away Program, the other person dies, thinking he or she is free at last. However, here's the catch...the Karma, Lessons, and Re-incarnation Programs kick in. Back again!

Now a repeat performance is commanded by none other than the person who did not resolve the issue and died and returns to play the Duality game again. Karma, Lessons, and Re-incarnation are not the solution. There are NO resolutions, only the repeated performances! So, if you are the victim and you have played that Role enough, you may return as the victimizer to get even. Or vice versa!

However, comprehend that the only person you are getting even with is your Self. And that is not even! Why? Because if in this Belief System you have to "make up" for the times you victimized others, you will definitely be the victim to pay your penance. You will make up for your "sins" so to speak and jump into the sacrifice, suffering, and punishment aspects of the Take-Away Program, beginning again with the Judgment Program. You even have the opportunity to skip the Lack Program and go directly to the Take-Away in your old/new script. This is how it works. Well, this could be something to look forward to…or NOT! Clear the Programs or Repeat them. Force your Self to suffer or Take Back Your Power.

Always embedded in the Take-Away Program are the ramifications of taking something away from your Self, not from someone else. The Take-Away Program is emotionally and physically painful. To Take-Away your own Power and give it away so unconsciously is as debilitating for the individual or group who accepts your Power from you.

Taking away and giving the Power up appear to be polar opposites of each other. They are not. The opposite sides of the Duality polarity are consciously and energetically bound together as though one. Whatever side of the pole you are on, the sides are exactly the same. It may not look like it, but both sides victimize and both sides represent the victims. Releasing your Self from this heinous Take-Away Program frees you on multiple levels of your Consciousness.

As you change, you provide opportunities for others to change or not. The more people who *see* and *feel* the disadvantages of the Take-Away Program and realize with "real eyes" how much time, efforts, creativity, and life are wasted, the quicker you and others will *see* the Truth of this madness, and together collectively we can release the Belief Systems of the Take-Away Program from this planet Earth and this Universe.

Taking Back Your Power provides the avenue
for Planet Earth to get her Power back too

From the group viewpoint of the Take-Away Program, only one person or group can rule over others. This establishes the rule of the elite, the ruler, and the rules.

In this paradigm, the separation is defined by the "haves" and the "have-nots". The "haves" give their Selves permission to Take-Away from others. No matter the facts of the situation of the Take-Away, the delusional "rulers" use all sorts of excuses, rationale, logic, and even reasonable explanations for their permission to have the upper hand. Excuses such as divine right, lineage, destiny, position, and even the right to force others to do their bidding to accomplish their rule as the rules! Their best logical illogic is "because my god is better than your god", which means "my dad can beat up your dad" says the Childish Adult Ego.

In the rationale of the Take-Away Program, the leader or leaders of the "right" group say they have the right to do the Take-Away Program with others. This is their "right" to make the controlled group follow their "rites" because they have the "right" to be the takers. What a Belief System!

In the process, the takers have the "right" to skew history as they slant it. Can you imagine how much real information has been lost, hidden, or misconstrued through this Take-Away Program? How many facts were lost? How much real history was destroyed? How much of the real history has been denied to you because a particular "ruling" group took away that knowledge in order to protect and perpetuate their Belief System? To make their Selves "right", the rights of others are denied and Taken Away.

Can you imagine how the legacies of certain civilizations were destroyed by the Take-Away Program? They were destroyed because the idea of one group's version of a god or deity was better than another's. Look what happens when the actions of a person or persons determine ownership over another. The relationship could be parent/child, husband/wife, master/slave, teacher/student, boss/worker, or religious group/government. This Belief System is the Take-Away Program in action. This Belief System stems from the fear of Lack which results in the Take-Away Program. The rulers, or those in control, are afraid of losing. And the losers, those who have accepted they have no Power, are afraid of never having any!

Through the Take-Away Program, the loss of identity has happened all through history. Any form of enslavement is the loss of identity for those enslaved. Whole civilizations throughout history have been forced to give up their identity. Whether it is a civilization, a community, or an individual who is forced to relinquish their life to the enslavement of another person or group, this is the ultimate Take-Away Program in action.

Loss of Self and the loss of identity force you, or your group, to give up your Power. The person or particular group who is in the position of enforcing the Take-Away Program for others gains by taking away whatever the "it" is they have determined "rightfully" now belongs to them. There is no concern regarding the consequences that the overpowered are having about their losses. This is irrelevant. What is relevant is the premeditated *force* that won the control.

You have to be careful not to enslave your Self because you *think* you are less. Slavery comes in many forms. You can enslave your Self to a Belief System because you *think* a particular group is your answer to happiness. This is exactly how cults and false hero-worship can enslave you. In a way, it is existing vicariously through one who is considered rich and famous, or a charismatic con man or woman, or a fast-talking manipulator who appears to know more about you than you do. No one does. You know about you. In other words, a "user" is the perfect implementer to Take-Away your Power and your life. You get enslaved in *their* life instead of living yours. It happens all the time.

Dependency is still another form of the Take-Away Program. Dependency in the "wanty-needy" venue is extremely debilitating. In the Law of Distraction, the dysfunctional attraction, many relationships are drawn together because of the low resonance of wanty-needy. More often than not, this is mistakenly viewed as love. The idea of love in this low-based frequency of dependency is the dysfunction of hoping, wishing, wanting, and needing validation outside of your Self, looking for someone to make you whole as a person, looking for someone to make you perfect. Looking for love in the wanty-needy resonance is love alright, the love that makes you less as you give your Power away.

Falling into the wanty-needy syndrome *hole* of the Take-Away Program, there is no *whole* element here at all. Most people are simply not aware of the ramifications of this Belief System which emanates from their Second Generative Sexual Creative Chakra. What is being generated from this Second Chakra is literally based upon a dysfunctional First Chakra's Belief System that someone outside of you makes you whole. This will be discussed later in the book.

This wanty-needy Belief System, whether coming from you, someone else, or from a group dynamic of dysfunction, is a trap. It is not about love. It is about getting caught up in a struggle for control with both sides being manipulated. Both sides of the wanty-needy are hooked. There is no Real Power, only an exchange of manipulation. The control goes back and forth between parties.

Wanty-needy has zero to do with love. It sounds good in a Country Western song, "I want you and I need you". However, it doesn't state the real agenda, which is "I want you to fix me. I need you to make my life perfect. I want you to do this to prove you love me. I need you to do this to validate me. I want you to give up your Power. I need you to give up your Power. And I want to give up my Power." Then no one has any Power. Both are wanty-needy victims. This is some Duality Belief System, B.S.! It's all about the trap and not about having a healthy relationship. Ever wonder why the divorce rate is over 50% or 60%? The trap of the dysfunctional, wanty-needy Duality Belief System creates the push-me-pull-ums, the back-and-forth victim relationship. This is called LOVE!

The programming runs so deep. The illusions of the Judgment, Lack, and Take-Away Programs are so dense and desperate. They do not allow the Consciousness of your energy field to *see* your Self as desiring, requiring, or deserving anything that would support you in your own Power. Before you can Take Back Your Power and heal your Self, you must be willing to make the commitment to your Self to consciously release the Fears of the Judgment, Lack, and Take-Away Programs.

All fears on this planet, no matter what the fear is labeled, are all versions of these. In the resonance of these Fear Programs, there is no room for the expansion of Consciousness. There is only room for the repetition of dysfunctional relationships and the dysfunctional behaviors that are the TRAP. No chance at being in your Power.

To Take Back Your Power and heal your Self at your Cellular Level core, the first step is to Trust Your Self, your Intuition, and your Heart.

As you read about the following five-step progressive process, the steps may appear to be out of order. They are not. There is a purpose to this order.

1) KNOWING

As a child or even as an adult, when someone labeled you as "bad" or "not good enough" in some way, inside of you at your core you knew that this label defined by some authority figure (a parent, a teacher, sibling, or whoever he or she represented) was not you or your Truth. But as a child, who are you going to believe? Of course, the authority figure. You don't believe at the time that you have choices or options. You are a child. Besides, the authority figure has, in your idea at the time, more knowledge, more experience, more education, more of everything than you do. Or so the perception seems.

You have no idea what happened to them in their past or where they are stuck in their past. Then a pattern is established, and the authority figure from your childhood becomes the spouse, the boss, the friend, the enemy, or the "grown-up" sibling. Whoever he or she is becomes the representative of the prior authority figure. The answer to the question, "Why do I continue to draw the same person or persons into my life?", now becomes evident. You have the evidence. This is why these situations happen repeatedly. There are no accidents.

You have been programmed. Until you get to the core of the conditioning and labeling, you are destined to repeat history. These are simply different versions of the Karma, Lessons, and Re-incarnation Programs in this lifetime. Seemingly different situations and seemingly different people, but nonetheless you are experiencing a variety of situations through the variations of people through the different ages and stages of you in lifetimes that are the same.

The label of the judgment becomes an interactive characteristic of your Belief Systems. The label affects your actions and re-actions of the repeated dysfunctional patterns of behavior. Even knowing that this label or judgment of you is not your deep Inner Truth as a child, because of this labeling, you did not *know* you had the Power to stop this pattern. You thought the label was you, or such was your reality.

Knowing is simply not enough to change or stop dysfunctional patterns. Knowing cannot empower you. You do not have the physical energy to change it at your Cellular Level just by knowing this label is not your Truth.

When a situation or person triggers the label, you are "hooked" emotionally back into the repeated pattern. You have to defend your Self, explain your Self, and again accept the powerlessness of the situation.

At your core, you want desperately to believe in your Self. The pattern attributed to the label is more believable because that authority figure supposedly knows more about you.

Because your *knowing* is still embedded in the Belief Systems of the Judgment and Lack Program, you remain stuck. Your *knowing* does not have the physical energy to change the Victim programming at your core.

The label imprinted into your Cellular Memory overrides your Truth, and you believe the label more than you believe in your Self.

Your knowing is not enough to free you.

2) UNDERSTANDING

Understanding is the second step in the process. The Consciousness of understanding is ambiguous. As a result of the variations in language, words, idioms, and their variety of meanings, the authenticity of the word "understanding" can be as varied as the words used to describe it. Many times, you *think* you understand something, especially from an intellectual viewpoint. You may identify with the meaning on a superficial level. However, it has no connection to what you are *feeling* at your core. You can rationalize the *what* is happening, but you cannot understand the deep realness of the *why*.

When your understanding has no *feeling*, there is no *real* core to your understanding. Underneath the *feeling*-less rational explanation of the *what*, the emotional issues of the *why* are still buried, still unaddressed. There is no clarity. There is no clarification. Therefore, there is no clearing or healing to the emotional attachment of the dysfunctional situation of the past. The judgment of the authority figure from your childhood is still there.

The reality of the understanding is therefore a perception. Perceptions have no facts. They are emotional and confusing. They have no Power. Excuses are perfect examples and expressions of perceptions and are completely emotionally debilitating for everyone involved, especially you.

When you truthfully connect to your *feelings* and begin to Trust Your Heart and Your Intuition, your *gut feeling*, you are beginning to understand the situations. You are connecting to your Self, not to your computer/brain. You are connecting to your Self through your Heart and your Intuition.

You can begin to understand that the individual, persons, or groups who *labeled* you as bad and wrong were talking about their Selves with all their insecurities and perceptions of all their past traumas. All of their emotional baggage was being dumped on you at whatever age or stage of life you were. These emotional perceptions even begin in the womb.

Allowing your Self to *feel* from your Heart releases the "hold" on you of the perceptions, allowing you to *see* the facts, which frees the energetic pathways so you can connect to your core Consciousness of Truth. You *feel* and your Truth clears the fears. Your connections to your Truth, and even Truths, become available to you without the fears of the Duality Programs of Judgment, Lack, and Take-Away.

3) *to be revealed*

4) CREATIVITY *and* 5) BEHAVIORS & ACTIONS

The fourth and fifth steps to Taking Back Your Power and healing your Self is your connection to your Clear Consciousness of *feeling* in your Heart what is correct to you. Now you can focus your creative energy to determine how you consciously create your life and how you now can consciously apply functional behaviors to produce beneficial results for *you*. What a concept! This is no concept…this is living!

You inspire your Self to consciously change your behaviors. Dysfunctional behaviors do not work anymore. The best factor of this is that they don't work for *you* anymore. You totally get what a waste of life it is to support any dysfunction. This is what being clearly conscious means.

You *respond* to life, instead of allowing a re-action or a repeated dysfunctional use of your creativity. The Duality Programs of Judgment, Lack, and Take-Away operate all around you. So what! You don't have to buy into them anymore. You are In Charge of Your Life.

You no longer have to waste your creativity, your productivity, or your time on the dysfunctional past or some label some unconscious and dysfunctional person pinned on you. You stop blaming them. You are now free to move on. You are free to create your life through Conscious Choices. You no longer have to settle for less. You are out of the labeled boxes. The Third Step is the step to your *realness*.

3) COMPREHENSION

Comprehension, the Third Step, is your key to empowering your Self and Taking Back Your Power! You now make your choices without the burden of dragging the dysfunctional aspects of your past into your present and future time frames.

When you Comprehend on all levels of your Cellular Consciousness, you Know and Understand you are the Creator of Your Life. You choose how you participate in life. You choose with whom you participate. When any relationships are toxic, you move on. You Know, Understand, and Comprehend dysfunctional situations do not serve you.

When you comprehend how these Duality Fear Programs work you over and over again, your entire body of Consciousness at the Cellular Level in all of your physical systems comprehends how the fears teach you to be a victim and then to victimize your Self and others as they do to you. This behavior is not love. This behavior is not loving.

The Fear Programs thrive on the dysfunctional Golden Rule, "Do unto others what others dysfunctionally are doing unto you!" The energy of force goes back and forth between the participants in this lifetime and in the Programs of Karma, Lessons, and Re-incarnation. FORCE is NOT POWER. Force is painful, emotionally and physically. Force is the experience of victimization.

In the Consciousness and energy of Comprehension, you have no judgment for your Self or others. You have practical enlightenment through the completion of the lessons you so brilliantly wrote in your scripts. You did all this to learn about your Self. Now you learned! Move on!

In the Consciousness of Comprehension, you become grateful and thankful for all your experiences and situations, and most of all for all those who jumped into your scripts and participated with you. When you *see* the brilliance, you can thank your Self and them. And where it is applicable, you comprehend the significance of the relationship(s) and even the lessons. You passed! You graduated! Now move forward.

Comprehension is the light bulb going on. You say, "I get it. Not only do I get it, I have it. I have the answers to the questions. Because now I know, understand, and comprehend how to ask the questions. No more asking me or anyone else what is wrong with me." There is nothing wrong with you. You were running the Fear Programs of Judgment, Lack, and Take-Away, giving your Power away and making your Self sick, wrong, and bad. Remember, these are how the programs work to keep you victimized.

Now you comprehend that the pain in your body is and always has been your body's attempt to get your attention. You don't have to cover up the pain anymore with drugs, prescriptions, or numb your Self with substance abuse or Self-denial abuse. You can ask your body, "What is my body telling me?" And you can respond, "I no longer ignore the intelligence and intellect of my body. I no longer ignore my own Cellular information."

**"I comprehend that I am connected to my Self.
My body responds to me.**

I comprehend my body, my Self, and my life."

There are no more reasons to rehash the lessons of the programming. There are no longer emotional hooks from the past dragging you back and forth. There is no longer a needy-wanty to expend your energy on blame, shame, guilt, or any other low-based, low-vitality resonance of fear-based Belief Systems. Comprehension is THE KEY to clearing the Fear Programs and the emotional issues attached to them both at your surface Consciousness and in your Cellular Memory.

Comprehension is the point of clearing. This physical and emotional change happens from the inside out, and then your world outside changes. Transcension from the Duality Programs is occurring. You are initiating the release of these manipulating Judgment, Lack, and Take-Away conditions. There are no reasons or computer/brain accusations of your Childish Adult Ego judging you. Judging others is irrelevant to you creating your life consciously. If someone or some group doesn't resonate with you, you move on without the emotional attachment of judgment or justification of why you are moving on. You don't have to emotionally validate the situation or those involved.

**When you comprehend that
your Self and your Life are up to you…
you are FREE to create your Life consciously!**

You become, by clear choice, the Master of your Consciousness and your energy. You choose how you participate or not. You comprehend that the Judgment, Lack, and Take-Away Programs *were* the teaching tools for you and your Childish Adult Ego to evolve no matter how many lifetimes it took.

At this point in your evolution of Consciousness, your Soul and Spirit begin to integrate and blend with the physicality of your body. Your Childish Adult Ego grows up in the Allness state of Consciousness with your divine mind and Cellular intelligence. You know this is happening because you can *feel* the change at your core and Cellular Levels of your Self. You know, you understand, and you comprehend your Self throughout your body of Consciousness. You *feel* your Self.

Your creativity is no longer based upon the old patterns of fear. You are in charge of your behaviors and your actions. New unchartered creativity becomes your potentials and possibilities. Now you can move even beyond the potentials and possibilities and make your dreams *real*. In a sense, this is a New Birth of *you* and *your Realness*. Re-birth includes all the old programs, all the different versions.

You take your stand to heal and empower your Self. You are not drawn back or sucked into the old patterns; they no longer have a hold on you. The old patterns of the dysfunctional law of dis-attraction are simply not relevant.

You know who you are! You understand your Self. You comprehend that your life is *your* creation. Whatever actions you choose, you are in charge. You are not stuck in the never-ending programs of decisions made through the dysfunctional programming. You make CHOICES. And you can change your choices at any time. This is evolution in action. Keep what works and dump the rest.

COMPREHENSION FREES YOU
from the DUALITY PROGRAMS and the FEARS.

TRANSCENSION IS YOURS!

Chapter 4

THE ALLNESS CONSCIOUSNESS OF YOU
MULTI-DIMENSIONAL

Levels of Consciousness,
Programming versus Awareness

"The intention of the Real Human Being is life
to the fullest of the Real Human's potentiality.

The Real Human is Multi-Dimensional, Multi-Faceted
and so is the Being of Allness Consciousness – unlimited.

The Real Human is coming out of the illusion –
to create the Dream as REAL."

-Sherry Anshara

Yes, Consciousness is awareness. You can, however, be *aware* of something, such as a person, a concept, or an idea, without being fully conscious. The question is…are you experienced enough to be fully conscious of the experience you are experiencing in the moment? Well, even though this sounds like double talk, it is not.

Unless you are fully conscious in the experience, you are not having total awareness of what is happening. When you are not prepared emotionally or physically for the experience, you forget the experience and that you wrote it in your script. Or, you do not even have a concept that you wrote a script. Don't judge your Self. The majority of the population on this planet is not prepared consciously for their individual or collective experiences.

What they are prepared for is the accepted paradigm of "life is tough", "life is the school of hard knocks", "life sucks", "kill or be killed", blah, blah, blah. How can anyone be prepared for any experiences under the circumstances of the programming that life is expected to be less? There is no reason to wonder why problems happen. These dysfunctional programs affect everyone on this planet, regardless of ethnicity, background, religion, politics, age or stage of life.

Your level of Consciousness is expressed through the use of your internal energy system. What this means is how you use your energy is conveyed through your behavior and patterns. Your patterns and behaviors are then represented by your words, language, and actions as determined by your Belief Systems and your state of awareness.

Awareness is not full Consciousness. For example, as a child, when you are riding in the back seat of your parent's car, you have an awareness of the car and your environment in the car. You do not have a full Consciousness until you learn how to drive. Through experience, you then become aware not only of the inside environment of the car but you become aware of the outside environment. This is both a metaphor and the Truth.

Being consciously aware of your internal environment in your body allows you to become aware of how you are creating and participating in the environment outside of you. When you are just aware and not fully conscious, you are not connected to your Self or to what is being created outside of you by You. Therefore, be clear about "what" you say about your Self, because what you say becomes the external expression of your life. And what you say about your life becomes the manifestation and actualization of your life. The importance is to be consciously aware. Being partially aware is not living fully conscious.

Your awareness is exhibited through your resonance. For instance, if you are running a Victim Duality Program, then your level of awareness is based upon your resonance to Victimhood. When you are clearly conscious, you know the difference in the resonance between being a victim and being in your Power. When you are in your Power, it's impossible to resonate to being a victim. You clearly *feel* the difference in the resonance.

How you resonate is the difference in how you create your life. How you create your life as you are being fully conscious makes it impossible to stay in the Fear Programs of Judgment, Lack, and Take-Away. You live. Survival is no longer a Duality option. You are a powerful Conscious Creator. No one can take away your Power. You do not resonate to *their* control and manipulation, whoever "they" are.

As you are becoming conscious, there will be times when you are more open and less fearful. You know it by the *feeling* of your own Power. During your journey becoming the Involved Powerful Conscious Creator, there may be times when you can be triggered by the Duality Fear Programs. And during these moments, you may experience being stuck and/or experiencing being immobilized.

Don't worry. Moving out of Duality is a progressive process. Cut your Self some slack. Don't judge your Self. Remember, you have lived in a continuing continuous continuum on this planet and in this Universe which resonates to the Duality Fear Programs. They were created to make you afraid of your own Power. At this point in time, it doesn't really matter who created Duality and the Fear Programs. What matters is you are evolving, no longer revolving in the resonance of Duality.

The Consciousness or the Belief Systems of you as a collective of your experiences and the collective Consciousness or the Belief Systems of the groups in which you participate through your life set the format for your behaviors and the creation of your "world". Their language of Consciousness or Belief Systems becomes your language. Their vocabulary becomes your Wordology Is Your Biology. So, the question to ask your Self is, "Are these *my* words or not?"

Here is the factor. So much of your Consciousness is unconscious to you. Therein lays the challenge. So much of your behaviors, thought patterns, and physical use of your energy come from your unconscious Consciousness. For example, consider your body as your house. Your garage or basement is your subconscious. This is where the psychology focus is. Your garage or basement is your left computer/brain. You know it has to be cleaned out at some point. So you tell the stories of your cluttered garage/basement/left computer/brain over and over again. This keeps you stuck in the past(s) retelling the same repeated stories going nowhere.

Connecting to your Heart, which is the most expanded resonance in your body, connects you to your body. **Your body is your infinite intelligence and intellect.** By accessing your body, you are now connecting to your Cellular Memory, which is the recording of all of your experiences in your entire continuum.

At this point, you are out of your computer/brain and into your body where all your answers are. It is how you ask your questions.

Question means "Quest" at your ion or Cellular Level of Consciousness. When you ask your left computer/brain what is wrong with you, your left computer/brain must come up with a dysfunctional answer. The Truth is that your left computer/brain does not have any answers, let alone a question. The Truth is that your body has the answers.

It is how you ask the questions. Being clearly conscious is the key to asking correct questions. Trust your body. Do not trust your left computer/brain. Your left computer/brain is Duality. Just as your desktops, laptops, tablets, and phones are programmed, so is your left computer/brain. All the keys to your Power, your answers, and to your freedom from Duality are in your body. So, formulate your questions consciously and you get conscious answers from within your Self.

In Duality, you do things and you don't even know why. This is why you say, "I have no idea why I do the things I do." The *why* is because you have been programmed with other people's ideas and with their collective Belief Systems instead of Clear Consciousness. This transference of Duality Belief Systems, instead of Clear Consciousness, becomes your behaviors and actions which are now generational from one generation of you to another generation of you.

This is called your continuing continuous continuum. You know, the Karma, Lessons, and Re-incarnation do-over lifetimes. They are from the beginning of your time continuum – where you lived, worked, played, and how you experienced your experiences and whether you benefitted from them or not. You and everyone else do not realize it is the perpetuation of the Duality Programming happening over and over again. The programming is subtle. The subtlety is enormous. Why? Because it is unconscious and yet it becomes your behaviors and actions without you being aware of what is really happening to you. Unconsciousness breeds more unconsciousness. Scary!

The programming is gradual and occurs over periods of time. Again, the programming is embedded in your Cellular Level over a singular lifetime and is ingrained in your unconsciousness over lifetimes. Sometimes the programming is deliberate and obvious. In the dynamics of cults, hate groups, and religious zealots, the programming is up front and intentional.

Although this type of programming may appear on the surface as having good intentions, it is very destructive to the freedom of *you* as an individual who doesn't agree and to others who disagree. You must agree to belong, even when it is at the expense of your free will. If you are in opposition, you are a threat. These types of groups deliberately indoctrinate their members by owning them. They control and manipulate their membership through the collective Belief Systems. Destructive force is their false strength.

The people in charge of governments, political groups, corporations, religions, and all factions have played this game of deliberate manipulation throughout the time continuum. Although there is the delusional illusion that their control and manipulations benefit and serve them, they are legends in their own minds. They appear to be able to control their flocks, membership, or converts forever. However, their lasting term of force is always temporary. Whatever the time period, long or short, it is always a temporary use of force. Why? Because there is always a shift in control! This is the exchange of a force. Even at the top, the enforcers force a change.

A rebellion within the ranks eventually occurs because deep within the Consciousness of you as a participant, or the participants of the group Consciousness in which you are, changes happen. South American governments have been affected by coups, revolutions, and rebellions, but what changes? Just a shift at the top. The Truth is that at the top you are not considered in the exchange of force. You simply must continue not to be manipulated.

Governments, religions, corporations, and groups appear to change currently and historically, yet there is no *real* change. The average person must "fit in" to the new and old rules, which are really the same. The top appears to change. Your life remains the same. The manipulation and control are also the same. Since you are considered belonging to the middle or the bottom, the manipulation continues. The surviving middle and bottom continue. The rebellion may not be understood at the time, but the rebellion always comes in one way or another. And life goes on.

Quite naturally, in fact, a shift takes place. How it occurs is through the paradigm, eyes, or slant of the overtaking force. This is how history is written and interpreted. Interpretation is not based on fact, especially for the lower rungs on the ladder in the shift. They have to keep going. They are called survivors. Their interpretation of the change is not a factor. The factor is what they are told happened or is happening. After the many battles of war on this planet, the civilian populations, whatever side they were on, had to come out of hiding, pick up whatever pieces were left of their lives, and keep going.

A paradigm has shifted nonetheless. The victory and the loss are only seen and experienced through the perceptions of the winner's and the loser's mentality. Independent opinions are not part of the game. You either go along with the shift in force or else! Sometimes it is difficult to see who the good guys and the bad guys are when your life is turned upside down. The shift of force happens this way in Duality. Individual Power does not factor into this change.

Victory does not always appear as the result of the battle, but in the shift of who is in control of the situation for the moment. The moment is however many minutes, days, weeks, or years the force of the "victor" remains intact. Browsing through "his"-story, more times than not, the rebel leaders and possibly the followers become the heroes. But keep in mind, these heroes are still considered the trouble-makers by those who have been overthrown in the shift of force.

Eventually, whatever the time frame is, the same questions begin to arise. Does this paradigm of the leaders' Belief Systems serve you? Does this collective Belief System have value? Does it serve anyone? Does it serve "us", those without any real input?

Look back through your own life. Recall those events where you recognized that your individual shift in your Consciousness did not fit with what was going on in that time frame. Do you *feel* you had little or no Power? Did you begin to realize with *real eyes* you were not willing to participate with the physical and even the spiritual dynamics of the current collective state of Consciousness surrounding you? These same questions rise to the surface regardless of the time frame, eon, century, or decade.

The winds of change in the collective Consciousness are blowing with gale force all over the planet.

The uncertainty of the un-direction is making itself obvious.

The reality of Duality is shifting.

The New Question is: What is Real for me?

Now you begin to ask your Self if you are *willing* to continue to participate in a Belief System which no longer benefits you or the collective Consciousness on this planet? You become the leader of your own rebellion. This is a gigantic leap in Taking Back Your Power. You are becoming conscious to what is correct for you and to what is not. The right or wrong no longer has the force of judgment over you.

What is correct for you? Ask your Self this question over and over again. Where does it resonate to you in your body? Do you *feel* some of your old Belief Systems are making your body feel sick? If they are, your body is responding to the question and is now asking you to pay attention. You are not experiencing that ill feeling for nothing. Your body knows you are experiencing a change of Consciousness at your Cellular Level. Your body requires you to be *aware*.

Recognize that the most frightening aberration of the control and manipulations of the "leading" ruling forces come in the guise of good intentions. Remember Hitler. Oh, Hitler's rhetoric sounded so good to the citizens of Germany. Remember those who blindly followed Jim Jones to Jonestown? It was called Jonestown for a reason. Remember the Branch Davidians? Of course, the good intentions sounded great, but the end results were suffering and death. What was the good? Oh, it was good for the leaders, but not so great for the ones being lead to slaughter. Remember, the leader knows best! This is *not* so!

You know best for your Self when you become Conscious to the Truth of your Consciousness

Look at the dynamics of family behaviors as you narrow the scope of the manipulation and control to familial Belief Systems. Imposing an idea over your free will and the Truth of you happens each day, without judging parents. Remember, they are products of controlling and manipulating Belief Systems too.

Remember the "sins" of the fathers (mothers) are continued to the sons (children). Forget about gender. The factor is the control of the Belief Systems. Why? The sins or the unconscious Consciousness is experienced over and over again generationally because of the embedded, limiting Belief Systems ingrained in the human experience. It doesn't matter the lineage of cultural, ethnicity, religion, political or group dynamics. What makes the huge effect is how much the Belief Systems of any particular group are *managed* by the rules of the rulers.

What matters is how much the collective or group consciously accepts the rules of the management and considers it their own. This is the importance. It was of the utmost importance that the James Jones followers accepted Jim Jones as the authority figure of the "father". This effect of the "father's" Belief System is what affects the dynamics of the relationships for the followers. The father can come in all sorts of guises as the authority figure for an individual or for the group.

The "do-gooder" can say "I do this because I love you". A small child, although at his or her deepest knowing of the Truth knows this is not correct, is conditioned to *belief system* that this is *love*. They have no choice but to take this form of love as reality. "I do this because I love you." This is the worst-case scenario of control and manipulation. Physical and sexual abuse is heinous. But it happens all the time. It is accepted all the time.

It doesn't matter what the background – social, financial, or religious. Physical and sexual abuse is the norm for the abused. The worst of the worst is that the behavior is horrendous and generational. This is the most horrific example of control and manipulation, and yet it continues. The victim becomes the sacrificial lamb, sometimes for the rest of the family to have a roof over their head, food on the table, and clothes on their back. The behavior is inexcusable but it is excused over and over again. Denial becomes the pardon.

Your First Chakra embodies all the manipulating, fear-based Duality Programs and their *reasonable* explanations to implement and defend the use of controlling force by the ruling factions. The 7 Chakra System is a dualistic approach to life. Chakra is simply a Sanskrit word meaning *circle*. Each Chakra is a circle of influence in your body which contains information.

The behavior and the results of this behavior begin when you are taught to Give Away Your Power. You are systematically taught to *believe* you have No Power. You are systematically embedded in your unconscious Consciousness that you are *less*, do not *deserve*, and must sacrifice your life to a Belief System to keep you in line. You are *taught* to be less. You are expected to be controlled and manipulated.

It begins in the womb with whatever fear or fears your parents have embedded within them. Whatever fears your parents have, they are transferred to you. You then *think* the limitations with which you are programmed are *your* collective Belief Systems. No, they are not. This doesn't mean you don't have your issues. Whatever you bring to the table that you have not cleared from your own continuum of experiences, they all belong to you.

Within the contract with your parents, biological or adopted, you choose the *perfect* couple to experience in order to heal your emotional continuing continuous issues. Each lifetime is the *perfect* lifetime to move through the debilitating, emotional issues, to heal them, and to get clearly conscious. The key here is being clearly conscious of who you are. Who you are *not* is the programming.

However, you don't realize this until you are willing and committed to realize with *real eyes* who you are *not*. Not wanna-be, wish-to-be, hope-to-be, but Who You Are without the detriments of the Duality Programming. You have to figure it out your Self. No one, absolutely no one outside of you can do it for you.

The insecurity and powerlessness from the Self-Debasing Duality Belief Systems move to your Second Chakra, the Sexual Generative Creative Chakra.

This Second Chakra, because of the fear embedded in your First Chakra, is so dense that the manifestation can only be powerless, sickly, and dysfunctional, exhibiting the behavioral patterns of being controlled and manipulated by the outside world. Your inside world becomes the outside product of the victim – the abused, the martyr, or whatever the description. And you will fit the description to a V. The capital V is the chant of the Victim Program. The capital V is the sign of the powerless.

There is no expression of Unconditional Love or Total Acceptance in this dense field of 3D Duality. The fear programming is too thick and viscous in this Second Chakra. It does however draw to you, in the Law of Dysfunctional Distraction, the perfect relationships to make you wrong, bad, and less. Always in the mode of seeking validation, you are caught looking for love in all the places that don't work. However, from a clear conscious standpoint, you now have the reason *why* you repeat these relationships.

DON'T KID YOUR SELF...

Dysfunctional repetition is NOT a learning experience
Dysfunctional repetition is Giving Your Power Away

Each lifetime, for you as an individual and for the group or groups in which you are an active or passive participant, has a purpose and a function in the development and the expansion of your Consciousness and your awareness of your Self. Overcoming the illusions of the programming, whether embedded in the Double Helix of your DNA or deoxyribonucleic acid, is the hereditary material in humans and almost all other organisms. The key word here is hereditary. Hereditary is part of your Cellular Memory. Hereditary begins in the womb. You begin to memorize the experiences you are having from the moment the sperm hits the egg. You are in!

Some of the programming you have in this lifetime is not yours. It is a by-product of your conditioning from your immediate family from the very beginning of *you*. You agreed to it in your contract with your parents and your family. You wrote the challenges to help you remember why you came here to Earth. You created the challenges to consciously overcome your emotional issues and the emotional issues you have with your immediate family. You can call your journey the road through hell or the road to enlightenment. You get to choose as you become clearly conscious. As you get clearly conscious, you begin to get your Power back.

Overcoming the Duality Programs may appear to be a complex process. In Truth, it is not. Emotionally hooked to past experiences and hooked to past relationships makes the challenges difficult. Why? The answer is due to the emotional attachments to the Judgment, Lack, and Take-Away Programs. The Duality deception is that you are not smart enough, strong enough, or never clear enough to overcome the programming. Your emotional hooks to the programming bind you so you can continue to be controlled and manipulated through your Self fears.

Making everything appear complicated is the perfect way to keep you and your energy confined and controlled within the low-based resonance of your First and Second Chakras of the old, tired, and run-down 7 Chakra System. Fear is the manipulating, comatose *belief systeming* which is driving the energy of this old system.

The confusion of Duality Reality produces behavioral patterns based upon what you *think* you know and upon your emotionally-driven fears. Your awakening, your wake-up call, is you taking a stand for your Self. Your awakening is you choosing to be clearly conscious. Your awakening is choosing to become more clearly aware of who you are instead of who you *think* you are based upon who you were told you are. You are so much more than how you have been defined in the Third Dimensional Limited Reality. You are so much more! That's a fact!

Transcending the old thought patterns, the old versions of behaviors, and the old limiting Belief Systems occurs when you expand your body's energy as you expand your awareness of your Self from your Cellular Level. As you connect to your Self from the inside out, the outside has a deeper connection to you. You also cease to be emotionally hooked on how the outside world affects you. In fact, the outside validation program has less and less effect on you. Why? You are now consciously creating the effect that *you desire.* Your world is up to you.

As you clear your emotional attachments, you become conscious of how you have been programmed to give away your Power. You begin to assess what means the most to you. The connection to your spiritual expansion of Consciousness within your physical body begins to take place. The spiritual aspect of you is physical and is connected to your intuition. Trust your intuition and spiritually you expand your connection to your Self, your world, this Earth, this Non-Duality Universe, and the Multi-verse, and to all life.

Spirituality is a clear state of your Consciousness, not a concept or some religious practice pretending to make you divine. You are already divine. You just have to accept this. You are special because you are you. Everyone is special in their uniqueness.

Spirituality is being grounded in creativity, which is your own Power based upon your Truth.

Your transformation and transfiguration are the physical alignments which release the oppositional Belief Systems of polarity within your human body. This physical change is the advent of becoming the Real Human. Why? You no longer "need" to be in opposition to your Self or be confined to the figure 8 of Duality's B.S. of infinity. You are releasing your Self from the limitations of the polaristic infinity resonance that is the trap of Duality.

This transformation and transfiguration are how you becoming YOU in your unlimited Humanness, spiraling with your Power, your Self, and your creativity into experiences that YOU create. Free of limitations…free of Duality…and free of Belief Systems. What does that look like? This is your opportunity to become the Real Human YOU.

So, how did you and all the you's in the human race get to be so unconscious in the first place? Even though throughout the centuries avatars and teachers showed up to give the message that you are more and not less? But the *less* and the *victim* programming continues to be the prevalent theme. The core reason to keeping the bar of Consciousness so low on planet Earth is FEAR! When you are unaware of any other levels of Consciousness within your physical body, or unaware there are other expressions of Consciousness, your behavioral patterns – good, bad or indifferent – result in repetitious patterns which are not always productive for a healthy life or lifestyle.

Not only do these ineffective behavioral patterns affect this life, but your other lifetimes have the same ineffective experiences because you have been taught to be less and to fear your own Power. These ineffective behaviors emerge over and over again from the programs embedded in your unconscious Consciousness, which are your Cellular Experiences. You create, do, and act upon what you *think* you know and not upon what you *really* know. As a composite of experiences, if you are not clear about who you are, you create from a database in your left computer/brain which only knows the programs. You cannot get clear about your Self in your computer/brain. Ever met a nurturing, loving computer? No!

The dysfunctional, individual behavioral pattern continues, and it plays itself forward into the group collective behavior. Why? Because like attracts like and dysfunction attracts dysfunction. This is the Law of Dysfunctional Distraction. Birds of a feather flock together and when the lead bird is out of whack consciously, so is the group. So, let's just follow that leader…into chaos.

How do you make the required changes to Take Back Your Power? Simply by your willingness to open your Self up beyond the taught and embedded limited Belief Systems and by your willingness to connect to all the levels of your Consciousness. Will it happen all at once? No. This would be difficult for the physicality of your body's nervous system. Your Childish Adult Ego is used to running to keep his or her job intact. Letting go of that survival/victim program is serious business.

The Shift begins when you intend to willingly expand your horizons, as in plural. In an expanded awareness, horizons are no longer vertical or horizontal. Your horizons are in all directions. All directions are expansive. With unlimited views of your Self, your world, and your abilities, you begin to recognize how Multi-Dimensional you are. Take it one step, one giant leap, or many steps at a time. Give your physical body the chance to keep up with your expanding awareness. It's a progressive process. Take the time. Why blow your nervous system's circuits, shut down, and regress? Be gentle with your Self. Stay open and enjoy the progression in your process. It is progressive. This is what expansion is. A progressive process.

As you allow your Self to develop your Multi-Dimensional Self, you become aware of what is best for you. Your behavior changes by your choices to be in charge of your body and your Self. Your behavioral changes are not determined by your physical and emotional pain. In the old programming, change is supposed to be painful, otherwise you didn't pay your dues. What a B.S. Program! Pain is not growth. Pain is pain. Pain is physical. Emotional pain is physical and triggers the physical pain throughout the physicality of your body. When you don't *feel*, you have become numb to your Self. There is no growth, no expansion of Consciousness, or well-beingness when you are numb. Numb is not alive.

As you develop your awareness, changes happen more naturally and less painfully. Sometimes in the changes, you change groups. You shift how you participate. If a group in which you participated, without judging the group dynamics, is not supportive of your growth and is a detriment to your growth, you know, understand, and comprehend it is time to move forward. This group and you are just not on the same wavelength. In Wordology Is

Your Biology, the word "group" means to GRO-UP. You are **gro**wing **up** and it is the time to move forward.

Each group in which you participated reflects your growing up process. Now it is not just a process, but a progressive process. The progressive process is a huge difference from the Karma, Lessons, and Re-incarnation Programs of being processed over and over. Picture a manufacturing rendering plant. You go through the Duality assembly line and come out the same way you came in. It's the same old baloney. But you do have a choice.

As you change your paradigms – remember, you are Multi-Dimensional – you recognize your thoughts are expressions of your energies based upon whether you're the clarity of your Consciousness or not. Your thoughts emerge from your Consciousness. Your Consciousness is your energy resonating at different octaves or on different wavelengths producing the various or different levels from which your Consciousness sends out your messages. From these various wavelengths of Consciousness, you create the attractions to individuals or groups which are vibrating with you. If you are full of fear, you attract fear-based people. If your wavelengths are from a clearer base of Consciousness, you attract more open, clear people into your life. This is how your Consciousness works.

As you awaken your Consciousness from your Cellular Level, initially to your Self, you will experience both subtle and dramatic changes in your Self and in your life. Sometimes the subtle shifts will be more noticeable than the dramatic changes. Why? Because the programming expects trauma-dramas. You are on the lookout for the trauma-dramas. You have been taught to expect them.

Whether they are trauma-dramas initiated by you or someone else, who can tell the difference between the spider and the fly? They're both caught up in the web of trauma-dramas. The trauma-dramas could be your families, your friends, your co-workers, or some group. You have been programmed to resonate with trauma-dramas. What a better way to keep you from being in your own Power!

On your course of waking up, you can get side-tracked. Why? Because you side-track your Self. You are testing the waters. You are testing your Self. Some of the tests may be amusing, but more times than not, they are not funny or fun. They are, however, experiences to show you where you are and where you are not. You are awakening on many levels of your Consciousness. Through your experiences, without Self-Judgment of good, bad or indifferent, you are giving your Self the opportunity to begin to integrate your Self. As you begin this connective progressive process, you are teaching your Self what resonates with you and what does not.

In the systematic development of waking up, everyone experiences in their own unique way their own version or versions of their personal system of awakening. No one has the right to be critical of anyone's version. Everyone is on their own timeline in their continuum of lifetimes. Each progressive process is exclusive to each individual.

Sometimes the process is not progressive. When it is not, it pertains to when you or someone hangs on to old Belief Systems which are really no longer relevant to your life. Holding on to the dysfunctional past, regardless of the time frame, whether it's this lifetime or previous ones, is a perfect example. The longer you hang on, the longer it takes to wake up and be fully conscious of your Self and for your Self.

Groups also have the opportunity to grow up and wake up together as a group. The dynamics are the same. The higher purpose of the collective Consciousness of the group is brought about by the expanded Consciousness of the individuals who are participating together for a great cause.

The path to Consciousness, the path to awakening, is very powerful through the group Consciousness. The group's resonance supports those involved in the group as well as the individuals supporting their Selves and each other. In this case, one person makes a difference, and then the dynamics of the group make a larger difference because all are on the same wavelength as contributors to life, the planet, the group, and to the individual members.

Mohammed Yunus is a perfect example of someone who made a difference locally, nationally, and globally. He created phenomenal successes by assisting people out of poverty through a Micro-Credit System. He is the banker to the "poor". He provides opportunities for a hand up instead of a hand out. He believed his system is a scalable and cost-effective way to reduce poverty around the world. He is one person who changed the collective Belief System about how the "poor" is viewed as "lazy and no good". Through the individuals he assisted, they in turn changed their own lives, their families, and their communities. A Shift in Consciousness happened.

There is no right way or wrong way to experience your individual awakening. The actual circumstances are up to you. The actual experiences may differ from individual to individual. Wherever you are, it is the perfect place to begin.

Whatever the circumstance, you Self-created the place and the circumstances. Whether through a major loss such as a Near-Death Experience, job, divorce, death of a loved one, illness, traumatic experience, or some event which changes your perspective about your Self and your life, the wake-up call sounds the alarm. "Time to wake up!" You have a choice. You can wake up or sleep through the alarm.

The purpose of the progressive process is to bring you out of the darkness. The darkness is the fear. Fear is yours and everyone's *lack of information*. Fear is the lack of information about how the Duality Systems works and works you over and over again. Duality is the ultimate manipulation program.

Do you think the ones in force at this time are any different than the ones in force at any other time? Of course not! They do not want you to be powerful within your Self! You wouldn't fit into the herd if you did! The idea is to be *of It*. "It" is being your <u>I</u>nner <u>T</u>ruth, and not the "true" of the manipulators.

Truth is your Truth. True is the programming. As long as you continue the Belief Systems of the B.S. Duality Programs, you are hooked. It is as simple as that. The goal is to be here fully alive on Earth and *not* exist in the Duality Programs of Earth. To be here without Duality is to create your life consciously and fearlessly. Isn't this a better way to be? You are in your Power.

With you and everyone else who chooses to evolve beyond the programming, there is the wonderful opportunity of creating a New Earth. Creating a New Earth cannot happen by existing in the seductive trauma-dramas of the Karma, Lessons, and Re-incarnation Programs. *Yes*, it *is* this simple!

As you get the facts and let go of the emotional validation attachment to the right and wrong programming of the conditioning, you *see* the light. Light is information. The information is found at your Cellular Level of Consciousness buried deep underneath the physicality of your emotional attachments to the Duality Programs, which are not Real. They are manipulative. When you are manipulated and controlled, you are *being* the Duality Programs. Therefore, the re-creation aspect of Duality continues to be re-created by you!

Where is the newness there? There is none, only the illusion of newness. Yes, the technology changes. However, the core fear-based Duality Programs remain the same, embedded in your physical body until you say, "enough is enough!"

**This old tired-out Duality paradigm of Fear Programs
and its dysfunctional behaviors
no longer serve you or humanity.**

**Ask your Self,
isn't it time to move on and get over it?!!**

Your expansion of awareness and integration of your Multi-Dimensional levels and spaces of Consciousness affect the evolutionary Transcension of your DNA, your biology, and your emotional attachments to the programming. This occurs as you develop and create for your Self new practices of thought, speech, language, behaviors and actions. The old behavioral games of conflict do not have to take up your time, efforts, or drain your energy.

Ask your Self, "Is it worth one molecule, one particle, or one cell of my life and creativity to be emotionally and physically hooked into the trauma-dramas?" If you answer yes, or if you don't know yet, then you are still hooked into the Judgment, Lack, and Take-Away Programs. If you say *no*, then you are willing to move forward. Then do it!

The games become irrelevant. The old control and manipulation games are worth nothing. Comprehend that what you *think* and what you *say* become your life. How powerful is this?! What you say about your Self in the moment is Who You Are and Who You Are Being. You can either use your language, words, and vocabulary which have force over you and keep you controlled and manipulated *or* you can use your language, words, and vocabulary to support you to be powerful and unlimited. At this point of becoming conscious, your "claim" to not knowing what's going on doesn't work anymore. You cannot claim ignorance. Ignorance is not bliss. Ignorance is lack of information. Ignorance is ignorance.

Here you are at a culmination or turning point to make the choices to release and dissolve the emotional hooks to your old practices and old behavioral patterns immersed in the old, non-relevant Duality Programs. Dysfunctional old behaviors and patterns are not worth your time, effort, or creative abilities. They are not worth you or your life! Your source of empowerment is not and has never been outside of you.

You realize with "real eyes" that you are so much more than what you have been programmed to accept by Duality's recycled programs.

You deserve so much more life!

As you begin to access your Cellular Memory, you comprehend that all of this Cellular information is your personal database of experiences from throughout your continuing continuous continuum. **Through your emotional body, you take all these experiences personally.** In doing so, your Childish Adult Ego's job is to play out the trauma-dramas with anyone and everyone who is written in your script. As the center of your world, you are the key player. And sometimes when you are not, you throw your Self into the trauma-drama conflict to get validation for your Childish Adult Ego's verification that he or she is doing their job. How perfect – or perfectly ridiculous – is this? Pretty ridiculous!

Look back to the times when you asked your Self, "How did I get dragged into this situation?" Easy! You picked up the vibes, emotionally jumped in to "fix" the situation, got trapped in the web of the trauma-drama, and stayed in it for as long as it took for you to extricate your Self.

The significant question is, how many lifetimes did it take you to realize with *real eyes* that you didn't have to jump in? You didn't have to replay the trauma-drama soap opera at all. As a matter of fact, as you wake up, you *see* what a waste of your creativity and time it has been to do trauma-dramas at all.

> **"Life is a matter of facts.**
> **So, stop living the fiction that doesn't matter!**
> **YOU MATTER."**
>
> **- Sherryism**

On the flip side of the coin, is it *your* trauma-drama you pulled others into? Or is it *you* continually throwing your Self into someone else's trauma-drama, instead of living a healthy, productive life? You have got to make a choice here. Wake up and smell the wonderful aroma of life. Or stay unconscious and life stinks!

When your Crown Chakra is buried up your First Chakra, if it looks like "it", smells like "it", feels like "it", and you exclaim "life is shitty!", then it *is*. The light at the end of the tunnel is your head sliding down your descending colon looking for a way out. Comprehension is the sound of the huge POP when your head comes sliding out! At last the light! What a sight!

The limiting boundaries of the Third Dimensional Duality Fear Belief Systems restrict your visions. No kidding. Now do you realize with *real eyes* where your head has been buried? The programming restricts and confines your imagination, your creativity, and your abilities to manifest the life you deserve. You do not deserve to settle for less.

Through these demanding, Self-Sacrificing programs, you and everyone else, rich or poor, famous or unknown, sabotage your Selves somewhere along the line. It happens not by chance. It happens because of the Judgment, Lack, and Take-Away Programs running unconsciously at your Cellular Level of Consciousness. These programs reinforce limitations. Regardless of acquisitions, material wealth, status, or money, a Belief System with limitations and time limits prevails.

Look around the world. Look around the U.S. Does what is happening look like the Duality picture? Of course it does!

As you give your Self permission to let go and release the programs, you release the restrictive density of the fear contained in your cells. As the physical density of the fear is released, your Cellular body has clean, open spaces. In these cleared, open spaces, there is room for a Consciousness which is Multi-Dimensional and unlimited.

The concept of the word "room" is irrelevant. In Third Dimensional terms, "room" would imply boundaries. At the Cellular Level, the clearing of the density is the physical releasing of the resonance of fear. Fear is heavy, dense, and restrictive. These are the physical properties of fear.

In the Transcension of your Consciousness, you are resonating at an expanded level of awareness. You are waking up!

As the resonance of your cells increase, so does the resonance of your DNA. Your biology and your health also experience an increase and expansion of resonance as you release the density and dullness of the Duality Fear Programs. In your expanded level of awareness, your expanded Consciousness becomes the resonance assisting you in creating a more unlimited way of living. Your world becomes larger! Everything in your life transforms. Imagine this!

Your Resonance is your Power!

You are the Life, the Power, and the Generator of *your* Resonance. Frequency and vibration are just by-products of Resonance. So, what's really important is how you are resonating. *Your* Resonance is the key to *your* Power.

You are In Charge of Your Life. When you have this clarity and the clarification, you can *see* the potentials and the possibilities becoming *real* in your life, instead of just dreaming your dreams, never to be fully actualized. You are becoming Multi-Dimensional.

In the process of clearing the restricting Belief Systems of Fear from your cells, your thoughts, your behaviors, and your actions become clear. What also becomes clear is the "how" you create, implement, manifest, and actualize your life. The more consciously clear you are of what you create, the easier the implementation, manifestation, and actualization. Clear implementation results from being clearly conscious.

When you're not clear, your implementation gets hung up in the Past, hooked to the Duality Belief Systems of being less-than and limited. So, it doesn't matter what the calendar date is. You are stuck in that dense Duality resonance of the Past, **validating the invalidation of your Self** again. You are disconnected from your Truth and your Realness.

Life is Real

It is NOT a Reality

Transcending, moving on, overcoming, and going beyond the old thought patterns and the old versions of the behaviors and the old Belief Systems happens as you wake up. As you wake up, you expand your awareness and become more conscious of all the Multi-Dimensional talents you have. Your energy field also expands simultaneously. You *feel* it. Everyone *feels* it. The "it" is your clear energy field.

Every thought, word, and idea is put into action by you through your behaviors. This is the expression of your energy. Your energy field is called:

- your aura by the metaphysical community
- your bio-energy field by the medical community
- your electromagnetic field by the scientific community

It's the same description, just different Wordology.

Through your energy field, you are expressing your Self. People are *feeling* your energy. Everything is energy and the expression of energy. Your energy is the movement <u>or</u> non-movement of your Consciousness. If you are stuck in a Fear Program, consciously or unconsciously, your energy is low, without vitality, and you are existing in the fears. You are not living life to your fullest. This is how your Consciousness and energy work together, or NOT!

If you are stuck and your head is up your First Chakra in a Duality Fear Program, then your energy is stuck in fear. What is happening in your energy field is you are creating some pretty icky experiences of fearful, stuck energy. Wow!

What a formula to attract relationships, wealth, and health when your head is buried up your… you get the idea?

Fear attracts fear without being conscious. This is how the Law of Attraction/Distraction works in Third Dimension Duality. Birds of a feather are stuck in the First Chakra together!!! How fun is that? Not quite!

In the beginning, humans grouped together or separated their Selves into tribes. These tribes regionalized into states, countries, nations, and now globalization. Through contemporary commerce, everyone has become linked internationally. The internet is *the* tool which has brought people together in ways never imagined even ten years ago. Through Facebook, Twitter, LinkedIn, Instagram, and the whole of social media, the look of the world has changed. What hasn't changed is that fears can still be promoted. Now it's not just through the media of TV, radio, and print, but instantly, with a touch of a keypad, the Duality Fear Programs can be transmitted around the globe.

The collective Consciousness is experiencing a paradigm shift, not over time, but in an instant. The issues are that the brain is a computer downloading information faster than it was constructed to do, the body is being bombarded with information at a rate faster than the body can physically process, and the instant access to information is challenging the physicality of the body. It is also challenging the emotional body. Waking up and expanding your Consciousness by comprehending your Self and how you choose to create, live, and participate in life is more crucial and critical than ever before in the history of humanity.

The old model to control and manipulate groups of people or individuals to be separate or separated from each other and promoting a disconnection between everyone was much easier to do in the past. This old "grid" of the collective is breaking down. It is about time and it is about timing. The old reality that says your personal life and professional life are separated is not viable. You *are* your personal life *and* your professional life.

The underlying separation patterns of thought in the past were used to keep people separated from each other. These old thought patterns perpetuated the control and manipulation programs under the separatism paradigm. The paradigm of more-than-less-than, haves-and-have-nots, and controller and controlled was so evident. Yet it was so ignored. This is just the game of the ritual of Duality. Whatever side of the board game you are on, the other side is always better. Remember the grass is always greener? NOT!

The rich against the poor, the boss against the employees, the religions against other religions, the countries against countries, the allies (whoever they are) against the enemies (whoever they are)… Notice how they change throughout history. The funny part of this shift is that it is the materialism aspect of Duality that infused the change. The projections to grow globally, to reach larger markets and audiences, and to determine what is acceptable and what is not created a wave from both sides of the game board wanting the same thing.

Now it is about wearing the right clothes, having the right shoes, carrying the right purse, and looking like everyone else. Knock-offs have become an industry. People are knocking their Selves off to look like the "haves"! Who can tell the difference? There is none because some of the "haves" are beginning to look like the "have-nots". The Truth is that there is no difference!

Take ten people in the front of a room, line them up, cut them in half, and look inside. They ALL LOOK THE

SAME! What makes them illusionally different is the perception of their Selves. Money has nothing to do with it. Whether rich or poor, the programs are all the same. The only difference is how each person creates their reality through the programs.

When you get down to the basics, the basics are the same. Judgment, Lack, and Take-Away from Self are the underlying Belief Systems of Duality in 3D. Just like a movie, 3D pretends to look Real. 3D is not Real when you are creating your life through the Fear Programs.

Whether you are a member of the have-or-have-nots, more-than-less-thans, or lower-or-higher-on-the-totem-pole in the delusion, everyone ends up at the same place, the end of the line. Religions preach that you came here to die. Some native cultures profess it is a good day to die. Some paradigms insist "the way it is, is the way it is". The 3D beat goes on and on and on through the centuries. Boring, boring, boring. Where's the creativity of newness? Sure, technology got better. So what? We can blow each other up in much better ways. The kill factor is faster and quicker.

The point is not how much quicker and more proficient you survive through the Fear Programs, but how much clearer and faster you become YOU as you Take Back Your Power and live your life as YOU choose to live your life. In 3D, you are one small aspect in a huge ocean of surviving. Standing in your Truth and accepting your Power, you are the determining aspect of you and your life.

There is no requirement to participate in the control and manipulating 3D experience. You consciously create your experience. Now you are the experience and you are the experiencer experiencing your experiences, instead of not having the experience to experience your experiences. It's a huge difference being in your Power no matter what is going on outside of you. Now, what goes on outside of you is how you choose your "outside" and how you choose to participate.

Right now, the deeper spiritual rise of Consciousness is surfacing around the world from within each of us. Spiritual has zero to do with religion. Spirituality is a Consciousness of clarity. Spirituality occurs when you *ground* your expanded, clear Consciousness of awareness throughout your entire body, in every cell, particle, and molecule, right down to the beginning source of you from your continuum. Spirituality is the practical aspect of your Consciousness which does NOT exist in Duality's Fear Programs.

There is no reason to Judge your Self that you Lack something and Take It Away from your Self and your life. Spirituality is living your life fully and fulfilled, connected to the Godness within your Self. Spirituality is being grounded in your body. Spirituality is consciously creating your life every day, being the Non-Emotional Observer (NEO), not getting caught up in the trauma-dramas, yours or anyone else's, and Being In Charge of Your Life and Creating newness, whatever that is for you.

In Quantum Physics, Quantum Mechanics, and Quantum Theory, in order to change anything, it has to be observed. To observe non-emotionally, which is not being stuck in the emotional experiences of the past, you can *see* your Role and everyone else's Roles in the experience. It doesn't mean that what happened was acceptable. However, by being the Non-Emotional Observer (NEO), you can move forward, letting go of the past. You can release victimization and start to Take Back Your Power.

Emotions keep you victimized. *Feeling* from the Heart frees you to be powerful. Emotion and *feeling* are not the same.

Their resonances do not match. *Feeling* is Clear Consciousness. Emotions are fear.

"Feelings are the Essence of the Heart in a Clear Conscious Moment...

Emotions are the descent into the traumatic past re-lived!"

-Sherryism

Spirituality is NOT being out of body and leaving your body to fend for itself! Spirituality is NOT suffering. That's the religious programs. Spirituality is not the more-than-less-than program, thinking you know more than someone else. Spirituality is not sitting on a mountainside waiting for a change and chanting about it. Spirituality is NOT being a victim of the Universe, or now the Multi-verse. Spirituality is NOT some ethereal "thing" bringing enlightenment through a tragedy or suffering.

"Spirituality is not a journey outside your Self, Spirituality is the connection with Self!"

-Sherryism

Spirituality is the practical applications of living life consciously. Spirituality is common sense. Spirituality is loving unconditionally. Spirituality is being connected to your Self and allowing your Self to be connected to others on the same wavelength, vibration, frequency, or resonance without judging others for their version of their wavelengths. Spirituality is total and complete acceptance of your Self.

Being spiritual means, you do not have to compare spiritual practices, that one is better than another. Spirituality is not setting intentions and then sitting around in this lifetime waiting for the Universe to do something for you. Spirituality requires *your* participation.

This is a physical 3D world requiring movement. So, when you intend something clearly, you have to participate. Get up off your First Chakra, and with the rest of your 7 Chakra System in alignment, get moving!

Participation is another important key to Taking Back Your Power. "No participation" means you are waiting around for something to happen. For sure things will happen, but not what you are expecting. You will get a whole lot of what you didn't expect simply because you stood around, waited around, sometimes for lifetimes, wasting valuable productive time, waiting for your intentions to happen.

STOP sitting around and get moving! Be the Power, not the force, that you require to implement your life.

If you don't implement your life consciously, someone unconscious will implement your life for you!

Step up to the plate! Stop feeding your Self the B.S. Programs of Duality. Stop being a victim and the victimizer of your Self. Stand up *to* your Self. You cannot stand up to anyone else if you don't Stand up *to* and *for* Your Self. This is not about conflict. This is about Standing for Your Truth, whether someone agrees with you or not. To Take Back Your Power, you must validate your Self. If someone validates you, this is frosting on the cake. You must be the whole cake. You must be all the ingredients for your Self and your life.

You can have the cake and eat it too. You are the cake that feeds you. Feed your Self what nourishes and nurtures you. If it is not your Truth in Unconditional Love and Total Acceptance for your Self and others, then it is CRAP!

Stay in your life. Participate fully. Stay out of Self-Judgment. Stay out of Lack. And Stay out of the Take-Away Programs.

Otherwise, you miss all the opportunities coming your way at whatever age or stage you are.

Becoming a Multi-Dimensional Being is the Consciousness of Allness within your Self. It is accepting, recognizing, and realizing with *real eyes* that all the potentials and the possibilities of your creativity are within you. Then and only then can you begin to bring the possibilities and potentials into the physical actualities of Realness.

You are Multi-Dimensional. Multi-Dimensional means multiple, not single. From Oneness, we are moving toward ALLNESS.

Before you can get to ALLNESS from Oneness...

- **You must get your head out of your First Chakra**
- **Examine your Belief Systems (the B.S. Programs)**
- **Let go of the victimization illusion**
- **Take Back Your Power**
- **See all your assets by being purposely Conscious**
- **Be the Non-Emotional Observer (NEO)**
- **Be the Conscious Creator**
- **Be in Charge of Your life**
- **Create Newness**

Now you are *being* who you are. Otherwise, you are stuck in **validating the invalidation of your Self** through the Fear Duality Programs over and over again as the victim of the B.S. Programs. Boring for sure!

ALL TIME - NO TIME

No matter how time is perceived from the view of the past, present, and future, time is really *This Moment*. Since your body holds at the Cellular Level every experience, every word, every language of every one of your backgrounds, whether you recall them or not, all of this information is stored as your Cellular Memory. In this recorded information are the sounds, smells, impressions, expressions, and experiences, whether you understand them or not, of your lifetimes and of your scripts. Your body stores the data as experiences.

Your left computer/brain is connected to the Male right side of body. It runs the Duality Programs of Judgment, Lack, and Take-Away through your Childish Adult Ego (CAE). Your CAE is the survivalist. Your CAE continues to run and re-manifest through the programs in your continuum, caught up in the loop of Karma, Lessons, and Re-incarnation. Your right computer/brain is connected to your Female left side, which is your Consciousness of creativity, inspiration, and intuition.

Why would the very forceful Childish Adult Ego (CAE) want you to clear and heal your Self? It will be unemployed and unemployable if you get clear. For this reason, your CAE keeps you in the continuous loop of the Duality Programs by continuing to block your connection to your body. After all, yours or anyone's Childish Adult Ego would wanty-needy to keep the long-term, guaranteed, continuous employment. Good grief or bad grief if you choose to get clear in the CAE's perception, which is the CAE's reception, deception, and conception.

Your Childish Adult Ego (CAE) will do anything to survive. It will even kill you because this amazing Childish Adult Ego knows you will return to 3D Duality. Your CAE knows full well you have bought into the Karma, Lessons, and Re-incarnation Programs.

Your Childish Adult Ego (CAE) is running the programs through your left computer/brain, manifesting the trauma-dramas, experiences, situations, and conditions through your Male side. This one side of Duality works continuously to your disadvantage. Repeating the dysfunction cycle is your CAE's claim to fame. It's a legend in his or her own mind, whatever your gender from whatever lifetime! Now you can *see* and "get" how this re-cycle bin of Karma, Lessons, and Re-incarnation works. Nothing changes.

**As long as you hang on to these
unreasonable 3D Duality Programs,
the unreasonable programs run your life unreasonably**

You are a compilation of all of your experiences. How wondrous is this! When it becomes wondrous it *is* simple. You do not have to wander continuously around wondering why you are always doing the same thing and expecting different results from lifetime to lifetime, year to year, day after day.

You have been taught to *belief system* you do not have the full ability to become your Self without the "outside" paradigm telling you who you are. Past, present, and future become the same time.

As you inter-face or inner-face with your Self and are willing to access your Cellular recordings as the Observer, you give your Self many opportunities to *see* for your Self all the why's of the what's you created. So what if you were unconscious at the time? So what if you were filled with fear at the time? That time is over, done, kaput! *This Moment* is what matters.

Prior to this moment, you were interfacing with your Self unconsciously because of the limiting Belief Systems, the 3D Duality conditioning, and most of all your Fear of not fitting in or belonging. **No one fits in**. The ones who did fit, pretended they did, and the ones who didn't fit in, denied that the ones that pretended to fit in, did fit in. In the meantime, everyone was having fits again and again. Come on, give it up.

One of the worst fears on this planet is the fear of dying. The fear of speaking in public is the first. So, let's address the fear of speaking in public.

As a human, you speak in public all the time. You do it when you go to the store, you do when you have company, you do it every day. You are speaking in public one way or another. When you go to Starbucks for a coffee, you speak in public, and if you are in the drive-through, you are speaking over a microphone. When you eat at a restaurant, you order your food. You are speaking in public. You are always speaking in public. Even a recluse speaks to his or her Self. The absurdity of it all is absurd.

Now let's address the fear of dying. If you believe in past lives in your continuum, guess what? You have died many times. As a matter of "fact", you are an expert at dying.

Let's see what happened in 3D Re-incarnation Duality. You died at childbirth, you died on the battlefield, you died through disease, you died because of this or you died because of that. You died. The programming of Duality's Karma, Lessons, and Re-incarnation demands you die and spend lifetimes fearing the "inevitable"! What a waste of your creativity, time, efforts, and productivity worrying about dying, especially over how it will happen!

Staying healthy, emotionally, mentally, physically, spiritually, and financially, is what it is all about. You came here to live, not die. Let go of the death programming.

Get this, please! The state of Consciousness you are in when you "die" is exactly the same place you pick up the next time around. So, stop going around and around, spinning on the Karmic wheel of Lessons and Re-incarnation which is fearful, non-productive, and not effective.

You are here at this time in the No Time of your continuum to Take Back Your Power, to be complete with your Self, to ascend, to expand your Consciousness, and to live a fulfilled life in your body in this lifetime. Otherwise, go back into the re-cycle bin of your left computer/brain and do the "it" of 3D Duality Programs again and again. You do have choices and options. Your choices and options are up to you and no one else.

This is the perfect time to get to the core of your issues, your repeated patterns, repeated behaviors and…yes…non-functioning repeated relationships. At this time in the No Time, you have no more time to waste trying to figure it out through your left computer/brain. You won't do it. Your left computer/brain does not function that way.

Your left computer/brain's job is to run the 3D Duality Programs that only your Childish Adult Ego (CAE), who is your survivalist, knows how to do, while the rest of you and your body is expected to suffer emotional trauma-dramas, illness, dis-ease, or whatever to validate your CAE's job! Your CAE knows how the 3D system works. When you are unconscious, your CAE is working you.

NOW is the time to comprehend how all aspects of your body of Consciousness works and how all the aspects of you can work together to clear, heal, and create consciously. Now this is a giant step in how you Take Back Your Power!

Through your *feeling* from your Heart and Heart Chakra, not your left computer/brain, clear your Childish Adult Ego's emotional attachments to the past at the Cellular Level in the Multi-Dimensions of your Self and your Consciousness. Clear out the "stuff"…all the molecules of emotions which have been taking up space in your cells and your body of Consciousness. Clear out the molecules which are stuffed with the programs of you being wrong, not good enough, and all the sabotaging language of 3D Duality. All junk! All fear-based Belief Systems.

At your core, there are no more maps, no more creeds, and no more philosophies preventing you from being your whole Self. From here forward, the directions come straight from the Truth of your Self, absent of the trues of the Duality Programs. The curriculum is revealed millisecond by millisecond, invisibly, yet *felt* intuitively, spontaneously, and lovingly.

As one of Thomas Meto's monks exclaims,

> **"Go into your cell and your cell will teach you**
> **everything there is to know.**
> **Your cell. Your Self."**
>
> *-Akshara Noor*

THE SET-UP

The happening! The Set-Up is the perfect situation, experience, or condition in your life that finally gets your attention. Of course, you created this incident for your own benefit, conscious or not! The life-changing event happens. At this point, the event is all about this lifetime now. Or, you have the option to wait until another lifetime, but that is up to you.

Now back to the Set-Up. Set-Ups are created and manifested through life-altering changes, such as illness, divorce, marriage, death, loss, business, job, money, position, or any radical change of circumstance. As a result, these changes, whether dramatic or subtle, change the way you view others, your Self, and the world. It "permanently" alters your life and your view of your life and who you are. The Shift can be gradual, you didn't see it coming, or it can be sudden, you didn't see it coming. You see, it is the same.

From this *perspective* (not the deceptive *perception*), permanency now means you can never go back to the old ways of the limiting Belief Systems. This re-cycle option may be too physically and emotionally painful for you, your body, and your Consciousness to go back. You may thinky-thinky you could go back, but what would be the point except for the lure of the trauma-drama. If the lure and the bait do not have more importance than *you* living consciously, then by all means resist the bait!

If you take the bait, it's your fate

With this physical change of Consciousness happening within your physical body, you do realize with *real eyes* your life has purpose and is on purpose. Being on purpose is Multi-Faceted, Multi-Dimensional, and Multi-versal.

The old operating 3D Duality Programs of your left computer/brain do not resonate with you anymore. You get "it". You get how destructive and non-productive they are in limiting your creativity and your ability to implement and manifest your life as you choose your life to be. Now you can use your brain as a tool instead of having your left computer/brain run your life.

In the Set-Up time, it can appear to be that you are totally alone, that you are abandoned, isolated, or lost. The fear of being alone and lonely may seem overwhelming. Not being understood and not understanding your Self is a part of the dynamics involved in the Set-Up. This process encourages you to look within for the answers.

At your clear core, beneath the rubble of the fears, here is where your Truth and Clarity reside.

You are coming home!

From an outside *perception* (deceptive conception), the Set-Up can appear as though your life has fallen apart. This is the part of the clearing process. Metaphorically, it is the spiritual roto-rooter in action. You cannot rise above the emotions and the emotional hooks to the past without clearing out the Fear Programs at your Cellular Level.

Remember, these programs have followed you for lifetimes. You thought they were Real. You may have even said in your metaphysical journey that "it" is all an illusion. How ridiculous! If you said that "it" is an illusion, why did you hang on to "it", whatever your perception of the "it" is?

For example, the abandonment issue is a debilitating fear which prompts repeated cycles of dysfunction. Abandonment...let me count the ways that I can unconsciously create this issue over lifetimes! Whether you play the Role of the abandoner or the abandonee, this is still the same fear-based issue of Judging your Self that you Lack something or other (perhaps "not good enough"), and you Take-Away from your Self by being abandoned. Even if you are the one who is doing the abandoning, the process is still the same. WOW, what a program of sacrifice, victimization, and blame and more, all rolled up in the abandonment re-cycle!

Whatever your personal script involves, you can re-create the abandonment issue at the beginning, the middle, or the end of your journey. When it is not resolved, you simply carry it forward or play it forward to the next lifetime. The

Truth is no one really wants to repeat this abandonment issue. The Truth is you do in 3D Duality.

Without comprehending this fear-based abandonment issue or any other emotional issue for that matter, this unconscious, deeply buried issue in your Cellular Experiences is repeated time and time again.

Where there is no resolution to an issue there is no solution

In the Set-Up, using abandonment as the triggering issue, when you choose to go to your core, you discover in every time frame your own Self-involvement in arranging the abandonment situation. "Situation" in Wordology Is Your Biology means "sit" U (you) at your "ion" or Cellular Level of Consciousness even when you are unconscious. Again, whether abandoner or abandonee, the fear is the same regardless of your Role.

The Set-Up is the vehicle allowing you to become conscious. The Set-Up provides you the opportunity to release the old pattern of behavior, let go of your Childish Adult Ego's emotional attachment to the "right" and "wrong" of the situation, and move on. You Take Your Power Back, which you lost in the events of your past, this lifetime or any other past lifetime.

In the Set-Up, you become aware and clearly conscious of your responsibility to your Self and your life. This is your life! You are clear that *responsibility* simply means your ability to respond to life or not, without doing the emotional re-enactment of the trauma-dramas. Responsibility is simply how you choose to participate or not! You have choices and options. You do not abandon your Self.

When you are at the core in the Set-Up time, you cannot ever blame anyone else for being responsible for anything happening in your life or lives. You cannot even blame your Self anymore. Blaming expends too much of your energy. Blaming burns you out. Your responsibility is knowing, understanding, and comprehending at your core that *your* life is in *your* hands.

The outcome of your life comes out in new and more creative directions, no longer based on the 3D Duality Programs. It doesn't mean the Duality Programs don't exist. They just don't affect you or your life. You are not hooked into the programming.

Embrace your Set-Ups. You wrote them into your scripts to become conscious. Your clarity comes as you allow your Self to learn about your Self without judgment through your Set-Ups. Your empowerment comes as you willingly and consciously Take Back Your Power on purpose with purpose for all the purposes of your life. You have many purposes. You are Multi-Dimensional, so how could you have just one purpose? How silly!

Your Set-Ups are designed by you to bring your issues to the surface from your core. By being the Non-Emotional Observer (NEO), you learn so much about the 3D Duality process which has processed you to death, to life, to death, and to life. You get the idea. In any given period of time, you have played out both sides of the programs: abuser, abused, haves, have-nots, controller, controlled, victim, victimizer. When you didn't have anyone to play the other side of the program, you did it to your Self.

This is how 3D Duality works.
3D Duality works you.
Now work for your Self.

Through all of your experiences, situations, and conditions, you have the opportunities to gain insight and wisdom. In the No Time, there is No Time like the present to move on. Why stay in the cycle of repeated offenses? Stop offending your Self.

Embrace all the experiences and *see* all the amazing things you have taught your Self. Be more amazed by all the things each person you wrote into your scripts taught you. Even the ones you disliked the most or even hated were and still are your best teachers. See it this way and wisdom comes to you.

**See your Self as the victim
and the victimizer will see you as the victim**

Change your Consciousness and you affect conscious changes in your life as well as others. Through the insight and wisdom, you gain from the Cellular Memory of your time continuum, NOW is the time to utilize this information, keep what serves you, and dump the rest. There is absolutely no value in hanging on to past experiences which have no relevance to a happy, healthy life now. Why hang on?

**When you make the emotional pain
more important than you,
you have no importance to your Self**

Now is definitely the time to design the life you require, desire, and absolutely deserve. Now is the perfect time to create, implement, and manifest your life from the expanded resonance of your Multi-Dimensional Self in the Consciousness of Allness. Being and living in the present moments also gives you the vision to begin to create your future consciously. Be your futurist.

In the present moments of the Now with your clear intentions set and your willingness to move forward with them, you are in the actuality of the movement of your energy through your Clear Consciousness to pre-sent or pre-send your intentions into the future. The past is one minute ago, and the future is one minute from now.

With this clarity that you are in charge of *your* life, *your* Consciousness, and *your* energy, the magic can happen. Your clear intentions are clarified to the Universe and the Multi-verse. Now you have set into motion what you actually require, desire, and deserve. You are now drawing to you the intentions you clearly sent out and now are deserving to implement and manifest into your life.

Be very clear about this. When you let go of the wanty-needy resonance of fear-based Belief Systems, your experiences of life change. When you say, "I need something," what you are really saying is "I don't have what it takes". The Truth is, at your core, you and everyone has what it takes. When you say I "want" something, the message goes out to your future, "well, maybe someday". In the wanty-needy program, you "lack" the energy to make it happen now or in your future.

In wanty-needy, you are projecting the very low resonance of the Lack Belief System into a reality where you probably won't get what you want anyway, so why bother? The energy then is so caught up in the resonance of the "want" that you never get what you want. The "want" is not tangible. Neither is the "need" tangible.

However, should your wanty-needy become tangible, it won't last. The fear of the Take-Away shows up and the physical Take-Away process happens. There is no strength, endurance, or Power behind wanty-needy. There is no drive of energy because wanty-needy is weakness. Wanty-needy is the perfection of the victim program.

The foundation of the "wanty" is the First Chakra's dysfunctional fear of not having. The First Chakra houses all the issues of relationships, families, money, and limiting 3D Duality Belief Systems. The foundation of the "needy" is the Second Chakra's dysfunctional fear of not being validated by others. The Second Chakra, the Creative and Sexual Chakra, is forced to create from a dysfunctional foundation of unresolved emotional issues.

Together, in a not so blissful dysfunctional partnership, the First and Second Chakra keep you in the repeated dysfunctional patterns of Karma, Lessons, and Re-incarnation. Until you get clear about the 3D Duality Programs, your Childish Adult Ego runs your life through these first two Chakras. Existing in the energy field of wanty-needy keeps you disconnected from your Consciousness of Allness within you. Duality rules! You are ruled. No exception to the rules, until you get clear. Once you get clear, the rules change. You make the rules for you.

Looking to a future of unlimited newness begins with Self talk. Through your energy, you produce your life with every thought you think, every word you speak, and every act you act out.

As you look at your future of new possibilities, potentials, and *seeing* your dreams become *real*, change the word "need" to require. "Require" has definite Power.

Change the word "want" to desire. "Desire" means to sire or birth your ideas.

Then know in your clear awareness you absolutely deserve to achieve your intentions on a regular basis. "Deserve" means to "serve" your Self first. This is not selfish. To require, desire, and deserve is to be in your Power. You are Centered in Self. You are NOT being Self-Centered.

When you don't take care of your Self first, you will enter into the resonance of the victimhood energy field. You will not be able to participate fully with your Self or anyone. You will be a drain as well as getting drained by life. You will be too weak.

Wanty-needy is so whiney. Wanty-needy is victimizing. When you are a victim of 3D Duality, you are wanty-needy. Great relationships – whether family, friends, business, or romantic – will not happen in this resonance of victimhood.

In the Consciousness of Allness, beginning with you, there is room for everyone. You have value. You are valuable. You have worth. You are worthy. This goes for everyone. No one is separate from each other. Only the 3D Duality Programs maintain separation. Everyone's essence is connected to Source, call it Godness or God. Everyone is connected at the core of Truth. The Allness of Consciousness transcends and embraces differences without judgment or opposition.

Separation takes a lot of energy to hold this resonance. Connectedness is easy. Connectedness flows inside of you. From the inside out, you become Allness. From the inside out, through Clear Consciousness, your energy is the Power Tool to Take Back Your Power and maintain the resonance to create and live your life on purpose with purpose for your purposes.

This is the purpose of your purposes…to create, implement, and manifest your best life on a continuing continuous continuum. Or, stay in the 3D Duality

Programs and re-do Karma, Lessons, and Re-incarnation. What do you choose?

Chapter 5

SELF CONSCIOUSNESS

Questioning, The Shake-Up, Fragmentation

**"The Spirits of truth and falsehood
struggle within the heart of man;
truth born out of the spring of Light,
falsehood from the well of darkness.
And according as a man inherits truth
so will he avoid darkness."**

-from the Manual Discipline of the Dead Sea Scrolls

Regardless of your religious idea, politics, creeds, codes, agendas, ideas and/or Belief Systems, encountering the information presented here can undoubtedly trigger questions, skepticisms, and even criticisms. This information is designed to rattle your cells, molecules, and particles to the sub-atomic level of you. If this information does not do this, then you are incredibly wondrously clear on how all the programs work and you do not get "worked" by the programs. You are definitely in your Power. However, if you are rattled to your core, congratulate your Self. You are open to *listen* and to hear your Self.

This book's message is to get you to question everything. If your Belief Systems are preventing you from believing in your Self, and if they are holding you back from achieving a healthy, productive life, then this is the perfect moment to ask questions. The purpose is to ask the questions in a productive way to get the correct answers for you.

The answers are all inside of you. It is how you ask the questions to your physical body of Consciousness that provides the answers clearly, without any doubt, and in complete trust of your Self.

**Support your Self by asking the questions
that give you the Truth instead of what's "true"**

Questions such as "what is wrong with me?", "why don't I have the right stuff?", "what's the matter with me?", "what the hell is going on in my life?", etc. only give you the incorrect answers, which are not your answers anyway. These questions elicit incorrect answers because they are based on the "outside" perceptions that something is wrong with you. Not the "right" education, not the "right" family, not enough of this or that – all the nots which turn into "knots" making you ill, such as the "knots" of cancer, heart disease, tumors, fibroids, arthritis, fibromyalgia, etc. All physical diagnoses begin with the emotional body of Consciousness, wrapped up tight in the 3D Duality Programs of Judgment, Lack, and Take-Away.

**Your body was designed to be healthy.
The programs are designed to make you sick.
They are particularly designed to make you sick
of your Self and then make your body sick.**

How sick is this?!

You require your Self, by your choice, to go beyond the 3D Duality Programs – the deceptional perceptions of right and wrong, good and bad, this or that – and be the Non-Emotional Observer (NEO). You require your Self to *see* your part and everyone's part in your script and theirs. You require to let go of the emotional hooks to the past. You require to look at the information as just that…information.

*"Stick to the facts
or you will stick to the trauma-dramas!"*

-Sherryism

See how the information either triggers or resonates to you. If it triggers you, then your body is giving you signals to look inside. If you resonate with it, then ask your body, "Why does this information make sense to me? What is it triggering in me to get me to look at my Belief Systems more deeply and less emotionally?" Either way, you are on the correct track. Not the right or wrong track, but a track speeding towards your answers.

Your journey on this planet is to become the Truth of Who You Are. How many times have you, or someone you know, run around this planet looking for "The" Self? You are busy running to "sacred" spots, seeking out the right guru (which means "gee you are you"), looking for the metaphizzler to heal you, wanty-needying all over the place in the search of finding "The" Self. When all along the Self is inside of you at your core Cellular Level of Consciousness!

Remember Dorothy looking for a way home, asking the delusionist man behind the curtain for her answers? Remember the Lion looking for Courage, the Tin Man looking for a Heart, and the Scarecrow looking for a Brain, while the wicked "outside" tried to destroy them? Looking for your answers outside of you is the delusional illusion the metaphysicians talk about all the time. Yet holding on to the delusion by keeping the illusion going, searching for the guru person, the perfect product, or the perfect way to provide the answers.

If you *belief system* that the "outside" has your answers, then follow the yellow brick road and you will come to the same conclusion as Dorothy. The path to your answers ends up at the end of the rainbow with YOU!

Aren't fairy tales great? No, they are just that...fairy tales. Ever wonder why it was the Grimm Brothers who wrote them and the fairy tales were so grim? If fairy tales are not real, then why do you or so many people buy them, searching for the fairy tale "outsider" to fix your issues, to make you whole by their half infringing on your space, or to gobble you up and spit you out? Living the happily ever after? It doesn't seem to turn out that way! Why? Because no one ever asked, "happily ever after what?" Wow, what a reality is the fairy tale nightmare!

Begin to question everything! Ask your Self. Question your Self! Why do you "think" or thinky-thinky the way you do? Why do you do the things you do? Why do you do the same things over and over again? Why do you repeat the same relationships over and over again? Why, Why, Why? **You cannot get to the *what* of anything until you know the *why*.**

Ask your Self what is comfortable to you. Why is it comfortable? Or is it the comfort of the discomfort zone because you know the pattern so well that you believe it is your reality? Question your values. Question what is your value of you to you? What is your worth? Are you worthy? Or are you running a Lack Program which labels you as unworthy and having no value. This appears to be a very deep-seated emotional Cellular issue.

Ask, ask, ask! Question, question, question! See what your body does when you begin to ask correct questions of your Body of Consciousness. Does your body re-act to what you are asking? Or is your body responding without the emotional hit? The emotional hit is the re-action of your body. Is your body attempting to get your attention and say, "Warning, warning, Will Robinson! Don't go there, you will have to deal with the issue, so let's pretend it doesn't exist"? If your body is re-acting, you are experiencing the "Lost in Space Will Robinson" syndrome, which is if you ignore "it", it will go away. It never does.

The Baby Boomers were weaned on the "if you don't talk about it, it doesn't exist" syndrome straight out of the 1950's. And yes, for sure, this denial Belief System affected the next generations. It is still going on in the Cellular Memory patterns of the Baby Boomers. They take the most medications, have the most body parts replaced, and have the most illnesses. They still *belief system* the 50's were the golden oldies and goodies.

They are oldy and moldy for sure! For sure it is time to grow up from the fairy tale nightmares. Shoving the emotional issues aside and denying anything "bad" went on is why the majority of the Baby Boomers are so physically and emotionally ill. Understand, this is not a judgment of the "if you don't talk about it, it doesn't exist" paradigm that happened all the time in the 50's. And if something did exist, some expert outside would surely solve the problem. Medicate, medicate, medicate. Location, location, location is the *where* the denial affected the health of the physical body. This paradigm made it so easy and difficult to shove the emotional issues even deeper into the cells of the body.

Ignorance and denial are NOT bliss

Ignorance and denial make you sick

Ask more questions and more questions…this is the avenue to Take Back Your Power. Accepting the status quo, accepting Belief Systems which limit you, and accepting anything which does *not* serve you to live a fulfilled life must be questioned. To trust and have faith in your own Self as your guide, even if you have been taught not to believe in your Self, is the way to start the Self-Consciousness Journey. From the inside out come the answers.

The Trust and Faith part of your quest is the most important part of the journey. The level of difficulty or ease your quest takes is up to totally up to you. It depends upon your Faith and Trust that the answers are indeed within you. Accept that the answers are never outside of you, as you have been conditioned to believe. The outside is the reference point only.

Question means…
Quest at the ion or Cellular Level for the answers!

The comprehension of your Self as being part of the Consciousness of Allness, being connected to the Non-Duality Universe and beyond to the Multi-verse, unfolds along your journey of Self-Discovery through the discernment. You must discern what *feels* correct to you.

If you have any concerns, apprehensions, or if any of the not-sures show up, then don't do anything until you have enough information to make a Clear Conscious Choice for something. Otherwise, step back as the Non-Emotional Observer (NEO) and collect more data and facts, for you may be jumping into a very familiar, non-productive situation.

Though it may appear there are challenges and tests, these are your reality benchmarks. As you comprehend that you create these benchmark challenges, you *see* that these "tests" teach you about your Self. Who else could teach you more about you than you? How you work through your benchmarks and tests is up to you. You can view them as challenges *or* opportunities, and as preventing you *or* showing you the way to your Truth. The choice is up to you. You are the creator of your Truth, and you are a contributor to your emotional issues.

The choice is Clear *or* Fear! You are the author of your life's scripts. You authored and accepted your part of the contracts. Though sometimes they are called divine contracts, most times they do not appear divine at all. But they are eye-opening if you open your eyes.

When you continue to create through fear, which is simply *a lack of information*, you discover your choices are limited or nil. Discernment is a key to making *decisions*, which are made for you, <u>or</u> *choices* with options, which you make for you.

When you discern between your Truth in the Allness of your Self and the 3D Duality Fear Programs, you determine the spectrum of making either clear choices for your Self or not. By making clear choices, you create what happens in your life and what options you prefer.

By allowing decisions to be made for you by someone else or some group who does not support or honor you or your Truth, you continue to exist in the limited 3D Fear Programs. This is a major turning point opportunity in Taking Back Your Power.

THE SHAKE-UP

What begins to happen in your discernment process is your 3D Childish Adult Ego and your world as you "think" you know it experiences a shake-up deep within your cells and your Soul. All your Childish Adult Ego's old patterns, behaviors, and values begin to be disrupted. Sometimes, it may seem you are falling apart and your world is crumbling. The Childish Adult Ego can only *interpret* through fear. The Childish Adult cannot *comprehend* anything in the resonance of fear. The Clear Perfect Child Within, the Christed Consciousness, is challenged lifetime after lifetime.

Make this your Fully-Alive-Time Lifetime

Though fear is a narrow band of a denseness, the energy emitted from this restricted band is an overpowering field of Self-Disempowerment. In the 3D Duality experience, fear is a resonance in your bands of Belief Systems. This is why you get caught up in Karma, Lessons, and Re-incarnation. You don't have a choice. Everything is decided for you until you choose to take the Shake-Up opportunity and use it as a means to free your Self. The key to this is being the Non-Emotional Observer (NEO).

If you really require to Take Back Your Power, then be the Non-Emotional Observer (NEO). You will teach your Self so much. You will access your Cellular Memory experiences. You will discern the information and select and choose what to keep and what to dump!

POWERLESSNESS is weakness at the hands of others.

You put your life in their hands
whether they know what they are doing or not!

The energy of fear feeds the Childish Adult Ego (CAE). Both are in tune on the same wavelength and on the same band of Belief Systems. This is how 3D Duality works. Is it really working for you or not? This low resonance feeds the CAE as a sick diet of junk food. When threatened, the Childish Adult Ego will do anything to survive. Remember, the Survival Program is the job of the CAE.

Your Childish Adult Ego (CAE) will even kill you. Why? Because your Childish Adult Ego knows you will come back and re-do it! Why? Because your CAE knows you have bought the Programs of Karma, Lessons, and Re-incarnation. Your CAE knows you know. And your CAE will fight for the ownership of you. Your CAE will fight with you to keep you in your left computer/brain under the control of 3D Duality. It's a partnership made in 3D hellish experiences with commercials in between called the good times!

In addition to the emotional hook of the rights and wrongs of the past, the other issue which leaves you in that state of powerlessness is when those around you – family, friends, associates, or whoever – have an idea of who you "should" be. They see as you see you! When you see you as being powerless, they act according to the unseen messages as well as the language you speak about your Self. They see you as powerless.

When you have dreams and aspirations that you keep hidden and contained inside of you, this is where your dreams and aspirations stay, buried deep inside. Why? Because you are NOT being the cause for your Self! You are *being* the being "they" or he or she wanty-needys you to be. So you be that!

"They" or he or she is comfortable with this arrangement. "They" or he or she wanty-needys you to NOT be your Self.

One huge factor in the dynamics of dysfunctional relationships is that if you don't know who you are, then "they" don't know either. Remember, on this planet very few know who they really are in their core. Everyone is existing in the programs and in each other's lives when you or "they" or he or she are not aware of their Selves in any situation.

The shift/change here is *you* connecting to *your* core to figure out how *you* are going to create *your* future. Otherwise your future is exactly the same, only less and less. You lose sight of the more and the more. This is why the future is the past. Same stuff, different day, different year, different decade, different lifetime, and same re-stuff!

**When you give your Power away,
you are not even aware of it most of the time.
Yes, some of the times you are.**

**When "they" are aware you are becoming aware
of your Self, "they" don't like it,
because "they" are afraid you will change.
And then what will happen to them?**

The Shake-Up time is your opportunity. Your big Ah Ha's are the point of the Shake-Up. The light bulb goes on. You hit your Self physically on your forehead and say, "Boo Dah, I am getting it." When it doesn't *feel* correct anymore to give your Power away, you are getting it. You are beginning to Take Back Your Power.

Embrace the Shake-Up, no matter who on the outside of you is expecting you to remain the same. Here's the kicker...YOU DON'T HAVE TO DO THE "IT" THE SAME WAY ANYMORE! Where and when the relationships, situations, or conditions do not serve you anymore, stop, observe, and ask your Self, "Is this worth one molecule, one particle, or one cell of my life and my creativity?" If the answer is "no", then stop giving your Power away.

If the answer is "yes", then the Shake-Up is working. You are rattling your Self to the core. Stop allowing others to feed you the food of Consciousness which is making you sick and has no relevancy to your life. You can choose to move forward even if they don't! You are not here to exist through someone else's life.

*You don't have to get a life.
You have one!!!*

The Take Back Your Power prevention specialist is your Childish Adult Ego's perception and masterless mind of your 3D unreality. A masterless mind of the temporary and of all opposition, the Childish Adult Ego (CAE) knows that the field of energy in which to manipulate and be manipulated is through the Fear Programs of Judgment, Lack, and Take-Away. When all the things the CAE thought were valuable no longer appear to have the same value, the CAE has to fight for survival.

MASTERMINDLESS...
the expertise of the Childish Adult Ego

The CAE will invent outside conflict to verify and vilify you at the same time. The CAE maintains control of your inside world and your outside world to keep you separated within your Self. As you become conscious of your own Allness and comprehend you are a Multi-Dimensional Human Being, the CAE loses his or her designated 3D driver status as being a separate identity to you.

The intent of the Allness of your Multi-Dimensional Self is the integration and blending of all the aspects of your physicality – Body, Spirit, Soul, Divine Mind (expanded awareness), Chakra Systems, Biology, Physiology, Anatomy. Everything about you is physical.

When you are disconnected from any aspect of your Self, you are physically disconnected from a part of your Self. Connecting to all facets of your Self is the purpose to Take Back Your Power. This is Transcension. You are transcending beyond 3D Duality as you are being your Inner Truth. Opposition to Self or to anyone or anything has no value when you are whole within your Self.

Being whole within your Self gives you the advantage. The advantage is that you are able to *hear* the programming running in others through their language and Wordology without judging them. You are able to *see* so clearly the programs running in others without being emotionally attached to their issues or trauma-dramas. You are able to *feel* their programs running without having to jump in and fix them, or enable them, or be part of their victimization mentality running in the background.

You become empathic. More importantly, you can remember when you bought, existed, and struggled in trauma-dramas just like "them". And of the utmost importance, you are in gratitude, gratefulness, and thankfulness that you don't have to exist that way anymore!

The Allness of your Multi-Dimensional Self allows for differences without opposition. There is no more room for conflict. You recognize it is a waste of your valuable life, your creativity, and your valuable time. You can even agree to disagree. What a huge difference between 3D Duality Programming and being conscious and valuing your Self and your life! There is no necessity to hurt, control, manipulate, or rule over another. The low-based resonance of 3D Duality is not worth wasting your life, your time, or your relationships!

You release your Self from the wanty-needy, dependency relationships, which go both ways. Comprehend that if you enable someone in the wanty-needy Belief System, you are the victimizer. Though the paradigm is perceived that the enabled is the victimizer victimizing everyone involved in the relationship regardless of the Role, the Truth is the enabler takes away the Power of the victim by supporting and enabling the victim to expect being victimized. The enabler supports the victimization. The enabler and the victim are victims of the repeated cycle, tossing the wanty-needy energy fields back and forth like a ball.

The infectious sicknesses of the 3D Duality Programs reply, demand, and perpetuate opposing forces – male/female, good/bad, right/wrong, high/low, top/bottom, rich/poor, my way or the highway. It doesn't work for the benefit of either the individual or the group Consciousness. If you are on the top, it appears to work. If you are on the bottom, it definitely does not appear to work.

3D Duality is war. It starts inside everyone with the 3D Duality Programs, infects you, infects the collective Consciousness, and infects the world. The results are evident in the strife and chaos throughout the world in everyone's lives.

The 3D Duality Programs are simply re-cycling the old patterns of control and manipulation in updated versions. They are basically the same when you get to the core of all of the programs. How you create your life through the programs is your unique brand of creations. You create your trauma-dramas, situations, conditions, re-actions – Act 1, Scene 2, Act 4000, and Scene 1200 – and then you add the leading list of characters with whom you attract to your stage of life.

To repeat the point...**all the 3D Duality Programs are the same**. How you live your life through them is your unique brand of creations. Now, Take Back Your Power and you are the Conscious Creator In Charge of *Your* Life, *your* creativity, *your* implementations, and *your* manifestations ongoing. Or, you can simply go on and go on and go on re-living the repetitious cycles of Duality. Re-sign up or sign off! Signing off does not mean you have to die. Signing off means you are signing up to live consciously and be clear!

Any of the old and supposedly new versions of the 3D Duality Programs – past, present, and futures – are wanty-needy. They are dependent upon the "hidden" agendas. Sometimes the agendas aren't so hidden; they can be obvious agendas such as in separatism, segregation, and apartheid (whether South Africa or not). The dynamics of all these Belief Systems are exactly the same.

Keeping you separated through fear from another or others is a perfect way to keep you controlled and manipulated through Belief Systems which instill bigotry, hatred, and prejudice. These are all examples of Belief Systems supporting emotional separatism without facts. History is then based upon the emotional experiences of winners and losers. The winners spin the history to favor their Belief Systems. The losers have no input. Why should they? They lost. Therefore, is history really history or a representation of the winner's version of how the events took place?

How the war was <u>won</u> is determined by the <u>one</u> who says this is how it happened. Yes, how it happened on the surface. Yet, what really happened? How did the conflict get started? What was the "real" cause of the war or conflict? Who determines the fact or the fiction of the "his"-tory or version of the experience? It doesn't matter if the war or conflict is political, national, or international. The experience is told through the emotional personality of the parties involved. The dynamics of war or conflict apply to marriage, business, politics, governments, sects, groups, cults, religions, gangs, etc.

The war or conflict is emotional, personal, and is all about control and manipulation. The winner has to take all. But remember, 3D Duality is temporary in its permanency! The winner, through the 3D Duality Program of Take-Away, eventually becomes the loser. The time arrives for another winner to come in to save the day to put the former winner in the place of the loser. This is the permanent temporary dynamic of war and conflict! Who's on first? It all depends whose "his"-tory is making the headlines!

The limited Belief Systems of 3D Duality itself is *dependency* in action through the Fear Programs. All the Fear Programs – Judgment, Lack, and Take-Away – are acted out and replayed through this lifetime and through the continuum of lifetimes. The influence in this low-based resonance, no matter how or what the fear is labeled is dependency and co-dependency. It's the wanty-needy resonance of "fixing". I "fix" you; you "fix" me.

The problem with this resonance is the focus on the fix and not on the resolution of the problems. Therefore, there is no resolution and no solution. There is only a continuation of the "fix it" dilemma. This dilemma is the running around from one dilemma to another dilemma, called a relationship, singing the Country Western song, "I am hoping, wishing, wanting, and needing someone to make me whole". And the second verse is, "Why am I always in the hole, fix-in' to find a way out?" The wanty-needy fix-in' song plays on and on and on.

Doesn't matter if it is the Grand Ole Opry or the New York Metropolitan Opera, the wanty-needy lyrics are all the same. As a matter of fact, it doesn't matter what language, stage, or place in time, the lyrics are always the same. I wanty-needy you, you wanty-needy me, and we wanty-needy together, until another person comes along, and the beat goes on to another wanty-needy relationship. This is the culture or the "cult-you-are" caught in this fix-in' fix-it program. Why am I fix-in' to find the perfect person to fix me? Am I in another fix again? No fixes here!

Dependency and co-dependency are exhausting. Dependency and co-dependency are the Victim Program. Is the victimizer the dependent one? Is the one being victimized the co-dependent one? To *see* the answer to these questions, look at the behaviors at the deepest levels of this aspect of the 3D Duality Victim Program. The perception is that the enabler is being victimized by the enabled. *Both* are victims in this scenario.

When the victim is enabled, though the intentions are well-intended by the enabler victimizer, the enabler victimizer is actually taking away the Power of the enabled victim. The enabled victim is giving his or her Power away to the enabler victimizer, blaming the enabler victimizer and despising the enabler victimizer for the help he or she is giving. The enabler is victimized by the enabled. The enabled is victimizing the enabler. This behavior is dysfunctional. Everyone is frustrated. Everyone is exhausted. Everyone becomes tired and resentful. The victimization behavior is in full force. No Power! Only force! Tiresome! Exhausting! Repeatable!

Those caught up in these victim/victimizer enabler/enabled behavioral patterns are prisoners, whether they chose it or not. They have no choice. The decisions are made for them by the victimizing enabler and victimizing enabled programming. Both are caught up in the crossfire. The victimizing enabler and the victimizing enabled are entrapped in the "let's pretend" trap, ambushing their children, families, and friends, and dragging them into the net.

The perfect example is the alcoholic ritual. The non-alcoholic enabler pretends the enabled alcoholic is just "having" one of those days, one of those "spells". Everyone not only pretends but denies anything is happening. "If you don't talk about it, it doesn't exist." The not talking about it is a definite hangover from the 1950's black-and-white era of Belief Systems.

The scenario is "what will the neighbors think?" So, let's just deny anything and pretend everything is alright. The absurdity of this is you had no idea you and your family were the neighbors and that your neighbors were saying that same thing, wondering what you were thinking. All of this behavior is the ludicrousness of the Judgment Program's dysfunctional conflict between the burden of denial and facing the freeing Truth. You cannot move forward without the pretense hovering over your life.

To keep you separate from your Self and others through limited Belief Systems is Separatism in action. Separation and separatism are financed at your expense through the Take-Away Program. Whatever the investment you have in this program – you are unworthy or have no value – you will continue to be a victim in one form or another. The 3D Duality paradigm is unlimited in versions of the Take-Away Program.

You can bank on the investment of your energy to be continuously dysfunctional when you continue to have a Belief System enforcing you to Take-Away from your Self a healthy, creative, and productive life. As long as you perceive you are less, unworthy, and not deserving, you will victimize your Self with the Take-Away Program in however many versions you can so unconsciously create to deny your Self a good life. You actually **validate the invalidation of your Self**. That's how you lose your Power to the Take-Away Program.

Ask your Self over and over again until you get this…

"Is it worth one molecule, one particle, or one cell of my life and my creative abilities to give my Power away?"

When you focus your life on Judgment, Lack, and Take-Away, you are doing your Self a disservice. When you do this, your energy becomes drained. You are constricting your resonance to a very low-based Belief System of limitation and victimization. You make your Self sick!

Living your life to your fullest potentials is utilizing your Clear Consciousness and energy in Allness from your inside out. Your outside life reflects the direct results of you deliberately creating, implementing, and manifesting your life as you choose your life to be. There are no limitations to your creativity. There are no limitations to what you can create that serves and empowers you.

When you are clear about what you require, desire, and deserve, you are living your dream in Realness each and every day. You are In Charge of Your Life. You are in charge of who you are. You make the meaning of life for you. You are the one who makes things happen. How everything happens is up to you.

FRAGMENTATION

When you have given away your Power to something or someone outside of you, the principle of fragmentation is set into place. You become disenfranchised from your Self. This is the ultimate separation of Self. You become in opposition to your own being.

Fragmentation is an implosion of your energy, a contraction of your Consciousness within you. The energy factor of your Consciousness eventually explodes to the surface by the intensity of your 3D Duality Fears. As these bands of energy, propelled by the unconscious and even conscious fears, are released throughout your body, a destructive stream of force emerges. As this force of fear is unleashed throughout the physicality of your body, your emotional body takes over. You appear to be going in all directions at once. Your physical body is taxed to the max. Stress is the verdict.

Your physical body, your Childish Adult Ego, and your emotions are running rampant without direction, focus, or common sense. Sensory overload becomes the abnormal norm. Your entire body of Consciousness, every aspect of you – Physical Body, Childish Adult Ego, Spirit, Mind, Soul, and Emotional Body – is out of balance. All the levels of your frequency are vibrating against each other. There is no connection of your Self to your Self.

Fragmentation is the breakdown and separation of your Consciousness. This state of Consciousness is debilitating, emotionally and physically. You are not present.

When this occurs, you go out of body. You slip out the back, Jack! You are wandering around somewhere, anywhere but here. You are not grounded. You are not in your body. You are fragmented! There is no awareness of the Allness of You. Being in Allness with your Self is virtually impossible. Your body breaks down emotionally, mentally, physically, spiritually, and financially. Putting your head under the covers looks inviting. This is an invitation to stop living! An invitation to exist! The programs running are "dead woman or dead man walking"! This is despair. This is not who you are.

In this fragmented state of Consciousness, you are fragile. In this state of fragility, illness, emotional disorders, and loss of Self are easily manifested in your body and in your life. Your energy is dispersed in multiple directions. This is not being your Multi-Dimensional Self. In this situation, your life becomes disjointed, chaotic, and confusing. Turmoil is the norm! You feel powerless. This is not who you are at your core Truth. This is the programming running through your left computer/brain, overriding you living your life productively.

Anxiety and depression rule your life. You are disconnected from your Self. You are, however, emotionally attached to incidents, occurrences, individuals, and situations in the past. The difficulty in this emotional state of Consciousness "feels" Real. This is **not** *feeling*. This is your emotional body run by the Childish Adult Ego, who is fighting for survival.

Your Childish Adult Ego (CAE) only knows survival. Your CAE only knows it will do anything to survive, even let you tank and be powerless in order to stay in control of you.

YOUR CHILDISH ADULT EGO ONLY KNOWS FEAR. Your CAE only knows how to operate in the 3D Duality Programs.

What is at stake here is *you*. Programs, which run on powerlessness, become the only path your CAE can take you down. The issue here is *take you down*. Your CAE knows how the programs work, knows how the up and down cycles work of Judgment, Lack, and Take-Away. When your body goes down too far, there is no coming back in this lifetime. You have to wait for the next one. Your CAE will do anything to survive.

Again, please comprehend that your Childish Adult Ego (CAE) will do anything to be in control, even to the point of your death, because he or she knows you will do it again through the Programs of Karma, Lessons, and Re-incarnation. Your CAE is a professional at re-invention, not newness.

There is no point in going down the tubes. You don't have to do it. You have all the resources to turn your life around, no matter what has happened. You have all the information inside of you to draw upon. You have been taught to be controlled and manipulated through the programs. You have been programmed to sacrifice your Self, your life, and to exist in servitude to the elite, whoever they are. It doesn't matter. What matters is that you say to your Self, "Enough is enough and I am worth more than just enough. I have worth and I am worthy. I am valuable and I have value."

If for any unreasonable reasons you find your Self at square one in the depths of fragmentation, you must believe that the light at the end of the tunnel is you. Allow your Self to *see* that you are not the programs, you are not the victim, and you do have choices and options. Although in the very throngs of the turmoil it may appear impossible, it is not.

The word "impossible" in Wordology Is Your Biology means "I Am Possible" (I M Possible). This is the giant step to take, whether it appears as a small step or not. This is the step to take. "I am the possibilities and the potentials. I am the only one who can validate me. I am the one. This is my life. The time is now to Take Charge of My Self. I didn't come here to this planet to suffer, to sacrifice, to be less, to exist on medications, or just to exist."

You are conditioned to be controlled and manipulated. You are conditioned to *belief system* the idea that serving your own highest and best is "selfish". The energetic Belief System of "selfish" is used to control you through guilt and unworthiness. The emotional hook of this band of energy is in your First Chakra of the old 7 Chakra System. The control and manipulation of this programming relies on the fear of not-deserving.

The Wordology of "selfish" and not-deserving exists in this First Chakra. The Second Chakra, which is your Creative and Sexual Chakra, emits the bands of energy embedded in a Belief System of sacrifice, attracting to you the person, group, or scenario outside of you to connect to your sacrifice band. You are **validated in the invalidation of your Self**, and the beat of suffering goes on. You project unworthiness in your relationships and in how you relate to life.

If you go back through history, do you really remember the martyrs who sacrificed and suffered their lives for the cause? Maybe you remember a few in your history lessons. However, the despots and the leaders of the cause continued living, while the martyrs gave up a perfectly good life. Who knows what they could have contributed if they had lived? This is not to say you cannot have a cause and support it, but is it worth losing your life? You have to make that choice for your Self.

It is not selfish to have a productive, healthy life. The Selfish Program is to keep you under control using your emotions to manipulate *you*. When you are Centered in Self, you are not Self-Centered or Selfish. There is a complete difference in Consciousness. When you are Centered in Self, you are In Charge of Your Life, and you are more open, more conscious, and you can assist others more effectively and willingly.

When you are in the low resonance of the Selfish Program, you are being manipulated and you manipulate your Self and others. You are resentful. You are not as effective in helping others because your energy is drained. You are drained emotionally and physically. You are Resentful with a capital R and the others you are helping know it.

"They" become emotional, and the bands of sacrifice and suffering go back and forth between you and the ones you resent. Then the Wordology Is Your Biology of "well, all I have done for you" comes out through the silent roar. Or, out of your mouth come these words of entrapment. You are angry because the other person or persons are not giving you the wanty-needy feedback of sincere gratitude. Resentment has no gratitude. How could it have?

No one is grateful. Everyone in the situation is resentful and no one wins. No one can win in the sacrifice and suffering and "don't be selfish" programming. Expectations run high. The resonance of this Belief System is low and disappointing. The disappointment is running on both sides of this energy-draining, resentful Duality band of fear.

The sacrificer is drained. The sacrificee is drained. The relationship is fragmented. Fragmentation reigns. Fragmentation affects not only you by draining your vital Power, it now drains those caught up in the trauma-drama. The scenario of this emotionally draining trauma-drama could last for years.

Ask your Self, "Is it worth it?" You have a choice. You can choose to be either Centered in Self *or* to be Self-Centered in the Childish Adult Ego (CAE). Your CAE is looking for the wanty-needy validation, even when the validation invalidates *you*. What a program! You are fragmented and being controlled and manipulated, while being controlling and manipulating without the awareness of what is happening. How perfectly awful is this dysfunctional relationship?

Self-Consciousness is a choice. You must question. You must question and ask the questions correctly to get the answers. Through your Cellular Memory of experiences, you find those answers already inside of you. Detachment is the key. Disconnecting doesn't work. In the state of disconnection, you are still attached to the past, emotionally in the right/wrong, victim/victimizer mentality of the Judgment, Lack, and Take-Away Programs. With disconnected attachments, you are fearful and full of fear-based programs.

Detachment means, as the Non-Emotional Observer (NEO), you *see* everyone's Role in the situation, event, and experience(s). This does not mean that what happened is correct. This does mean that what happened was hurtful. Yes, the past dysfunctions are hurtful.

YOU CANNOT CHANGE THE PAST.

What you can do is be detached as the Non-Emotional Observer (NEO) and *see* the past for what it is. Then release all the physical emotional molecules of the experience. Let go of the experience, the person(s), place, or situation involved with you. Whether physical abuse, emotional abuse, or sexual abuse, all abuse is physical.

You cannot heal through your left computer/brain. Your left computer/brain is run by your Childish Adult Ego, who tries and tries and tries, trying to rationalize, logicalize, and make sense of what happened. Your left computer/brain is a computer. It cannot heal you through rationale, logic, or sense.

Your computer/brain has no sense. If it did, you would not keep repeating the same dysfunctional patterns and subjecting your body to these dysfunctional experiences. **Your body is your infinite intelligence and intellect.** Your computer/brain only knows how to run the ingrained neuronet programming through the un-leadership of your Childish Adult Ego.

This is how the programs work. Who cares how the programs got started or even how they are used to manipulate you by the Powers that be. Why care at this point and waste more time thinky-thinking about it? What the point is now is YOU CARE ABOUT YOUR SELF. In this moment, and there is only this Moment, realize with *real eyes* that this is the time to take a stand for your Self. Detach! Take Back Your Power!

You deserve to do it for your Self. When you change your life, your world changes. When you hang on to the past, you are living the past again and again. Then this Moment Now doesn't matter. If your *now* is based on your *then* – your emotional attachments to the past – your current *now* is always *then*. Make your Now be *this* Moment's Now!

**"I came to this planet to live,
to create on a continuing continuous continuum,
to live productively, have great relationships
and to be healthy and in the form of prosperity
that I choose.**

Anything else is the programs running.

**I am not running anymore
and the programs are not going to run me!"**

INTERVENTION:
HAND-OUT OR HAND-UP?

Take a look at the government and welfare systems. These are perfect examples of intervention and manipulation. These interventions are cloaked in the concept or idea of what is "best" for someone or some group of people. These programs fuel the trap of servitude and mastery. This is not the Mastery of your Self, but the mastery *over* you or the group. This serves no one, not even you as a contributor to the servitude aspect of the programming. There is no ideal in servitude. Expect to serve the ones doling out the servitude. Perhaps this is job security based on the insecurity of others?

This serves no one, least of all the individuals, families, and groups it is supposed to serve. For example, those who are on welfare are judged as lazy or no good and who continually and constantly drain society. This sets them up for existing as the labels they are given. This sets them up for a future of continual failure. This paradigm expects them to exist in this failure program. This is what is expected of "them" and the expectations of failure are the results. This is the Belief System which ingrains this low resonance into the system.

On the other hand, those who are administering the welfare programs appear to have job security. Their security paradigm is based upon the insecurity Belief System of those on welfare (well-fare). How fair/fare is this working model? Depends on what side of the fair/fare you are on. Both versions are illusions. They only appear to be *real* from the 3D Duality perception of opposition as the manipulated and the manipulators.

This paradigm does not support a Consciousness of growth, abundance, and prosperity. This paradigm does not support the education of Consciousness. This paradigm supports limited Belief Systems of suffering and less-than. Those on welfare have no well fair. There is nothing fair about it. This paradigm only perpetuates Judgment, Lack, and Take-Away. It also encourages Self-Defeating entitlement. There is no Power in Self-Defeating entitlement. Only resentment builds on both sides of this no-well-fair program.

The misconception is that anyone, group or institution, can do anything "to" or "for" someone else. The Truth is you cannot do anything "to" or "for" someone else. Whether individually or as a group, everyone equally participates *with* each other, even when it is dysfunctional and the behavior is powerless. Whether anyone in the exchange of "to" or "for" is aware of it or not, the behavior of "to" and "for" is very disempowering.

The concept of doing something "to" and "for" someone else results in control and manipulation. "To" and "for" is the Set-Up for an expectation-driven result. The person or group who is expecting their version of doing something "to" and "for" someone or some other group doesn't achieve the expectation. Why? Because the individual or the group on the other side of the "to" and "for" are emotional for many reasons.

They think they are being victimized, don't have a chance, are stuck in this hand-out paradigm, and that they are *less than* with no way out – all the results of the dense resonance of their Belief Systems of being victimized by the system. They lose initiative. They become the "why bother". Take the dole and suffer. The other side of this Duality Band is that "they" are lazy or no good. The Truth is both sides of this dysfunctional band of *belief systeming* have accepted this as the reality.

The 3D Duality Programs are layers and layers of Belief Systems from all your lifetimes and everyone's lifetimes. Opposition, not deserving, insufficiency, separatism, fragmentation, and victimization are simply versions designed to keep you off balance, out of focus, and disconnected from your Self and your own Truth. You are conditioned to *belief system* that you are not In Charge of Your Life. You are conditioned to *belief system* that there is no other way. The Truth is, there is no other way or ways in 3D Duality Reality.

Give your Self the opportunities – yes plural – to *feel* the essence of your Self. Get to know your Self from the inside out. Get to know Who You Are, not who you thinky-thinky you are or what you have been told or labeled in the programming. Begin to connect to your Truth at your core Cellular Level of Consciousness in your Cellular Memory. Begin to ask your Self questions the *correct* way.

Ask your physical Body of Consciousness. Ask your Self. Ask your Cells.

1. Why is there pain in this area?
2. What is the pain telling me?
3. Why do I re-act this way?
4. Why do I get emotional?
5. Why do I give my Power away so easily?
6. Why is my life not working?
7. Why do I re-create the same relationships?
8. Continue to ask the "Why's"

YOU Cannot Change the WHAT
Until YOU Get to the WHY

BE OPEN TO THE ANSWERS

DO NOT ANALYZE or LOGICALIZE
Do NOT Listen to Your CHILDISH ADULT EGO

FEEL **the ANSWERS from YOUR HEART**
TRUST THE ANSWERS

TRUST YOUR INTUTION

TRUST YOUR HEART

THIS IS THE ONLY PLACE TO START!

What does the term "lightbody" mean? There is confusion about this term. As you connect to your *light*, which is simply at your core Truth of Consciousness underneath all the 3D Duality Fear Programs, you now comprehend your experiences as the Non-Emotional Observer (NEO), without the emotional attachments to the past as being victimized, controlled, or manipulated. You *see* the facts of the experiences for what they are. These experiences are direct results of the 3D Duality Fear Programs of Judgment, Lack, and Take-Away, regardless of the timeline in your continuum. This is a 3D Duality World. This is the world we change as we get conscious and *you* Take Back Your Power.

Your body actually experiences a physical lightness. You release the heavy burdensome *weight* of these dense emotional molecules which are stored in your body as the unconscious Cellular Experiences. As these dense, viscous, emotional molecules physically lift up and out of your physical body, you *feel* lighter. This is the explanation of the so-called *lightbody*.

Even the term "light worker" has become convoluted. This is another Program of Separatism. This group, though well-meaning, separates itself in opposition to others. No one group has the answers to enlightenment. No group!

The enlightenment comes from you letting go of limiting programs. You do the letting go of the physical emotional molecules from your body. You are the one who detaches from the dysfunctional past, which is no longer relevant to your life. Regardless of what group you choose to participate in, it is up to you to *enlighten* your Self.

"Stop looking for the light at the end of the tunnel.
You are the Light, which is information.

By connecting to your Self,
you end your Duality tunnel vision...
and you clearly *see*...

YOU ARE UNLIMITED!"

-Wind Ohmoto

Your light is your information. Your light is your personal knowledge without taking it personally. Ask your body for the information and your body will enlighten you. The light is not outside of you. Your answers are not outside of you. The life you create outside of you begins inside of you.

You are the creative writer of your scripts, contracts, relationships, the play, trauma/drama/comedy, and your life.

Be in charge of you and your life.

This moment, this lifetime, this life…

TAKE BACK

YOUR

POWER!

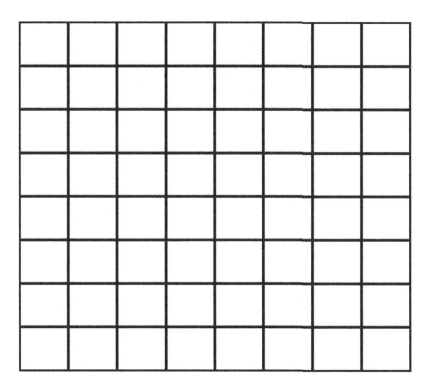

Matrix/Template of Limited Consciousness:
Grid of the Seven Chakra System

This is a continuing process of recycling same old same old
programs, patterns, and behaviors regardless of time.

Chapter 6

IS TRUE ENOUGH?

The Old Consciousness -
3D Duality Belief Systems of the Seven Chakras

"Healing occurs
with the shedding of Duality
as you align your Self
with the Allness of your Power."

-Sherry Anshara

The question to ask your Self is "How and why did I get so enmeshed in these old 3D Duality Programs and patterns?" The answer is very simple. The 3D Duality Programmed Belief Systems are embedded, not only in your cells, but also in this outdated system of 7 Chakras.

Chakra is a Sanskrit word meaning "wheel". These 7 Chakras illustrate the flow or non-flow of your energy in a clockwise circular motion within your physical body of Consciousness. The flow occurs when you are open and focused on being clearly conscious. The flow is disrupted when you are caught up in the 3D Duality Programs of Judgment, Lack, and Take-Away. When the flow is disrupted, your life is disrupted. The ups and downs of life have a direct correlation to your 7 Chakra System.

Most people are completely unaware how their bodies really work as a physical body of Consciousness. Now let's complicate it with an unseen energetic system which is supposed to work in unison with all your other systems. And you ask your Self, why am I out of alignment? Well, hello…you can't help your Self. The 3D Duality System sets you up. All of your physical systems are easily misaligned by all of the fears imposed upon your life here on this planet and in this Duality Universe.

Both the Earth and the Universe are in a 3D Duality dimension. The ideas of enlightenment include becoming conscious, getting "it", seeing the light, being the light, and it goes on and on. Metaphors can go on for centuries, but the objective is to get over Duality and Take Back Your Power. So, moving forward...

For thousands of years, this 7 Chakra System has been accepted as the primary centers of specific energy fields of Consciousness within your physical body. From the 3D Duality limitation paradigm, this system is not supposed to be seen physically but experienced through your interactions and relationships.

This group of seven separate states of Consciousness is assigned specific characteristics pertaining to particular traits which influence your experiences during your lifetime. When your 7 Chakra System is in alignment, your life is considered balanced and healthy. However, the majority of the time, this system works in opposition to itself.

The challenge of this system is keeping these energy fields in alignment with each other. The issue is how do you do it? Being clearly conscious is the goal to keep these seven separate systems working together for your benefit. They cannot, however, work for your benefit if you are in opposition to your Self. When these 7 Chakras of Consciousness are in opposition to each other, you are definitely not benefiting from this misalignment.

These seven separate systems of awareness cannot be in alignment if you are out of alignment with your Truth in the first place. How can you be in any type of alignment when you are faced with fearful experiences each and every day of your life? The news, TV, radio, and periodicals are filled with the fear of this and the fear of that. Who in the heck could be in any type of alignment with your Self with the odds stacked against you? If you are off balance, not in your Power, you are very easily controlled, manipulated, and forced out of balance with your natural state of being.

When you are out of alignment with your Self emotionally, mentally, physically, spiritually, and financially, your Chakras cannot align. The reason is that you are running the 3D Duality Programs of Judging Your Self that you Lack something, and then you Take Away your abilities to be in alignment with your Self. These seven areas of Consciousness are problematic when you don't comprehend how they work. The realities which are plugged into these energetic fields become your Self-oppositional life. This system is Duality.

This 3D Duality System is not designed to work together. When you are truly willing to be In Charge of Your Life, you must Take Charge of this 7 Chakra System along with every physical system in your body, including your computer/brain. When you stand up for your Self, your systems begin to align because you are choosing to make them work for you instead of them working you.

When you are in charge of your Self and your life, you can work this 7 Chakra System to benefit your life and well-being. These 7 Chakras are experienced when you physically connect to each and/or all of them. At this point, you are able to access this useful information, which is compartmentalized in each of these areas of your body. All of the 3D Duality Programs of Judgment, Lack, and Take-Away and the patterns of your behavior of limited Belief Systems are embedded in these 7 Chakras, as well as encoded in your cells.

Your cells register your experiences and store them in your cells. Your 7 Chakra System internalizes the experiences according to what each Chakra is assigned as a collective body of Consciousness. Your Childish Adult Ego, in control of your left computer/brain, runs the 3D Duality Programs. Your emotional body, burdened by your Childish Adult Ego's survival and victim programs, influences the stability of all your body's physical systems, especially when you are overcome by the Fear Programs in any of the particular areas of your body, which correlate to each or any of your 7 Chakras.

Of course, each Chakra is affected and influenced by one, several, or all of your 7 Chakras. When you are emotional or out of alignment with your Self, a domino effect takes place. You become the domino and your alignment is off. In the worst-case scenario, you physically, emotionally, mentally, spiritually, and financially take the hit. Then depression, anxiety, and illness happen quite naturally. Although this is not natural to a healthy body of Consciousness, this is what happens. Illness becomes "natural". How ill is this?

Your body can go on for years with the Fear Programs running your life. Eventually your physical body can't hang on anymore. So death happens...you have left the building.

When the Consciousness and the flow of energy of your Chakras are not in alliance, neither is your physical body of Consciousness. For example, when your spinal column is out of alignment, you might go to a chiropractor for an adjustment. The purpose of the adjustment is to re-align your spinal column. Proper alignment makes you *feel* better; your spinal column is operational again, and your energy is flowing, benefiting your well-being. However, it is only temporary unless you get to the core issues in your spinal column. To address the core issues, you require to consciously identify which Chakra and which corresponding physical system is misaligned. What is causing the blockage of energy? What 3D Duality Belief System is affecting the particular area of your spinal column and the related Chakra? Finding the answers to these questions is easy if you are willing to search out the answers within you. You must be the Non-Emotional Observer (NEO) and not judge the answer or the question.

An initial first step in Taking Back Your Power is acknowledging that you have been programmed to be afraid of your own Power. It is okay to acknowledge that you do get off balance. It happens to everyone, even to those you thinky-thinky are smarter than you, more conscious than you, more "something" than you. This is not the Truth.

You and only You connect your Self to your Self. Your search always begins inside of you. The outside search is not where you can find You. You cannot get thrown out of alignment by the "outside" because "inside" you are beginning to know your Self. This progressive process of connecting inside your Self initiates your journey of balance.

The 3D Duality Programs focus on treatment of the body to find the answer to the illness or dysfunction. Treatment does not make the connection to the root of the issue which is supporting the illness. Yes, we have been taught to support illness. Treatment is just that…treatment! Until you are willing to connect non-emotionally to your Self on all levels of your Consciousness…physically, emotionally, mentally, spiritually, and financially, and to your Body, your Childish Adult Ego, and your Soul, you will continue the cycle of the old Fear-based 3D Duality Programs in this lifetime, and in the next, and the next, and the next. 3D Duality propagates continuing re-cycles of function, dysfunction, function, dysfunction, function, and dysfunction. The only way to stop this cycle is to choose to end 3D Duality Belief Systems within your Self. You do not know what that is…yet!

The most powerful position you can have in your life right here right now is *being* the Non-Emotional Observer (NEO). When you detach from the traumas and dramas throughout your life, you can *see* from this Non-Emotional Observer (NEO) perspective that *you* created all of the events in which you get involved. How absolutely delicious…not so much!

From this point of observation, without all the judgments and the emotional attachments to the situations, the individuals, and the jobs, you can begin to *see* how hilariously some of your trauma-dramas outshined the writers of soap operas. When you are in the full-blown emotional circumstances of the event, you cannot *see* or even *hear* anything that is going on around you. You are swirling around from the inside out, stuck in the emotional tornado which is throwing you around like a rag doll. In these dramatic moments, there is no way you can really *see* what is going on, especially when you are in the Victim Role of the situation.

The only "salvation" or solving it at your ion/Cellular Level is by stepping into this powerful position of the Non-Emotional Observer (NEO). You have to observe your Self first. You cannot detach and get all the facts until you observe your Self! This is a have-to moment. The only way to move above, beyond, and forward from the past is *to be* this Power-filled position of the Non-Emotional Observer (NEO).

As the rational, Non-Emotional Observer (NEO), you can get the facts, *see* how everyone in the situation participates, and *see* your part. Even if you don't like the part you played, metaphorically and physically, the past is over. It is the have-to-move-forward time. The call sign is "over and out" of the past.

Your Non-Emotional Observer (NEO) position is your ticket out of the trauma-drama theater, off the soap opera stage, and *for* creating a new script which best serves your life. It's time to get over whatever has been holding you back. There is no point in re-living, re-traumatizing, or re-enacting the same scripts, the same repeated situations, and especially the same recurring relationships. Don't re-up; this is not the Army.

It is so time to move forward. Embrace your Non-Emotional Observer (NEO). This is your get-out-of-jail-free card. Yes, the past may have been filled with incredible, horrific experiences, but you are here *now* and alive. Stay out of the past. Begin to live your life as *you* desire. You deserve it. Be the Non-Emotional Observer (NEO) and practical miracles happen every day. You are alive, so LIVE!

You do not *change* the 3D Duality System.
You *release* it from your Consciousness…

YOU RELEASE IT OUT OF EXISTENCE!!!

THE SEVEN CHAKRAS

The 7 Chakra System is based upon Duality. This system is a system of realities and oppositions. As you clear these 7 Duality Chakras, you *see* and *feel* the difference between a reality, realities, and what is REAL for you. The REALNESS of how, why, when, and where you consciously create in your Power is what becomes your REAL and your REALNESS. It is created, implemented, manifested, and actualized by you. REAL and REALNESS have no resonance connections to Duality's limited realities. Becoming a REAL Human is ascending beyond the limitations of Duality in your body in this lifetime.

All the Consciousness in your body is connected to your 7 Chakras. The Consciousness of your Chakras are influenced by the 3D Duality Programs, recorded and embedded in your physical biological systems in your DNA (deoxyribonucleic acid template) through the conditioning of Judgment, Lack, and Take-Away. Your Chakra System is only as clearly conscious as you are. If you are emotionally blocked or stuck in the past, so is your Chakra System. This is how it works.

When your resonance is constricted because you are fearful, your Chakra System is vibrating at a low frequency of fear. When you resonate to fear, you attract fear and fear-filled experiences. The resonance of your Chakra System – whether expanded or contracted – depends upon the resonance of your Consciousness. Where you are emotionally, mentally, physically, spiritually, and financially is where your Chakra System is in the same regard. This is how it is. The lower the resonance of your awareness, the more intensely lower is the resonance of your Chakra System. The more fear you have, the more the vortices of your Chakra System are dense and closed. When the energy vortices of your Chakras and your awareness are more open and expanded, there is no sense of being "stuck". You are in the flow.

In your physical biology at the Cellular Level is the history of your experiences throughout your continuum, this lifetime and other lifetimes. Up to the present moment, your history is being recorded in your cells in every part of your body, including in all of your systems and in every part of your physical make-up, as well as your aura/bio-energy field/electromagnetic field. These are three different words that mean the same thing. These records of your experiences and your measurable levels of awareness include Cellular Memories, Cellular Memorizations (this lifetime), and the Cellular Sounds pertaining to the experiences.

Even if you and your computer/brain have forgotten, your body records, stores, and remembers the experiences. However, in the remembering, you are always influenced by your emotional body, especially when you are running a victim/victimization program.

As these experiences are recorded in specific areas of your body, they relate to specific Chakras. Your entire physical body of Consciousness is connected and interlinked within itself to your Chakra Systems. Without Consciousness or awareness of the inter-link, there is no awareness of the inter-connectedness living within your body on all the levels of Consciousness. When you are not connected and inter-linked within your Self, you cannot be healed on these levels of Consciousness. When you are not connected and inter-linked on all levels of your Consciousness, you cannot be fully and consciously participatory in life. The dense resonance of the 3D Duality Programs challenges you to *not* make these connections which you require to be in your Power.

An extraordinary experience or burst in the expansion of your awareness can occur through a Near-Death Experience, an out-of-body experience, or a Self-revelation/realization experience. The challenge is maintaining this growth spurt of awareness. The difficulty is that the 3D Duality Reality is very physically dense in its resonance. Therefore, the challenge to hold the expanded resonance of Consciousness for longer than short periods of time takes determined efforts. You cannot buy back into the 3D Duality Fears that you cannot be more than you are. Short episodes are acceptable.

To be confidently conscious and In Charge of Your Life on a regular basis is the nemesis of the 3D Duality Fear Programs. Your Childish Adult Ego's job is survival. Your Childish Adult Ego (CAE) becomes more deeply afraid. He or she wanty-needys you to survive. Anything over and above the survival resonance just can't happen!!! Your CAE will do anything to keep his or her job even at the expense of your health and wellness. Job *in*-security will not do!

However, these Self-created experiences by your expanded Consciousness which manifests these bursts or glimpses above the 3D Duality resonance of fear are always life-changing incidents to get your attention. Though these incidents can contribute to your frustration and anger, they have great purpose to your life. In the frustration, simply calm down and ask your Self this defining question, "Why are these experiences seemingly so temporary?"

You begin to connect to your deepest knowing that there really is much more to you and your life than what you have been taught to believe. These bursts and glimpses of insight from the inside of your core are the experiences of the *More*. These *More* experiences expand your resonance.

Even if these *More* moments are short in a linear time frame, they are enough of a resonance change to shift your Consciousness. In these moments, your body *feels* and distinguishes the difference between the heaviness/weightiness of 3D Duality Reality and the lightness/clarity of the expansion of your awareness/Consciousness. You are now experiencing the *More* of your own Conscious Evolution of your Consciousness. You are beginning to expand beyond the resonance of the 3D Duality Programs of Fear.

Your DNA programming is a collective environment for both your lineage and your birth-time as you are born into a particular collective Belief System. During your gestation period in your mother's womb, the minute the sperm hits the egg you immediately begin to process your own experiences from the continuum of stories you bring to this current lifetime. At the same time, you are influenced at your Cellular Level by your own parents' Belief Systems, which become an integral part of your Consciousness.

Remember, you and your parents co-signed the contract. You chose your parents…the good, the bad, and the ugly! In the contract, you also are influenced by the Cellular Experiences of your ancestors. Now you have it! Here you are! Now, what was that again?

You are affected and influenced at your Cellular Level of Consciousness by your experiences from your continuum. You are affected and influenced by your parents' Cellular Experiences of their 3D Duality Programming. You are affected and influenced by your ancestors' Cellular Experiences of their 3D Duality. You are also affected and influenced by the collective Belief System in the decade in which you are born. You are further affected and influenced by each decade of the collective Belief System in which you live. So, you wonder why you and everyone on this planet are having such a difficult time finding their Selves? There are so many places to look!

The best place to start is your First or Base Chakra. One of the ways is to make sure you take your head out of your First Chakra so you can *see* where you are in this 3D Duality mess. By becoming the Non-Emotional Observer (NEO), you take away the emotional attachments or emotional hooks to the past. You detach your Self from the trauma-dramas, the B-lame Game, and begin to *see* all your experiences, your contracts, and your situations as the tools of experiences to find your Self and Take Back Your Power in real, practical ways. No fluff, no woo woo, no outside validation…just connecting to your Self. You are looking for the facts, not re-telling the stories.

To reiterate, every era holds a collective Belief System since the beginning: the 1930's economic Depression, the 1940's "World at War"; the 1950's "if you don't talk about 'it', 'it' doesn't exist"; the 1960's Camelot and the hidden agendas; the 1970's "tune out and turn on" and the search for meaning; the 1980's Me Generation, "greed is good", and excessive "big" hair, shoulder pads, cars, etc.; the 1990's confusion, and the prelude to the end of "whatever" with Y2K and 2012 and whenever the next end(s) of the world is predicted.

Since everything is resonance, the Consciousness of each decade, each century, and each eon also has a resonance of the collective Consciousness. Since fear is the major resonance of 3D Duality, in the perfect disorder/order of life here on Planet Earth, there is a balance. Although the balance may not seem very balanced, there is an order in the disorder. For example, in the 1930's the Belief System of Lack permeated the world. This Belief System was at that time defined as the Great Depression.

The children born during this period of time were embedded with this Fear Program which permeated the world during their gestation period in the womb. Their parents' experience of the Depression was the ultimate fear of scarcity, uncertainty, and powerlessness. This heavy, depressive, collective Belief System became the Cellular Experiences of those born in this era. The memorization of their parents' experiences of the Depression became the embedded Cellular reality of the babies. The children/adults of the Great Depression became depressed, fearful of not enough, and, in the worst-case scenarios, became hoarders, whether it was of money, things, or food. They were afraid of not having enough.

In this sense of powerlessness, a resonance was created to offset the heavy density of the fear. This resonance was music. The 1930's music was fast-paced ditty music which didn't always make sense. The songs included "Happy Days Are Here Again", "Puttin' On the Ritz" and "Ten Cents a Dance". This type of music was created to help people release the incredible losses of Power. In the 1940's, the romantic music of love helped offset the horrors of a World at War.

The black-and-white, flat-lined, "if you don't talk about 'it', 'it' doesn't exist" 1950's music was challenged by the 1954 hit "Rock Around the Clock" by Bill Haley and the Comets. Elvis Presley's music hit the charts. There were hearings in Washington, D.C. that the 1950 morals of the teenagers were in detriment. The 1960's, the 1970's, the 1980's, the 1990's, and the 2000's all had a particular resonance for each of these decades' stylistic music to seemingly balance out the resonance of the collective Consciousness. The adults were irritated, and the children and teenagers seemingly had something of their own. It was music. Music is a resonance used to counterbalance the resonance of the collective Consciousness in a particular era.

By the way, in the idea of children, there was really not a Consciousness of childhood until the early 1900's. Before that time, children were property. They were treated like little adults. If you look at paintings from Europe's history, the children of the upper classes were dressed as miniature adults. Children were married off at young ages regardless of their status. Poor children were property of the elite. There were no rights and little to no education for poor children until the turn of the century with the shift in Consciousness by the brilliant Maria Montessori, when she introduced the concept of childhood as we know it today. Before that time, childhood simply did not exist. You were either privileged as a product of the privileged or you were poor and the property of the privileged. And in both Duality versions of childhood, both were property. As a privileged child, you were programmed to do your duty. And as a poor child, you were programmed to do your duty.

All of the decades represented their own structure of a collective Consciousness in which everyone participated. Whether anyone was aware or not of the collective Consciousness in the decades in which they lived, everyone participated in their own unique way. Reflecting back, most people would say their pasts were the good ol' days! The question to ask without judgment is "What good ol' days?"

As you can see, each decade had its own unique characteristics. Certainly, in the 1950's, the dysfunctional program, "if you don't talk about it, it doesn't exist", had a direct impact to infuse the rebellion swelling in the 1960's. The rebellion swelled even more in the 1970's with the Flower Power of the hippies looking for nirvana through drugs, free love, and "tuning out and turning on". The 1980's turned the rebellion around, and the rebellion took a turn to greedy capitalism. Of course, the 1990's had its own form of confused rebellion with the concept of "where is all this going when the world ends in 2000?" The 2000's speculated another end of the world in 2012. And in 2016, the threat of Duality is the New World Order.

Perhaps it is the end of the world of what we have known as Duality and its illusional reality of control and manipulation. To end Duality is creating your world as what is Real to you. Ending Duality is a personal choice. If you are hooked into the trauma-dramas and the illusions, then by all means stay in Duality and the re-do illusions. If you are looking for freedom and to be in your own Power to create your life consciously, then by all means you can opt out of Duality.

You can choose be free of the illusions and the dysfunctional realities. Non-Duality is freeing your Human Spirit and Soul in your physical body to create your life as the Masters you are meant to be. This is the advent of becoming conscious without the limited Belief Systems of the 3D Duality Fear Programs.

Non-Duality is simplicity at its finest without the emotional and physical illusional dysfunctions. You are unhooking emotionally and physically from Duality. You are on your journey to freedom while living in your human body. You don't have to die or wait for the next lifetime in hopes to get free. You are exiting the Duality do-over trap in your continuum. You are freeing your Self. At last! Your Childish Adult Ego is growing up with your Perfect Child Within. You are becoming a Master.

Can you *see* and comprehend the perfection and simplicity of the Allness Consciousness where everyone and everything on Earth is connected? In this connectedness, why would there be a wanty-needy to war with each other?

Wanty-needy in any type of relationship is the ultimate victim-victimizer program running. There is no difference in the relationships between individuals, groups, or nations when wanty-needy rules. What is the point of controlling and manipulating each other in the wanty-needy resonance? What a waste of valuable time, effort, and creativity! What a waste of relationships! What a waste!

Perhaps the physical death of the 3D Duality Belief Systems is the perfect beginning to lay a new foundation for the New Earth! Ask your Self, is it worth continuing this madness and the long-lasting, dark night of Soul? Is it worth making your life so complicated that you deny your Self a great, healthy life?

Life does not have to be complex. Making everything so complicated only provides your Childish Adult Ego with the perfect excuses to validate the dysfunction of the 3D Duality System as a reality. The goal is letting go of the complications, the outside validation addictions, the trauma-dramas, and the waste of your valuable time and life.

Clear and conscious simplicity is the objective to create and manifest a collective Consciousness of Allness, which is Multi-Dimensional in functional operation. You have a choice as you move forward in your future. Dysfunctional complications or clear creative simplicity? The choice is yours.

In the Allness of a unified Consciousness within you, life is creative and free-flowing. In the 3D Duality Programs of Judgment, Lack, and Take-Away, everything is complicated and dysfunctional. As you integrate and unify your own Clear Consciousness within your Self, the magnitude of simplicity becomes evident. You simply create your own life consciously.

Your parents' Consciousness, whether clear or filled with fear, were influenced at their Cellular Level not only through their own individual Cellular Memory of experiences throughout their continuum, but also by their own memorization processes during the decade in which they were born. They were, just like you, subjected to the collective Consciousness of each decade in which they lived.

At the time of your conception, your parents' memorization processes significantly impacted your Cellular Experiences in the encoding in your DNA and biology. The encoding and the conditioning began the moment the sperm hit the egg and you're "in". As mentioned previously, your DNA was affected by the collective Belief System in the decade in which you were born. In each additional decade in which you live, you are also affected at your Cellular Level of experience by the collective Belief System.

Your DNA also includes being connected to your family members and their issues, which may be expressed as dysfunctions, diseases, disorders, addictions, as well as the contributions to your predispositions for health, wellness, and longevity. Your DNA affects your physical and emotional levels of Consciousness, whether you are aware of this or not.

Since DNA has a resonance and a field of energy based upon your Consciousness, it can be changed. Everything about you and your life is changeable, mutable, and variable. Roles change, scenes change, costumes change, relationships change, lifetimes change. Now it is time for a Consciousness change!

Duality is the Permanent Temporary

The Permanent Temporary is the permanent continuation of Duality in the temporary of lifetimes

As you evolve consciously, you evolve your DNA. Therefore, if you have a disposition of a physical disorder in your body through your genetics, you have the ability to change your DNA through evolving your Consciousness. For example, if your family has a history of diabetes, the old diagnosis is that you will have diabetes. However, as you become more conscious about diabetes, you clear your emotional attachments of bitterness, take care of your Self, and eat the proper nutrition. You do not have to continue the programming of diabetes. You Take Back Your Power and Take Charge of your life, your health, and your well-being. With knowledge and information instead of fear, you heal the emotional and physical issues of diabetes. You have a choice. Re-live the gene pool of your genetics *or* create a new healthy life.

Your biology is another receptacle which retains your history of experiences. On a daily, moment to moment basis, your history is recorded play by play, experience by experience, trauma-drama by trauma-drama, and sound by sound in your body.

When you are not in tune with your body, you have no idea most of the time how each of these experiences impacts your health and wellness. Every cell in every part of your body records, retains, and processes each experience. Every system of your biological make-up is affected by the recorded information. Where your body is physically and emotionally the weakest is where your body is challenged by illness and disease.

These records of your experiences are documented as your Cellular Memories or Memorizations. Even the sounds equated to these Cellular Experiences are recorded. Your body is constantly downloading, uploading, and sometimes just plain loading up on information, data, and experiences. Even if you are not aware of what is happening, or your computer/brain has simply forgotten the happenings, your body never forgets.

When the experiences are too much for your body to handle, your computer/brain shuts you down. You are on overload. However, it doesn't matter because your body continues to record what is happening in your life. When you are unconscious and your Consciousness is somewhere else – out-of-body, astral-traveling, or completely blank – your body is still recording the information. As these experiences are recorded, they are embedded in the various areas of your body to which your Consciousness is connected in the events.

For instance, over-responsibility affects the shoulders and upper back. Not being supported in any way affects your ankles and wrists. Your body is brilliant in its function to store the information. The intelligence and intellect of your body expect you to catch on someday. When you don't, your body breaks down and you get sick. So, with memories from your continuum or memorizations in this lifetime and with the sounds connected to the experiences, not only do your cells record the specifics in your body's various localities, your experiences are also connected to specific Chakras.

Your body of Consciousness is both connected and inter-linked within itself and its Chakra System to every frame of time and experience you have ever had. Whether your experiences are as an individual or as a member of a group, you are both a collective Consciousness of experiences and a part of a collective Consciousness of a group. Allowing your Self to detach from the 3D Duality Programs gives you the empowering opportunity for you to actually recognize and connect to this inter-link of Multi-Dimensional Consciousness that you are within your Self.

Without the Consciousness or the awareness of this inter-link, you cannot be hooked-up to this inter-connectedness which is within your body on all levels of your Multi-Dimensional Self. When you are not connected and inter-linked within your Self, you cannot be healed on all the levels of your Consciousness. When you are not connected and inter-linked within your Self, you cannot be fully and consciously participatory in your life. The dense resonance of Duality is definitely the challenge in making the connections with *all* levels of your Consciousness.

The conditioning is so accepted that it is mistaken for your Truth. There is a fine line between true and Truth. Another challenge for you and your body of Consciousness are the 3D Duality Fear Programs through the Belief System conditioning in this current lifetime. The conditioning is so obvious that they go unseen and undetected in hidden agendas of control and manipulation. Powerlessness is their key ingredient to take your Power away from you.

"True" is the accepted Belief System of the time. "True" is used to manipulate and control. In any religion, there are man-made interpretations of what will happen to you if you don't follow the specific rules and guidelines, making you afraid of "god". The greatest "god" fear is being punished for eternity. Yet this program of conditioning doesn't seem to be working very well with the crime rate, murder rate, and abuse rate being so high. Something is off kilter. The only thing not off kilter is the fear.

"Trues" change over time and lifetimes. The "trues" are dependent upon the illusional control which they have over an individual or a group. The use of "trues" can be extremely manipulative, especially for economic gain. The "trues" are extremely important to the 3D Duality Programs. The "trues" provide the means in which to manipulate the collective group Belief Systems. These "true" dogmas usually do not allow for any type of questioning. The "trues" demand only absolute followers, no questions asked!

The "trues" are not wrong or right. They are just what they are…true in their context of limitation.

Embedded in the "trues" are the unseen fears which are the perfect blockers or preventative measures to keep you in line and not asking any questions. This is the obvious hidden agenda. Like the purloined letter in the Edgar Allen Poe story, the fears are obvious but no one is allowed to talk about them.

As a result of the fears, there is no flow of energy because your Consciousness is directed to be fearful. With no flow, your Consciousness cannot be expanded beyond the limitations of 3D Duality.

Truth is Multi-Dimensional. Truth is Allness in action without opposition. Within Allness there is room for everyone. Truth provides the open space to agree to even disagree without going to war, without killing, without controlling and manipulating someone else's Truth.

Living out of the box of 3D Duality may be the opportunity of heaven right here on Earth. Perhaps when you have the opportunity to live your Truth, you will be too busy to run the 3D Duality Programs of Judgment, Lack, and Take-Away. You will have the time to create, implement, manifest, and actualize your life as the Conscious Creator In Charge of Your Life, creating newness on a continuing continuous continuum of productivity.

The Female creative brain is in the right Male side of the head and is connected to the left Female side of the body. Your Female side is your Power and your Creativity.

The Male brain is in the left Female side of the head and is connected to your right Male manifesting side. The 3D Duality Programming implies that the intelligence and intellect in your brain all stem from your left brain. The effect of this is that you are only using your left brain to be smart, though not so smart. As the left brain continues to run the 3D Duality Programs, your Female side, in fact, your entire body has to go along with the repetitious cycle of re-creating the same old same old. Even speaking the word *re-create, re-create, re-create* is nerve-wracking. You require using your *entire* brain, not just the left brain, for creative and manifesting balance.

Your brain is just a computer. Your REAL intelligence and intellect are in your body, not in your brain. Your body contains all of your experiences.

3D Duality's foundation is for the opposing polarity of your energy fields to be in opposition to each other and to your Self. The Female left-side Creative Consciousness is always in opposition to your Male right-side Manifesting Consciousness. Your upper Chakras are in opposition to your lower Chakras, and then each Chakra is in opposition to each other.

"Negative" is labeled bad and "positive" is labeled good. You have both negative and positive poles. "Negative" and "positive" are Duality terms and descriptives to keep opposition oppositional, which means *to keep you separated within your Self.*

When you go to the ocean, you *feel* the resonance of the negative ions coming from the water, and you *feel* good. So how can "negative" be bad? Without the negative and positive working together, you would not be who you are or be whole.

Balance is all aspects of your Self "being" in Allness with your Self from the inside out. Then the outside comes into creative and productive balance.

Balance is not standing still. Balance is movement. Balance is your Female Creative side in connection with your Body and your Clear Perfect Child Within implementing your creativity with your Male Manifesting side moving forward through your world bringing your creativity into fruition and actualization from your Heart, which is the most expansive resonance field in your body, into your physical tangible life. This is the Godness Consciousness progressive process of YOU living a full life.

Your Female (Creativity), Male (Manifestation), Perfect Child Within (Implementer), and your Heart through your hands into Actualization…is your Godness Consciousness progressive process in action:

1. **Create**   Female Left Side/right brain organization
2. **Implement**   Solar Plexus/Perfect Child Within (the *real* law of attraction)
3. **Manifest**   Male Right Side/left brain organization
4. **Actualize**   Heart (most expansive resonance field in your body) through your hands

This is moving forward in Multi-Dimensional directions in your continuing continuous continuum each and every day. This is stability in action!

When you are programmed that "negative" is bad and "positive" is good, there is no stability. You have a never-ending cycle of peaks and valleys. In Multi-Dimensional Truth, there is no opposition starting with your Self. So, ask your Self, "What is the point of always being in opposition instead of focusing on creating my life with clarity, focus, direction, and purpose on a clear path of creating, implementing, manifesting, and actualizing?"

Consider a shift of Consciousness that "negative" is not labeled bad and "positive" is not labeled good. Based upon

Consciousness, **it is the appropriate or inappropriate use of your energy which is the key to your results.** If you are fear-filled, what you manifest is fear-filled experiences. If you are clear how the creative progressive process works, then you clearly create the life you require, desire, and deserve. You have the choice to Take Back Your Power.

"If you don't like what is happening in your life, then STOP!

Create a new happening that you do like!"

-Sherryism

The Truth is…how you use your Consciousness and the Power of your Resonance is what makes the difference to your life and to all of those with whom you participate. When you clearly comprehend the difference between your Truth and the 3D Duality Belief Systems, you do indeed have a choice of how you live. At this point, you begin to balance your polarity into the Allness of your Multi-Dimensional Self. This is the Shift.

You are beginning to align all aspects of your awareness from the inside Cellular Levels of Consciousness. You are beginning the progressive process of unifying your Multi-Dimensional Self through the Shift of becoming Who You Are and Taking Back Your Power.

The clarity of your resonance is *felt* not only by you but by those around you. Alignment is occurring within all aspects of you, your DNA, your biology, your physiology, and your Chakra System. You are becoming YOU in the Allness Consciousness of Truth. In this resonance, there is no time or space for the 3D Duality Programs.

Before we delve into the Chakra System, there is a misconception that an open Chakra is a good thing. This is not necessarily the Truth. If one or all of your Chakras are open and you are NOT conscious of your Self *or* the 3D Duality Programs of Judgment, Lack, and Take-Away (the dogmatic fear-filled limited Belief Systems), you can actually hurt your Self emotionally, mentally, physically, spiritually, and financially by giving away your Power un-knowingly.

Until you are aware how your Chakra Systems work, be vigilant. For example, if you wear your Heart on your sleeve figuratively, you actually have an unconscious, open Heart. Wonder why you get emotionally hurt? Wonder why you attract the same abuser or victimizer into your life? This is why!

Getting your Chakra System consciously in alignment with your entire physical body of Consciousness involves not only understanding how your systems work together or in opposition to each other, but also comprehending as a Multi-Dimensional human being how everything works together from your inside out. If one or several aspects of you are out of alignment and not conscious, then you are out of balance. This is how your systems work or don't work together.

The 7 Chakra System is no different than any other system in your body. It is both energetic and physical. It is physical since everything about you is physical, no matter whether it is seen or unseen. Each Chakra is a center of information.

The First Chakra:

Base Foundation

Your First Chakra is located at the base of your spinal column or tailbone and includes the pubic bone. In this First Chakra resides all of your Consciousness. All of your physical 3D Duality bands embedded with your fears, ideas, Belief Systems, agendas, and issues about your life or lives are located here. Your physical 3D Duality bands connected to your biological family and your personal and professional relationships – past, present, and future – are located here. Even your ideas about your Self, good, bad or indifferent, are housed here in the First Chakra of Consciousness. Whether you are aware of this information or not, this is the place it all begins in the 7 Chakra System.

All of your interactions and behaviors with your Self, your family, friends, associates, co-workers, strangers, and perceived enemies begin with the resonance of your Consciousness. The more constricted the resonance of your Consciousness and awareness, the more frequent the trauma-dramas and dysfunctional relationships become the "norm" in your life.

As a result of this resonance of your awareness, on-going personal emotional, mental, physical, spiritual, and financial challenges continue to plague you. These challenges are usually labeled "failures" from the 3D Duality perception. The lower the resonance of your Belief Systems, the more difficult and emotionally challenging the problems continue to be.

When the foundation of your First Chakra is infused with the Belief Systems of the 3D Duality Fear Programs of Judgment, Lack, and Take-Away, your life is filled with fear. There is no other way in the resonance. When the foundation of your Consciousness is FEAR, the foundation of your life is FEAR-filled. Every interaction, every relationship, every situation, and everything about your life is affected and infected by FEAR. Every form of emotional fear – less-than, undeserving, guilt, shame, blame, inadequacy, abandonment, and the list of fears in every form of Judgment, Lack, and Take-Away goes on and on –

impacts your life on a moment to moment, day to day basis. FEAR influences how you create, implement, manifest, and actualize your life.

The Karmic Programs of Lessons and the 3D Duality Fear-based B.S. Programs imprison you in this First Chakra to be chained to the cyclical loops of ups and downs. As long as you buy into these programs, you are caught up in the dysfunctional cycles.

Let go of the never-ending 3D Duality Lesson Program. How many times do you have to "do" abandonment or any other dysfunctional program? Abuser/abused, victim/victimizer, and the list goes on and on. The Truth is the only lesson to know, understand, and comprehend is that YOU are love, lovable, and deserve to be loved unconditionally. This resonance must start with you in your First Chakra. Otherwise, you sentence your Self to exist in 3D Duality Programming lifetime after lifetime.

All of the programs located in the First Chakra of this old system are what this one and only lesson is all about. It is loving your Self unconditionally, accepting your Self completely, and letting go of the fears which have kept you hooked into the emotional controls and manipulations of these programs. Any and all of the energy you expend on inappropriate behaviors and actions are fueled by these fears.

All versions of the fears are just that – versions of the same thing regardless if they are labeled fear of this or fear of that. They are the same. The different labels are given are to keep you unbalanced. Fear is unbalanced living. You can label the fears what you will and attempt to find the logic in the labels. Fear has no logic, intellect, or intelligence. Fear only has control and manipulation as its agenda. Are you willing to continue to be ruled by an agenda, or are you willing to Take Back Your Power?

This First Chakra houses all of the versions of the Lack Program: the fears of inadequacy, not good enough, and not measuring up. They are all the fears **validating the invalidation of you**. They state, "You don't have it and you don't deserve it", whatever the "it" issue is.

The Big Lack Program embedded in this First Chakra is the relationship to money. "Money is the root of all evil", "money doesn't grow on trees", "throw good money after bad", "filthy rich", "rich people are not happy", "money buys happiness", "money can't buy happiness", or whatever the version hooking you in that money has more value than you. This keeps you from having money. The Truth is money is a form of energy. Give your Power away to money, and you drain your energy. You become weak.

The energy of Consciousness that you attach to money determines your relationship to it. The correlation between the energy of money and the concept of money as a force over you keeps you in a fear-based mode of being controlled and manipulated by a product called money.

The Truth is…money does not have Power over you. You simply have been programmed to *belief system* that money is more valuable than you. You "think" you believe money is not available to you. This is a Belief System and not what you innately believe. When your fear of lacking money, or any fear of lack from the Lack Program is housed in this First Chakra, you can manifest physical pain and lower back problems. Colon cancer, hemorrhoids, fissures, rectal bleeding, rectal cancer, etc. are manifestations of emotional and physical issues in your First Chakra.

As you comprehend that money or anything is a form of the physical manifestation of energy, you detach from the emotional issues attached to the Lack Program. You Take Back Your Power from the Belief Systems that money, "things", or people control your life. Money and things are not entities. They are manifested products of energy. They can't control you unless you allow your Self to be controlled. Be In Charge of Your Life. Let go of any form of control. Control is debilitating for both the controlled and the one doing the controlling.

Giving your Power away to anything or anyone is giving your Life away

Your *real* wealth is the clear knowledge and comprehension you gain from your experiences throughout your continuum without the emotional attachments to the 3D Duality Programs. The wisdom of your wealth is gained by letting go of all of the versions of the Fear Programs instilled in you that your worth is determined from the outside of you.

Healing begins when you comprehend in your First Chakra that these burdensome Fears of Judgment, Lack, and Take-Away can no longer take up valuable space in your body. When you accept that your worth and value come from within you, the worth and value of your life become paramount.

Relationships in all forms – family, friends, business, acquaintances, and all aspects of your life – become more open, more joyful, and more satisfying. An important factor in this change is comprehending that living your life based on the fears housed in this First Chakra is what keeps you powerless. A life full-filled, a life worth *life*-ing, begins to happen the minute you choose to unlock your expanded awareness/Consciousness by releasing the Karma, Lessons, and Re-incarnation Belief System that you "have to" exist in these programs again and again.

All judgments, all misunderstandings, and all the emotional and physical pain in relationships were, in the past, expressed through the debilitating behaviors involved in your relationships. These behaviors were expressed because you were not aware of how these 3D Duality Programs embedded in your First Chakra affected your entire life and lives. You were not even aware how these embedded programs affected those with whom you were involved.

In Duality, relationships are NOT *real*. It doesn't mean you aren't involved in relationships as a reality. Ask your Self, what is *real* about your relationships if they are based upon how you would like them to be? Are you including how the other person or persons involved would like you to be?

If this sounds like double talk, it is. Do you really *listen* in the conversations, or are you only hearing what you thinky-thinky you wanty-needy to hear? Now ask your Self, what exactly are you saying and what is the other person or persons saying? Are you *listening* to each other(s), or are you just hearing what you don't want to hear?

Changing your foundation of Consciousness in your First Chakra opens the pathways of transition and transformation to the other six Chakras. As in any organization, the top, or in this case, your expanded Consciousness is only as strong and inter-linked as your foundation of Consciousness which begins in your First Chakra. Shit does NOT happen…it begins in your First Chakra.

All the fears of any kind housed in your First Chakra impact the entire Consciousness of your physical body, emotionally, mentally, physically, spiritually, and financially.

Your Childish Adult Ego, your Spirit, your Soul, your Divine Mind (expanded awareness), in other words, all of *you* is connected to your First Chakra.

The illness, disease, and/or dysfunctions in your body are the direct results of the Duality Belief Systems of fear spreading from your First Chakra to the other Chakras and extending to all the other systems of your body. Where your body is the weakest is where the illness, disease, or dysfunction begins to manifest, based upon the fears locked in the foundation of your Belief Systems within your First Chakra.

Limited Belief Systems (B.S.) or Clear Consciousness in the foundation of your First Chakra makes the differences in how you create your life through your Creative Sexual Generative Second Chakra.

B.S. begets B.S.

Clear Consciousness begets unlimited creativity.

Begin by focusing on totally accepting your Self and unconditionally loving your Self beginning in your First Chakra. This is not being Self-Centered. Being Centered in Self is a giant step to becoming conscious. Becoming conscious is being fully aware that you have not been fully aware of how the 3D Duality Programs have stopped you from being you!

Begin as the Non-Emotional Observer (NEO) by examining all your ingrained Belief Systems, whether political, religious, cult, metaphysical, science, medicine, etc. See if they resonate with you.

Are you asking your Self over and over again any of these questions: *What am I doing here? What am I supposed to be doing?*

What is my purpose in life? What is this all about? Why am I repeating dysfunctional relationships? Or are you simply asking: *Why am I not happy?*

If you are continuing to ask your Self the same questions repeatedly that do not seem to have answers, then somewhere buried in your First Chakra of 3D Duality Programs you are running <u>unconsciously</u>, not subconsciously, programming which prevents you from finding your answers.

Fear…Fear of your own Power…
is "the" prevention program which keeps on ticking
and "prevents" you from getting your answers

The 3D Duality Programs control you by reaffirming to you that the answers are outside you. There is no "outside of you" that you don't create. Whether you believe it or not, the 3D Duality Programs wanty-needy you to *not* Believe in Your Self! Continuing to *not* Believe in Your Self is the perfect way to control and manipulate you by any group, guru (gee you are you), authority figure, etc.

As long as you remain in the Belief Systems of less, "they" (the controlling authority figures) will always be "more" than you. This is what the Belief Systems in the 3D Duality First Chakra is all about. They keep you from Taking Back Your Power.

Becoming Clearly Conscious to all the Belief Systems
and the manipulation of the 3D Duality Programs
is how you set your Self free
and Take Back Your Power!

This is your Paradigm Shift out of 3D Duality. Be of "it", your Inner Truth, and not in "it", Duality! Clear the old paradigm out of your First Chakra. The clarity begins. So does your Real, Newness Life begin! Take the initiative and begin to establish in your First Chakra that *you* Believe in Your Self, *you* trust your intuition, and *you* trust your Heart. This is the first place to start.

The Second Chakra:

Creative, Generative, Sexual

As you make the conscious choice, and only you can make that choice to release the old 3D Duality Programs from your First Chakra, you create a dynamic Shift beginning with this new, clear, powerful Consciousness which produces an upward, well-structured movement of your energy into your Second Chakra. Your Second Chakra is your Creative, Generative, Sexual Chakra.

How you create your life – your relationships, your professions, your income, and all of your entire outside world – is generated from this Second Chakra. The issue is *how* you *created* your life, because what determines what, how, and why you create your life as you do is directly connected to the Belief Systems in your First Chakra.

You must make the choice! Do you continue in your continuing continuous continuum of the 3D Duality Programs of Judgment, Lack, and Take-Away? Do you hold on to their First Chakra puckering dysfunctions of limitations?

Or, do you now choose to delete these programs and replace them with believing in your Self, believing in your intuition, and believing in your unlimited, creative abilities? Is there really any other choice to make? Do you decide to keep embracing the pain and the emotional delusions? NO!

Now, with a clear comprehension from the First Chakra of clear believing in your Self comes the genesis of your seed or ideas. Your seed of creativity can generate the physical child you birthed. Or, it can be the idea from the creative inventor within you who is fully in charge of what you are choosing to create, produce, implement, manifest, and actualize in the physical world outside of your Self.

Every person, every situation, every event, and every condition are created, produced, implemented, manifested, and actualized by YOU. Are you getting the picture of how powerful you are? Are you comprehending that you are the only one that can be In Charge of Your Life? There is absolutely nothing in your life you do not create, whether you are conscious, or aware of it, or not!

No matter how your "outside" life appears, you are the one making it "appear" before your very eyes. When you realize with *real eyes* that you are the one who creates your limited Realities <u>or</u> your unlimited Realness, you are accepting that you are sovereign within your Self and have sovereignty over your own life. You are the head of your state of Consciousness. How you choose to play in the outside world is the Role of your Self.

Everything in your physical world is the manifestation of *your creative ideas*, which are embedded within your Second Chakra. For example, your state of Consciousness says, "This is my worst fear". Now consider how many times you created in your life your worst fearful experience.

This is not a judgment or commentary on your ability to create from your Second Chakra. This is simply a fact about how you have utilized your creativity to create your life based upon either limited Belief Systems <u>or</u> Believing in Your Self, your Truth, and your natural abilities to manifest the life you require, desire, and deserve.

Ask your Self, "Is my creativity a physical manifestation of my fears? Or, is the physical manifestation of what I require, desire, and deserve clearly what I am getting in life?"

Your First Chakra is, again, what you *belief system* or what you Believe for Your Self. The issues of relationships from your First Chakra connect to your Second Chakra with your Sexual, Generative, Creative ideas about your Self. They produce the dynamics and behaviors from the level of Consciousness in these two Chakras. Scary or clear?

As another example, if you are fearful of being abandoned, the relationships you create outside of you match your fear with the other person(s). Abandoner meets the abandonee. Victimizer meets the Victim. Controller meets the controlled. Your Consciousness and "their" Consciousness match. The list could be casts of thousands. You could call this mis-match.com. However, you must comprehend this is the perfect dysfunctional match. You draw the perfect person(s) to you who will validate your wanty-needyness to **validate the invalidation of your Self**. You will be abandoned, victimized, or controlled. How wondrously dysfunctional! This is your First and Second Chakra in action.

You can count the ways you have been abandoned, victimized, and controlled. Stop counting and don't count on this dysfunction anymore. Or, if in your cleverness you are tired of being victimized, abandoned, and controlled, you can play the *other* Role. You still have the option of Re-incarnation to get even. Or you can make a choice to stop!

You can stay in the Victim Program, whichever Role you play, and enhance it with the Blame Game. The roots of the Blame Game go deep. The programming that the person(s) outside of you have abandoned, victimized, or controlled you provides you with an excuse to give up your Power. The Be-Lame Game is crippling. This game becomes the dysfunctional exchange of draining energy in the relationship resulting from your unconscious Belief Systems.

You use up your vital energy and drain your creativity. You become exhausted, anxious, and depressed. You are deeply disappointed in life. All the drugs in the world cannot clear the disappointment issue that is labeled depression. The only thing which can clear depression is getting to the core of the disappointment.

By identifying the situation as the Non-Emotional Observer (NEO), you comprehend "how" the disappointment became embedded in your Cellular Memory as the result of an emotional experience. You were not able to clearly process what was happening at that particular time of dysfunctional emotional state of unconsciousness. You did not have enough information or facts. You took the experience personally because you did not know there is another way to see it. You gave your Power away.

In this giving-Power-away experience, you lock into your Cellular Experience the emotional attachment to the person(s), situation, or condition of the experience. You become stuck and you blame and you re-live the Blame Game over and over again. The situation or person(s) may change, but the dysfunctional re-enactment becomes the "norm" as the blaming Victim. You, in your Second Chakra, then re-create the dysfunctional experience repeatedly. This is a behavioral pattern established in your Cellular unconsciousness. You accept the dysfunctional outcomes as "the way your life is"!

When there is a Victim Program of Judgment, Lack, and Take-Away embedded in your First Chakra, the behavioral pattern becomes the unconscious sick reality. Your Second Creative Generative Sexual Chakra then attracts, through the Victim band, the perfect Victimizer. The bands go back and forth. The push-me-pull-ums. The Victimizer victimizes! The Victim is the Victim.

When there is no current Victimizer, then the Victim victimizes his Self or her Self. This is the way of the 3D Duality Programs in the Victim/Victimizer Roles. This is the Game of Force. There is no Power. There is only control and manipulation. In many cases, the Victim is the one who forces the Victimizer to victimize. This is not judging the individuals involved. This is simply how the bands of the Victimhood Program operate.

In Quantum Physics, there is a string theory that everything is made up of strings vibrating at a certain frequency. The Truth is there are invisible energy bands with information on them going out from your body and connecting to the energy bands of another person or group. If your band sends out information that "I am a Victim", then you will attract the Victimizer. This is why the Law of Attraction becomes the Law of Distraction, unconsciously creating and existing in 3D Duality Belief Systems. What you say, spoken or not, makes your day.

You unconsciously create all the trauma-dramas in your life and repeat them both in this lifetime, previous lifetimes, and in lifetimes to come. Give your Self the opportunity to consider how incredible your life can be if you choose to release the fears and be an active, conscious participant in the creative process of your life.

You can choose to draw friends and a supportive community to you through the *real* Law of Attraction using your clear, conscious, and fearless First Chakra working in unison with your Second Creative Chakra. Or, you can continue in the Law of Distraction sending out dysfunctional fear-based bands to attract more traumas and dramas in your life.

When you are clearly conscious, is there any other choice? Unless you love being the Victim and love 3D Duality dysfunctional relationships along with the emotional pain and suffering programs, then by all means continue on in your continuous continuum. By the way, if you believe being a martyr is the way to go, ask your Self, how many martyrs in history are remembered? The despots are remembered; the martyrs are only numbers without faces or names, if that!

Being fully participatory in all of your creativity and creativeness is what life is all about. In the beginning, there was nothing. Then from the nothingness came the something. When you are in alignment with your Godness Consciousness within you, devoid of the 3D Duality Programs of Fear, you have ascended your Consciousness. You are fully participatory. You are using the fullest potential of your creativity to create your life consciously. You are creating Multi-Dimensionally. Get it?!

God created! YOU, as your own Godness Consciousness, create from the nothingness into the somethingness of whatever it is you are creating. The distinction is Consciousness. You are Multi-Dimensional as is God.

Look around at everything and at all this planet has to offer. Look at the diversity of people, places, terrain, weather, religions, politics, groups, and on and on and on. Is this not Multi-Dimensional creation at its finest *or* at its worst?

Clear, deliberate, and focused Consciousness is creative. So is unconscious, fear-ridden, unfocused, undirected

Consciousness creative. See how it works? You do have a choice!

So, it's either the powerful Godness within you creating your experiences or it's the limited you disconnected from your Godness Power who is creating your experiences. You are the one who determines how you create your life. Connection or no connection! Your life is up to you. When life is not turning out the way you "think" it should, then what are you "shoulding" on? Your Self? Blaming it on God? Are you not accepting it is you who has emotionally disconnected from the Godness within you?

There is no connection to a God outside of you. The connection begins inside of you. If your First Chakra is afraid of the connection to God, then your Second Chakra is out of alignment with your Godness Consciousness. Now all you can create for your Self are the trauma-dramas, such as being less, being the Victim, and all the stuff that goes with this crap stuck in your First Chakra!

The illnesses connected to your Second Chakra include colon cancer, IBS (I bull-shit), polyps, intestinal issues, Crohn's, uterine, cervical, prostate cancer, hip replacements, lower spine issues, and the list goes on. Your Second Chakra is directly related to the past, whether this lifetime or other lifetimes.

There is also a direct connection of your Second Chakra to your Occipital Bone. When you begin to release the tightness and tension in the Occipital area, there is also a physical and emotional release in the abdomen.

Your hips, housing your abdomen, are also connected to your jaw. TMJ is a physical manifestation of not able to speak your Truth. You clinch your jaws and your hips tighten. Since you can't speak your Truth it is most difficult to create your life, and your hips will misalign. Even when you replace your hips or have surgery on your jaws, the emotional issues are still buried deep inside these areas of the body.

The disconnection to your Truth is still there no matter how many times you have something replaced. Until you replace the old programs, they are still unconsciously running at your Cellular Level.

Consciousness is the solution
Consciousness is the answer

As long as you allow your Self to be controlled and manipulated by the 3D Duality Programs, your life is filled with trauma-dramas, illness, dysfunctional relationships, and disconnection to your Self.

Being connected to your Self from the inside makes your outside life happen so much more productively. Fully participatory means you are fully participating in all aspects of your life. You are not emotionally and physically drained of your vital energy. You do not allow your Self to be controlled and you do not have to control. You are not manipulated and there is no requirement for you to manipulate. You can *see* what a waste of your valuable time it is to NOT create from this Second Chakra clearly and consciously.

Ascension is not some mysterious or mystical occurrence. Ascension is rising above the emotional turmoil of the Judgment, Lack, and Take-Away 3D Duality Programs. It is saying, enough is enough of the Fears. And it is taking charge of your life and your creative process each minute of every day. These are *your* minutes, hours, days, weeks, and years…you get the idea. You absolutely deserve to have a great life.

Here in this Second Chakra, you can stop playing the emotional, dysfunctional love relationships of manipulation. What a waste of valuable time to play left computer/brain head games which are connected to your Creative Generative Sexual Chakra!

Relationships don't happen. You send out the bands of either wanty-needy or clear bands of what you require, desire, and deserve in a relationship, whether romantic or not. Relationships are not accidents. Confused bands beget confused relationships.

If you don't know your Truth or where you stand, don't expect anyone else to understand where you stand or what is your Truth. Relationships are dysfunctional because your Belief Systems are dysfunctional.

Clarity attracts clarity. Dysfunction attracts dysfunction. How fun is this? NOT!

Your Childish Adult Ego (CAE) is your Master Manipulator of your Second Chakra. Your CAE is your survivalist. It only knows how to survive. Survival is all your CAE knows. Why? Because your CAE, from lifetime to lifetime and time frame through time frame, kept you alive, if you call that alive.

As you become conscious, your Childish Adult Ego (CAE) has to grow up and get conscious. All your CAE has known is keeping you alive, which is not always living. So, love your CAE unconditionally. Let he or she know they can't kill you this time. Remember, the CAE's behavior is "well, if life doesn't work out, let's die because the return clause of Re-incarnation is written in the 3D Duality Contract".

It is time for your Childish Adult Ego (CAE) to grow up and live. It is time for your CAE to stop running your

Second Chakra, re-creating the trauma-dramas to validate you existing in survival mode.

The Survival Program is exhausting and it prevents you from living life to the fullest. How can you fully thrive if you are always just barely surviving? There is no Thriving in Surviving.

Your Childish Adult Ego knows the 3D Duality Programs. You and your body just go along for the ride of your lifetime(s). Your Childish Adult Ego sets you up for re-creating all the various versions of the same 3D Duality Programs. Different time frames, different costumes, different scenes, different Roles, and yet the same.

Appearances are deceiving when you are not conscious in your Consciousness. There are no surprises here. Your Childish Adult Ego knows so well how to access your Cellular Memory, Cellular Memorizations, and the Cellular Sounds associated with the events and the issues residing in your First Chakra.

How clever your Childish Adult Ego is to always re-create from your Second Chakra the different versions of trauma-dramas. Though they appear to be different, they are basically the same re-productions and re-enactments. Your clever little Childish Adult Ego knows how to survive and drag you along.

Periodically there are reprieves when life looks great. However, your Childish Adult Ego knows it is time to create an ax to fall on your head to validate that life cannot be great all the time. So, watch out for the ax!!! As long as you are unconscious, your Childish Adult Ego will run your show/life!

The energy emitted from the unconscious imprinting in your Second Chakra of the victim/victimizer, abuser/abused, manipulator/manipulated, and master/slave programs is part of your Cellular Memory or Cellular Memorization which has not been cleared. You can guarantee that in whatever 3D Duality Program you are holding on to, you will absolutely play out your part in the scene or scenes. You have no other choice until you choose, as the Non-Emotional Observer (NEO), to go "into" the Consciousness of your Role and *see* who has played and replayed with you. Otherwise, you are locked into the programming, re-living your Role or Roles.

Now, as this Non-Emotional Observer (NEO), you have the opportunity to release your emotional attachments and hooks to the issues. Let them go! This is the time for you to forgive the issues in your tissues and those who are attached to the issues, including your Self.

Forgiveness simply means for *you* to give *your* Self this opportunity to be the Non-Emotional Observer (NEO), witness the events, *see* all the players, and give *your* Self permission to let go of the emotional attachments or hooks.

Don't give any more energy to the past issue or to what happened. **You cannot change the past.**

Release the issue from your Cellular Memory, Cellular Memorization, and the Cellular Sound connected to the experiences. This is the time to move forward, free and clear of the past which no longer serves you. You can do this.

Your commitment to healing and being free from the issues and fears begins in these first two Chakras of the old 7 Chakra System. Remember, the 7 Chakra System is the 3D Duality of the Judgment, Lack, and Take-Away Programs.

All of the diseases, dysfunctions, malfunctions, and physical and emotional pain in the lower areas of your body are caused and created from the unconscious Consciousness buried in your cells within the locality of these Chakras. When your life force is not being supported, your creativity is not being nurtured. You are not honoring your life because of the 3D Duality Programs of Fear.

Your life force is weakened and you become ill or diseased. The physicality of problems as previously described of cancer, intestinal tract problems, and bladder issues is the result of not being conscious in your First and Second Chakra.

The Second Chakra is the correlation between your left side and your right side. Your left side is the Power of your Female Consciousness of creativity, inspiration, intuition, and guidance. Your right side is your Male manifesting side.

In actuality, the physical body at this point in time on the planet is Male. This has nothing to do with gender, sexuality, or sexual preference. This is simply the physical embodiment of the Male left brain Consciousness of Duality.

All the gods are Male. All the gurus are Male. All the wars are manifestations of the left computer/brain Male Consciousness of 3D Duality. Fight or flight. The Male Duality Consciousness is Force.

Your Female Consciousness is your Power. The energy of your Female Consciousness gives birth to your idea or seed. It's your natural creativity. Your Female Consciousness is the foundation of the new paradigm of the physical establishment of the Thirteen Chakras. Your Spirit is the igniting "light" of the expression of your Female Consciousness.

However, in your 3D Duality Body of the 7 Chakra System, the Female embodiment of your Spirit is suppressed. Your Spirit of creativity is shut down by the Belief Systems of Fear, and then Karma, Lessons, and Re-incarnation take over and over and over again. There is no Power in these manifestations of the do-it-over-and-over-again-and-again programming without resolutions and definitely no solutions.

When your left-side Female Consciousness is shut down, your Male manifesting right side can only manifest the same dysfunctional behaviors. There is no alignment in this fear. Therefore, the repetitive scenarios continue. Your Female and Male Consciousness then remain, regardless of your lifetime or time frame, in opposition to each other within your physical and emotional body. Opposition and internal and external war are the rule and the "force" of this powerless Duality Consciousness.

This time of transformation or Transcension is the clear connection and alignment of your powerful Female Creativity in union with your Male Manifesting Consciousness. This is the *real* sacrament of marriage which takes place within you. This happens in your sacrum based upon sacredness and not upon the sacrifice promoted by the 3D Duality Programs. This is both the metaphoric description and the Realness of the new paradigm.

Without this union, healing your Childish Adult Ego is not possible. Healing both the Female and Male 3D Duality emotional and physical issues allow the Childish Adult Ego to grow up, to stop running the old programming of re-cycled survival, and to move forward in life creating and experiencing *real* newness.

The sacredness of healing the Male, Female, and the Childish Adult Ego into a blended Consciousness of

Beingness is the Allness of your Multi-Dimensional Self. This connection and expansion of your Consciousness, beyond the confines of the 3D Duality Programs of Fear, empowers you to ascend your Beingness into the Allness of your Multi-Dimensional Self.

In the Newtonian paradigm, it is cause and effect. This is the trap of 3D Duality. In Quantum Physics, you affect the cause because you are **being** the **cause** for your Self. "Because" is no longer an excuse of why you can't do something or anything.

Grounding this newness of your Power through your physical body unifies the physicality of your Soul and Spirit, releasing the density of the old 3D Duality Reality. More new dimensions and new creativities are now your possibilities and potentials being generated from your dreams into Realness. Your choices are unlimited. Your creativity is unlimited. YOU are UNLIMITED. You Take Back Your Power.

The Third Chakra:

Solar Plexus
Perfect Child Within and Childish Adult Ego

As you continue to heal your Self by addressing and liberating your Self from the physicality of your emotional issues in your First and Second Chakras, your Clear Consciousness frees the Power of your energy to move up through your body. You are actually physically "ascending" your empowered energy in an upward movement.

You are clear about Believing in Your Self in your First Chakra. You are in charge of your creativity in your Second

Chakra and you absolutely know how to participate in life or not participate.

You are in Clear Choice mode. You are no longer emotional, powerless, in fearful decision-making mode, or in survival re-action mode. You are connecting with your Self and with life. You make choices.

As you integrate through this sacred Male/Female marriage of your Consciousness and energy in your physical body, you literally birth a new child in your Solar Plexus. In a physical and metaphorical sense, you are birthing the child of your Godness Consciousness within you.

In your Solar Plexus also resides your Childish Adult Ego (CAE), who represents all of the children from all of your lifetimes who existed through the 3D Duality Programs, especially the survival game program.

Your CAE is your survivalist. This is the profession of your CAE to assist you to survive until you die the 3D Duality death and return to survive again and again. Being rich or poor is not the issue. The issue is how you create all the 3D Duality versions of survival and death!

Your CAE experiences throughout your continuum going in and out of relationships, repeating relationships, changing genders, exchanging your bands of Belief Systems, playing out different Roles, and *existing*. The lifetimes where you became detached are the lifetimes you truly lived. These are the moments of non-emotional clarity when you are detached from the trauma-dramas. However, since 3D Duality is the continuation of Karma, Lessons, and Re-incarnation, most of your lifetimes are in the survival mode of existing.

You were programmed to exist for the elite, whoever they were or are in this lifetime and whatever the definition of royalty — the authority figure, the leader, the athlete, the rock star, and the person or persons or group or groups who are defined as "better than you". These elite are the "illusional royalty" defined by a 3D Duality society. This is sick, ill, and dysfunctional. If you cannot live up to the delusional standards of the royalty, then your Childish Adult Ego must do anything and everything to be identified with "them" and give your Power away again and again, lifetime after lifetime. How absolutely 3D Duality!!!

As you become clearly conscious, your Childish Adult Ego (CAE) begins to grow up. This is not always an easy process because your CAE only knows how to survive in the programs.

Your CAE fights you becoming conscious, sometimes even fighting you to the death. As you become conscious, your CAE does not wanty-needy to be put out of a job. Your CAE knows you have bought into the Karma, Lessons, and Re-incarnation Programs. So, big deal. You die and you will return! Your CAE knows you can't really die; you will just transition to another time frame. Your CAE is an expert and knows 3D Duality Programs from your core!

Your Clear Child, or your Perfect Child Within, waits patiently for you and your Childish Adult Ego to become conscious. This Perfect Child Within represents all of the children from all of your lifetimes of experiences and relationships, events, and situations in which you participated. Your Perfect Child Within, as the representative of these children, holds the memories, memorizations, and sounds of the joys and the traumas of all your times. This Child is your resource for healing the Fear Programs of Judgment, Lack, and Take-Away and your emotional attachments or hooks to your past experiences, which are held within your body at the Cellular Level. The time is here to bring this Perfect Child Within into the Light!

Your Perfect Child Within, through the connection with your Conscious Female and Conscious Male, is the Conscious Power Source of **implementation**. In other words, this is how it works. Your Female is your Power and your creativity. Your Perfect Child Within is the implementer who attracts your sources and resources you require. Your Male side is the manifestor of your creativity. Together, they create, implement, and manifest the actualization process of your creativity.

This Perfect Child Within remembers the pursuit of discovery without fear. This Perfect Child Within remembers how to imagine and how to dream without fear. This Perfect Child Within remembers how to vision, how to connect in your physical body with your Spirit and your Soul without questions. This Perfect Child Within remembers the pursuit of discovery with joy, excitement, and enthusiasm. Your clear inner Perfect Child is your Light.

Light is clear information without any emotional attachment or baggage from the past. This Perfect Child Within is the Godness connection within you. This Perfect Child Within is your Christed Consciousness.

Through the eyes of this Perfect Child Within, you *see* the many aspects of your participations. You are no longer hindered by the limitations of your 3D Duality views of life.

Your Solar Plexus is the place underneath your Heart Chakra where your Perfect Child Within lives. When this Child is forced to exist through the embedded fears in your First Chakra, the creative process from the Second Chakra is extremely painful for your Perfect Child Within. The deep, cyclical, emotionally and physically painful experiences shut down the Perfect Child Within. Your Childish Adult Ego has to step up to the plate, defend you, and make sure you are in the limited survival mode.

The physically draining, illness-making, emotionally painful experiences of your stories force your Perfect Child Within to hide deep inside you. Your Childish Adult Ego (CAE) pops to the surface to take control and manipulate you and also to be manipulated by the 3D Duality Programs. Your CAE is your false protector. Your Perfect Child Within is manipulated by the emotional attachments to the dysfunctional past and by the 3D Duality Programs. Your Perfect Child Within has very short windows of opportunities to come to the surface.

A life-altering, life-changing experience is usually the opportunity for the Perfect Child Within to come to life. When the opportunity presents itself, you are shaken at your core Belief Systems in both your First and Second Chakras. When the foundation of your limited Belief Systems (B.S. Programs) are uprooted, your Perfect Child Within knows, understands, and comprehends you are in a paradigm Shift of Consciousness.

Your Perfect Child Within is your empowerment. Your Perfect Child Within assists you to remember your Truth. Your Perfect Child Within supports you to let go of the programming and the "trues" of the B.S. Programs, which are so manipulative.

Comprehend that all childish behaviors are the re-active, repeated, dysfunctional behavior patterns in which your Childish Adult Ego (CAE) is programmed to deal with situations. Your CAE doesn't know he or she has a choice to do anything differently. The reaction is the cover-up and the illusional protection of your CAE in your adult body.

The Childish Adult Ego (CAE) and the "adult" operate dysfunctionally together, both wanty-needing to survive and to be "right". According to your CAE and your "adult", being right is much more important than being clear. 3D Duality rules dysfunctionally and continually!

The Perfect Child Within allows the Childish Adult Ego (CAE) and the "adult" to *think* this duo is "right" and even righteous. The Perfect Child Within provides the space, patiently standing by, waiting for the CAE and the "adult" to continue the journey in his or her search of healing and clarity, even if it takes a million lifetimes. The CAE and the "adult" think they are in control. Control is manipulation. Control is an illusion.

The Truth is realized with *real eyes* when the Perfect Child Within is recognized and acknowledged as the fully-functional Power Source in collaboration with the Clear Adult Male and Female in conscious connection. Empowerment is now the source of this connection in the Multi-Dimensional Allness of Clear Consciousness.

Now the journey can be continued without being powerless and fear-filled, burdened by the 3D Duality Programs of Judgment, Lack, and Take-Away. Survival is the behavior of the past. Creativity, implementation, manifestation, and actualization are the dynamics of the unlimited Clear Consciousness on a continuing continuous continuum.

"The Self-Image of the Childish Adult Ego is small.
The imagination and creativity of the
Perfect Child Within is unlimited."

-Sherryism

With the emotional scars and fears cleared from the First Chakra, the Clear Consciousness propels the empowering energy to rise into the Second Chakra. The creative Power is open and expanded to create into your physical world new ideas, new visions, and newness as the rule of thumb instead of being ruled under the thumb of 3D Duality Programs.

Your life is productive, exciting, and worth living. You have worth and value. You comprehend that you are worthy and valuable. There is no room for the Belief System of Lack and Survival in Clear Consciousness. Your Childish Adult Ego grows up and your adult becomes adult. In other words, your adult grows up.

Your conscious Perfect Child Within's powerful energy is now connected. Your conscious Perfect Child Within is integrally linked with the Consciousness of your Female creativity and the Consciousness of your Male's ability to manifest what your Female is creating. Your Perfect Child Within is the implementer.

This is the Consciousness of Allness. Through this connection, your Consciousness, your energy, and your entire body are synchronized with the Non-Duality Universe and Multi-verse. In this resonance, your Consciousness expands to meet your Heart.

The Fourth Chakra:

Heart

Our Father, who art in Heaven, hallowed be Thy Name. The physical body is Male and is the producer who manifests into the physical what is created through the Female creativity and implemented by either the Perfect

Child Within or the Childish Adult Ego. There is a huge difference when the manifestation is implemented by the Childish Adult Ego who reigns in fear.

From a physical perspective, the Heart Chakra includes the esophagus, trachea, lungs, bronchi, heart, scapula, spinal column in the back of the Heart Chakra, the arms, elbows, wrists, hands, fingers, chest, sternum, thymus, the muscles, tissues, blood vessels, etc. All of these areas, when the Heart Chakra is under duress, are affected by the emotional hooks to the unchangeable past.

All of the diseases, afflictions, and dysfunctions in the Heart Chakra – such as heart attacks, respiratory problems, lung issues, circulatory problems, etc. – result from your Heart being "broken". Your Perfect Child Within takes the "hit" physically as well as emotionally. Your Childish Adult Ego **validates the invalidation of you**, continuing the patterns of you not being worthy of Self-love or love from an outside source.

When your Childish Adult Ego (CAE) has had enough, the escape clause in your script is activated. When the emotional stress is too much for your physical body to handle, your CAE will absolutely manifest a lethal Heart Chakra attack. Both your Childish Adult Ego and your Perfect Child Within know you will be back. Again, your Conscious Perfect Child Within awaits for the next opportunity when you will take a stand for your Self, heal the 3D Duality Programs, and have a great life. And most importantly… grow-up your Childish Adult Ego.

The Belief Systems of not being worthy of love, not being lovable, and not being validated make you sick in the Heart. When your Childish Adult Ego is controlling and manipulating you in the survival mode, you have no choice but to be sick.

Whatever your paradigm of the causes and effects of your biology, your genetics, or even your conditioning which stem from your Belief Systems, you become sick at Heart. By becoming clear of your emotional issues and baggage, letting go of the past, and being in your Power, you heal the particular area within your Heart Chakra and your Heart Chakra itself.

When you look at the word Heart, you see it spells "He-Art". Through your Heart, which is the most expansive resonance in the body, when you clear and heal your emotional issues through the integration of your Male (physical body), your Female creativity (Spirit), and your Conscious Perfect Child Within, you create a life on purpose with purposes on the canvas of your life.

You are the creator, the artist, and the canvas. You choose how you paint your life. You are In Charge of Your Life. You are the Conscious Creator (Female Power Source), the implementer (Clear Conscious Perfect Child Within), and the manifesting agent (Male producer) of your life.

On your canvas of life is the "hallowed be thy Name". Directing your Clear Heart resonance into the creative energy from your Second Chakra with a new First Chakra foundation of Believing in Your Self, you are fearless and powerful. Clearly In Charge of Your Life, you are with purposes on purpose. You create from your Heart with the resonance of your Godness within you. How divine are you!

Being full of life, your life is full. In creating, whether you do it spontaneously or with planning, there is no inner turmoil or conflict coming from your Childish Adult Ego, no matter what your adult linear age is. No matter what is happening outside of you, you are the Non-Emotional Observer (NEO) In Charge of Your Life. You begin to create newness in minute to minute, day by day, week by week, year by year moments in your time frames.

> Matters of the Heart
> Love is all that Matters
> We are the Matter
> Of all living
> Matter that you live
> Your living Matters
> To all. We are all.
>
> *-Wei Chen*

As Wei Chen, an ancient Chinese poet, expressed in this beautiful poem, all that really matters is what matters to you from your healed Heart Chakra. Your Heart is the practical resonance of magic which infusing life into your creativity. How luscious!

The four chambers of the heart metaphorically represent the four dimensions of the Consciousness of your Male (physical Body), your Female (Spirit), your Clear Conscious Perfect Child Within, and the Heart of your Soul resonating Unconditional Love and Total Acceptance from within you. The four chambers now vibrate with your personal resonance of Unconditional Love and Total Acceptance.

When you utilize your Heart as the energizing Power from a clear foundation of Consciousness and infuse into your creativity the openness of your Clear Conscious Perfect Child Within, you are expressing your life, your creativity, and the implementation of your manifestations and actualizations with Unconditional Love and Total Acceptance. There is no requirement to allow old emotions and old 3D Fear patterns of behavior to interfere with your life and your creative process. All directions from your Heart Chakra are open. You are free and open to participate in the expression of your artistry.

The rise of your energy, powered by your Clear Consciousness from your healed, powerful Heart Chakra into your Fifth Chakra (your throat), provides the vocal pathway to speak your Truth. The resonance of your words, language, vocabulary, and the way you communicate change exponentially. Fearful words, language, and vocabulary are no longer relevant.

The Fifth Chakra:

Throat

The Truth shall set you free. Speaking your Truth absolutely sets you free. When you are speaking from your Heart, your words are without any judgment.

The judgment of others is judgment of your Self. What's the point? This is the Truth. When you speak your Truth without the wanty-needy to be validated and to be right, the shift in the resonance of your Throat Chakra expands naturally. You speak clearly and with kindness and compassion. As this occurs, the resonance is *felt* both by you internally and also by others externally as you speak to others. You speak with a powerful and empowering continuity.

The words and vocabulary of fear, control, and manipulation, regardless of language, have a very low, dense resonance. When the resonance of the vocabulary is so low, the words are painful. The body re-acts. The body gets sick. The words are not only pain-filled for you, they are pain-inducing to others.

The diseases and dysfunctions occurring in the Throat Chakra and related areas include thyroid cancer, tonsillitis, cervical issues, degeneration of disks, throat cancer, teeth issues, tongue cancer, and gum disease to name a few.

When you cannot speak your Truth, the force of your stressed energy jams up in your jaw resulting in TMJ. Jaw issues such as TMJ are related back to the Second Chakra. When you cannot speak your Truth, your Heart is closed, your Childish Adult Ego is in re-active mode, and your creativity in your Second Chakra, the hips, is blocked. Your hips get locked. You are not flexible either in your body or your life. This also affects your sex life.

Between your hips is your abdomen, which is connected to your occipital bone. The abdomen and occipital bone are connected. When there are problems in these areas, the issues are the emotional hooks to the past – the right and wrong, good and bad, victim and victimizer – and the beat of the past goes on. Irritable bowel syndrome, colitis, cancer, digestive colon issue, etc. are the results. Your body is all connected. The issues are connected. All of the issues – emotional, mental, physical, spiritual, and financial – are connected to all the parts of your body.

All the issues are physical. All the dysfunctional issues are physical and emotional. This is why you get sick. Sickness is "what" happens when you do not comprehend the "why" of what is happening inside of you.

You cannot change the "what" until you get to the "why". Every aspect of you is inter-linked. The confusion happens when the inter-link of information is dis-oriented. When one or multiple aspects of you are disconnected from each other, illness happens.

It does not happen from an outside source. It happens because you are not clearly conscious within your Self.

How can anyone be clear with the 3D Duality Programs running on for lifetimes, embedded in your cells through your experiences, whether you are conscious of them or not? Without the knowledge to comprehend how your systems work, you get worked over and over and over again by the programming. If you think you get out of paying taxes with death, get over it. You will return. Your body will continually be "taxed", enmeshed in the Judgment, Lack, and Take-Away Programs. This is the way of Third Dimension. You are continually being "in" it, the Duality Programs, and not "of" it, your Inner Truth.

When you are disconnected, you are not connected to your Self. It is as simple as this.

Detachment is the key to the progressive process to Take Back Your Power. **No emotional attachment.** You must be non-emotional and *see* everything for what "everything" is, and not what your Childish Adult Ego says it is. You must *see* the facts of the situations or conditions. Expand beyond the dense resonance of the 3D Duality Programs. You must do this.

Trying and trying to find your answers in a state of emotional distraction is impossible. The thick molecules of emotions are just that…thick, viscous, and gelatinous. Your gelatinous emotions cloud your ability to *see* clearly what is going on in your life. You have been taught to keep quiet and shut up.

Here is the absurdity. Everyone can hardly wait for the Perfect Child Within to say his or her first words. The child is encouraged to talk. What happens after that? Shut up! Everyone can hardly wait for the Perfect Child Within to take his or her first steps. The child is encouraged to walk. What happens after that? Shut up and sit down. DAH! This is why "they" say by the time the Perfect Child Within is between 3 and 5 years of age, they are already tainted. The programming doesn't just happen at this early age.

Do you "thunk" this confusion sets a lifelong pattern of not being able to speak your Truth or walk your Truth? You bet it does. The programming even begins in the womb, which is situated in your mother's Second Chakra.

During your gestation period, you are being imprinted moment by moment with experiences of what and how your parents are experiencing *their* experiences. Of course, you wrote the contracts with them. What you like about your parents, you have cleared. The emotional issues you are having with your parents and family are, in fact, the issues you wrote into your contract to work through, get clear, and move on.

However, when the physical and emotional issues are so difficult, you must realize with *real eyes* that YOU wrote these challenges into your script and into the contract with your parents and family. In a past life, you could have been the parent or sibling.

The minute and the very moment you begin to become the Non-Emotional Observer (NEO) is the minute and the moment you begin your own personal progressive process to Take Back Your Power. Then, and only then, is when you begin to discover how you can speak your Truth without getting into the emotionally draining aspects of the 3D Duality Programming.

You are able to speak your Truth, always with kindness and compassion. You speak from your Heart, and not from your left computer/brain. You gain the physical strength to love speaking your Truth. You empower your Self. You can use this ability to empower others. You speak Truth, not the Judgment, Lack, and Take-Away Programs, which only instill fear, control, and manipulation. The more you speak your Truth, the more you realize how much productive time was wasted in the past trying to figure out what to say or by simply not speaking at all. Is it a wonder that relationships are so strained?

When no one is allowed to speak their Truth, there are no *real* conversations going on. There are only imagined conversations: "What did he, she, or they say?" "What did that mean?" "What do you 'think' was said?" Yadda, yadda, yadda. These shallow words continue to be spoken.

The hoping, wishing, and wanty-needy low resonance language is being thrown back and forth in relationships. Everyone is in their heads and not connected with their Hearts when speaking in the dense resonance of 3D Duality language. It is always emotional and never factual.

When your First Chakra is not clear and is embedded with fear, the words spoken from your Throat Chakra are also fearful and not clear. Your Childish Adult Ego rules your language. He or she has to do it. You are in the survival mode. Your Heart Chakra is shut down. Your Creative Chakra is shut down. Your Solar Plexus and your Perfect Child Within are shut down. This is called "shut down". Get it?!!

Your Throat Chakra can only express the continuation of fear and the words that express fear. The language of your relationships is fear! "What will they think of me?" "Will I be accepted?" "Did I say the right or wrong thing?" Judgment, Judgment, Judgment of Self. Giving your Power away is the rule of the thumb in this resonance. You are speaking Self-talk in the emotional language that has no basis of facts, only emotional turmoil and misunderstanding.

When your Throat is closed because of the 3D Duality Fear Programs, which do not allow you to speak your Truth, physical issues arise from the emotional issues of being dis-empowered. When you don't speak your Truth, you actually say "I am stuck". No kidding. You definitely are stuck. You say "I am blocked". Yes, you are blocked. Block means you are **B**-eing the **lock** that has you jailed in a Childish Adult Ego's perception which prevents you from speaking your Truth.

Your Throat Chakra is connected directly to your feet. If you cannot speak your Truth, you cannot move forward in life. Your feet move but they do not move forward. Your feet are stuck in the past as you continue to "hang ten" vested in the emotional baggage of luggage, which you bagged in the past and are still lugging around.

Look at the feet issues: bunions, feet on your tippy toes, the out-of-body syndrome, plantar fasciitis, broken bones, broken toes, bone spurs, in-grown toenails, swelling, you name it! The physical issues in the feet are directly related to your Throat Chakra. You can't speak your Truth and you can't move forward in life consciously. Linear time passes, but you are still standing in the past, hanging on to the past issues stuck in your throat because you cannot speak the Truth about them. You can only keep quiet, explode from time to time, shut up, and continue through the cycle of speaking the 3D Duality Programs, which keep you afraid of your Power and speaking your Truth.

The words you speak consciously or unconsciously from your Throat Chakra, when attached to the Fear Programs, become statements of Self-prophesy. "I don't deserve." "I am not good enough." "No one will ever love me." "I don't have the right." Such words of Self-deprecation and Self-sabotage continue to fall out of your mouth.

Whatever the declarations your Throat Chakra declares, whether silently unspoken, stuck in your throat, or spoken out loud, you speak your reality when you are stuck in Duality. When you are out of Duality, you speak your Real Truth.

Though your Heart Chakra is the most expansive resonance in your 7 Chakra System, your Throat Chakra is of the utmost importance. No matter how open your Heart is, if you cannot speak your Truth, you will attract Heart stabbers, Heart grabbers, and Heart breakers directly to you with your open, *unconscious* Heart.

When you speak your Truth with kindness and compassion, judgment is released and, at the same time, your Chakra centers are open. Your entire body *feels* the resonance of your Truth through the language, words, and vocabulary you speak about your Self and others. Your cells *feel* what is going on. Your entire body *feels* the freedom. Speaking your Truth speaks to you to Take Back Your Power.

You empower your Self by accepting Who You Are. What you have to say has meaning and purpose. You have meaning and purpose on purpose.

As you clear your Consciousness and expand your resonance through speaking your Truth, you heal your body. Your body now knows what to do.

When you get out of your own way, you can verbally thank your Childish Adult Ego (CAE) for being a great teacher and for helping you survive in sometimes unimaginable, seemingly not survivable conditions. By speaking your Truth, without the interference of your fearful CAE, you Take Charge of Your Self and your life. Speaking your Truth into the physical world is the resonance which empowers you.

You are now speaking from a clear foundation of Believing in Your Self. You speak your creativity. There are no longer on-going reasons to block your Self. Your Perfect Child Within is empowered to implement the creativity of your Female Power in union with your Male's ability to manifest what is created by your Female and implemented through your Body and your Perfect Child Within. All aspects of your Self on all dimensions are beginning to integrate.

Is this an on-going process? Of course it is. Can there be challenges stemming from outside influences? Of course there can be. So What! As long as you stay in your Truth, you do not have to give your Self up to the 3D Duality Programs.

Duality is fading away. The time has come. This is your opportunity to move on and forward at the same time. This is the time for the collective Consciousness of the 3D Duality Programs to be deleted from your left computer/brain.

Yes! This is a process. Make your process *progressive*. Otherwise, you are still in the process plant coming out on the same other side as the same old encased baloney. Move on and up. You have the choice or not!

Remember, the old paradigm of the 7 Chakras uses the Throat Chakra as the means for you to speak, sing, yell, laugh, swear, cough, and make sound, especially in the form of words, language, and vocabulary. A deeper purpose of the Throat Chakra is to provide a vocal avenue for Cellular Sound releases for all the parts of your body to express their Selves.

For instance, during a situation, you may not have had the experience to experience the experience at the time. You may have been frightened, shocked, traumatized, or even felt joy and happiness. No doubt you have been asked in the past whether you are having a good time or if you are happy or if you are sad or if you are whatever. However, because of the "shut up" and "be quiet" programming, you could not express your Self. This programming says: "You are NOT supposed to speak or you could embarrass your Self! You are NOT supposed to fully express your Self."

Your unexpressed sounds of the experiences of those specific times, whether of trauma or joy, are memorized in the different areas of your body associated with these situations. Your emotional attachments to the experiences affect your molecules and your cells.

Your body becomes strained because you have been conditioned to NOT express your Self. You could draw "negative" attention to your Self. Or, you could draw any attention to your Self, good, bad or indifferent.

There is no way you could have your Self be seen or heard under the circumstances of the Fear-filled Programs. You are definitely not worthy to be seen or heard. Remember, "children are to be seen and not heard"? Do you think it is any different for "adults" who are stuck in their childhood?

Clear Self-expression is discouraged. Emotional, dysfunctional Self-expression is acceptable. This is the way you are conditioned to act. Dysfunctional Self-expression is the way in 3D Duality. It is embraced, publicized, and encouraged.

Self-medicating, whether legal or illegal, can make you even more unconscious to your Truth. You can't Take Back Your Power under these circumstances. But it is very acceptable for you to be ill, sick, and dysfunctional and to continue to look outside of your Self for your answers.

There are many programs that tell you they have your answers. If this is the Truth, why are so many people sick, dysfunctional, and not enjoying supportive relationships? Do you "thunk" something is off? Do you "thunk" perhaps it is the foundation of the 3D Duality Programs which encourages the dysfunctional emotional and physical issues?

When a sound is equated to a trauma, the sound is stored as a Cellular Memorization of the experience. During your healing process, using your Throat Chakra as an instrument to express the sound from that particular area of your body now provides the physical expression for the sound to be released. The trauma is released through the physical acknowledgement and the physical sound relating to the trauma.

Most of the time, you are not allowed to express sound. The minute you express the sound of pain, you are given a pill to suppress the sound. The particular area of the body traumatized continually suppresses the painful experience stored there and it is not able to be released from the body through the Throat Chakra.

This is a sound planet. Your body is sound. Each of your systems has sound, whether you are aware of it or not. When you are hungry, doesn't your stomach growl? Is not your body telling you something?

If, as an example, you are in an accident and hurt your leg, your leg memorizes the accident and the trauma of the accident as does your whole body. The sound connected to the accident is memorized by the collective Consciousness of your leg. When the physical healing occurs, there is still the painful memory of the experience embedded in your leg.

By releasing the sound and resonance of the pain through the physical Cellular Sound release utilizing your Throat Chakra, a deeper level of healing occurs. Your Throat Chakra is the avenue to heal the trauma by acknowledging and allowing the sound to be released. In this case, the emotional and physical trauma to your leg is acknowledged and released.

Using your Throat Chakra to support your healing process, the other 7 Chakra centers also benefit through this natural tool of your body to use sound to heal. Your body is now releasing the sound of the trauma and the sound of the pain. Healing is sound. Healing is a resonance.

Everything in your body – your cells, your molecules, your systems, your Consciousness – has its own resonance of sound. When your resonances are out of balance, your body is out of alignment. Your words even reflect it when you say "I am out of balance", "I am off today", or "I am out of kilter". You are out of alignment from your Cellular Level of Consciousness. When you are, there is a program running.

You naturally make the sounds of being out of alignment. You sigh. You moan. You groan. You exhale noisily. Your body is making sound. Pay attention. Where is the sound emanating from in your body? Connect and *listen*. Your body requires releasing the embedded sound or sounds in that particular area of the body. Your body knows how to heal. Your left computer/brain does not! Neither does your Childish Adult Ego. If the Childish Adult Ego did, then ask your Self, why are there so many sick people on this planet, especially at this time?

Your Throat Chakra is of the utmost importance to your body. Your Throat Chakra expresses your words, language, vocabulary, and sounds which are either supportive to you or not. When your words are spoken in the resonance of fear, such as Self-sabotage, Self-loathing, and less-than, your body reacts to this dense resonance. You are making your Self sick. Your Belief System is now focused in the sound of depression and illness. Dis-ease eventually becomes disease.

The resonance of your vocabulary impacts your life, your relationships, your health, and your wealth. In the 3D Duality Programs, polarity is described as either positive or negative. The Consciousness of your energy has nothing to do with negative or positive. It does have to do with the focus of your Consciousness and your energy being in alignment.

Your energy is a by-product of your Consciousness. Your energy is either the movement (flowing) of your Clear Consciousness *or* the non-movement (stuck) of your limited Belief Systems. When your Belief Systems are fear-filled, your energy is fear-filled. And you attract fearful experiences in your relationships, both personal and professional. There is no flow. It's called stuckness. Stuckness is Duality.

REAL freedom to create your life consciously is Non-Duality. The objective of Non-Duality in your Throat Chakra is to speak your freedom and embody your freedom to speak your creativity.

The Throat Chakra in the 7 Chakra System speaks the Duality "true", yet never speaks your Non-Duality Truth. When you can't speak your Truth from your Heart, you can't speak your Truth. You can only speak the Duality Programming. The 7 Chakra System is old and outdated.

Your energy, which is a projection of you, creates every experience of your life. The clearer you are, the clearer are all the directions your life takes.

Now consider the use of your energy based on your awareness of Consciousness as either the appropriate use of your energy or the inappropriate use of your energy. Your energy expresses your Consciousness. What this means is…what you are creating or how you are participating in life is how you are using your energy based upon your Consciousness. If you are fear-filled, your energy attracts fear-filled experiences. If you are clear, your energy attracts clear experiences.

So ask your Self, what do you clearly require to attract into your life? Or do you unclearly wanty-needy to attract more wanty-needy experiences to you?

There is a significant difference in the results. In 3D Duality, the results are usually the physical manifestation of the Law of Distraction, which is the dysfunctional Law of Attraction working not so well through the 3D Duality Programs.

By focusing on the expanded resonance of your Consciousness fearlessly, you change your life. You speak differently. There is no language of victimization.

You can't change the circumstances of the past. You certainly can change the circumstances of your present time. In turn, you change your future.

Your past is one minute ago. Your future is one minute from now. What you do in that split second between these 2 time frames changes the results of your life from this very moment of the present time.

When you give credence to your Self, you speak the vocabulary, words, and language of Unconditional Love and Total Acceptance, first to your Self and then to others. Your life, your experiences, and your relationships are experienced through this resonance of your Truth. Your Throat Chakra is instrumental in this progressive, one-clear-step-at-a-time process.

The creative process of your actions and behaviors are now predicated upon the resonance of your words, language, and vocabulary. The resonance expressed from your Throat says volumes about where you are emotionally, mentally, physically, spiritually, and financially in your life. The sounds and words that come out of your Throat Chakra is your Consciousness.

Healing your Throat Chakra gives you the opportunity to heal your entire body through the physical resonances of sound. The Consciousness of Allness happens through sound, in whatever form the sound happens to be. Speaking your Truth is vital to your life. Speaking your Truth gives you vitality.

By speaking your Truth with Unconditional Love and Total Acceptance, you initiate the resonance you require in order to make the Shift out of 3D Duality. Then you can be of "it", your Inner Truth, and not in "it", the Fear Programs of Duality. You resonate Non-Duality.

From your healed Throat Chakra, your body resonates with clarity. Your cells respond. Your molecules no longer have the emotional attachments to the past traumas. You keep what serves you and you dump the rest.

The sound of clarity to heal your Self is from your Throat Chakra, doing the job it is meant to do. Now you can *listen* with your Heart, instead of just hearing through your left computer/brain ears. And you even begin to *see* more clearly. Your resonance is ascending beyond Duality.

The Sixth Chakra:

The Third Eye

From your Third Eye come the visions of your expanded Consciousness. You are resonating with your expanded awareness instead of Duality's "Higher" Self and "Lower" Self.

When your Third Eye is closed down, your intuitive sight and the guidance from your more expanded vision of and for your Self is shut down. Your field of limited sight is directed by your Childish Adult Ego through your left computer/brain.

Remember, your Childish Adult Ego's job is survival. With an expanded vision of your Self, there is no requirement to exist in survival mode. Survival is existing. It's not living consciously. Survival has too many repeated caveats of trauma-dramas. Through your Third Eye, you now realize with *real eyes* that living fully is NOT about existing. In existence, there is no creativity. Only re-do's.

The more closed your Third Eye is, the more your life is ingrained in fear. You cannot *see* clearly, let alone have a clear vision for your Self and your life. How can you envision being the Non-Emotional Observer (NEO) and the Conscious Creator In Charge of Your Life? With your Third Eye closed, there are simply few possibilities for the quality of life you deserve. There is no vision for desire, require, and deserve. There are only the limitations for the vision of your Self and your life.

Your Childish Adult Ego (CAE) is terrified of your Third Eye. Why? Because if you *see* the Truth of Who You Are, your CAE has to grow-up, has to let go of the 3D Duality Programs, and has to let go of being your survivalist. Who wanty-needys to lose his or her job?

Limited Belief Systems are the paradigm of your Childish Adult Ego (CAE). The Limited Belief Systems (B.S.) in your First Chakra are the only things your CAE knows. This is the only paradigm that provides the credibility and acknowledgement to keep your CAE employed by you. Pain, suffering, sacrifice, less-than, and not good enough are the perfect ways to keep you under control and powerless. The CAE is afraid of losing his or her job. Sound familiar?

Your Childish Adult Ego (CAE) sets you up. Your CAE sets you up for the continuing patterns of making you right to make you wrong to make you right to make you wrong. The pattern continues lifetime after lifetime until the perfect situation occurs. The perfect situation could be a Near-Death Experience. The perfect situation is the life-altering, perception-altering, life-changing experience in which you begin to *see* things in a different way. The experience of the situation may take some processing in linear time for you to actually *see* with new eyes what your life is all about.

Your Perfect Child Within waits patiently for your Childish Adult Ego (CAE) to set you up. It waits knowing an opportunity will be presented for you to wake up and *see* for your Self how you have been manipulated and controlled in the re-cycle bin of your left computer/brain with the direction of your survivalist, your CAE. How perfect is this relationship for 3D Duality existence! Now your Perfect Child Within, connecting to your Third Eye, provides you with this Set-Up opportunity to *see* a new vision of your Self.

The situation which activates your Third Eye usually is identified as the illness, the accident, or the "big one" which changes the game and the rules. When your Third Eye opens, your view of the world changes. Your view of your life, your relationships, and your view of everything changes. You may begin to *see* auras, visions, angels, and beings. You may have inter-dimensional experiences. The unexplained will have new explanations. You may experience realms around you that you cannot define by 3D Duality limited views.

The "New Kids on the Block", those described or identified as Indigo, Crystal, Blue Ray, or Double Heart children, already have their Third Eye open. They speak openly about what they are *seeing*, experiencing, and *feeling* until they are shut down by the parents, school system, or religious organizations.

Many of these children are given prescription drugs. Many of them end up taking illegal drugs because their sensitive systems become accustomed to the drugs. Their brains become toxic as a result of both the prescription and the street drugs. Sad but the Truth! Their Third Eyes and all their Duality Chakras are systematically suppressed.

It is not unusual for them to talk about imaginary friends who are not imaginary. They *see* the auric fields, yes plural fields, around people's bodies. Many have all sorts of visitations from deceased loved ones, even those they have never met here on Earth in this lifetime. This doesn't preclude other lifetimes in which they participated with each other. They are naturally intuitive, sensitive, and Multi-Dimensional.

As *your* Third Eye opens, you may remember, as these Clear Children do, these types of experiences from your own childhood, which were suppressed because of Duality's Fear Programs. Your parents could not comprehend anything happening outside of the limited Belief Systems. The Duality Fear Programs have no room or Consciousness for anything other than fear and the fear-based god programming.

When your Third Eye is not connected to the rest of your body and the other Chakras, the vision for you and your life is very limited. You exist in boundaries and restrictions in a very narrow band of limitations. Nothing is as it appears. An illusion for sure! Yet why continue the Belief System paradigm that 3D Duality is an illusion? If it is an illusion, then let's get over it and move on.

The fear is so great. The fear is so dense. The fear is so viscous. In giving up the illusion, you would empower your Self to live greatness. Now that is something to require, desire, and deserve. Do you "thunk?"

As a child, your Third Eye was purposely closed down. You are so much more controllable when you don't have a vision for your Self. If you do, the 3D Duality Programming won't work so well. So you get worked on to keep your Self in check. God forbid you should have a wonderful, healthy, wealthy life! If you have it for a while, then you must give it up. That's the re-cycle bin of 3D Duality. Have it, lost it, have it, lost it…do-over, do-over, do-over.

Your Third Eye is closed down through the conditioning of fear. With fear permeating your Third Eye, you cannot *see* anything else but the Judgment, Lack, and Take-Away Programs. As long as you are willing to continue this limited view of your Self, of your life, of the Universe, and of the Multi-verse, you are limited. How simple is this?!

You don't have to create a life-threatening, life-altering situation to open your Third Eye. You can open it by your willingness to get out of your own way and consciously connect to it.

First direct your Third Eye into your clear First Chakra. You are not buying into the limiting Belief Systems (B.S.) anymore. As you do this, you courageously know that those painful experiences, previously housed in your First Chakra, are not there. You give your Self the clarity to *see* that your new foundation of Clear Consciousness in your First Chakra gives you the platform to create newness.

The more Light or knowledge you place in your First Chakra, the more vision your Third Eye can show you. You are in the mode to Take Back Your Power. Hooray! Fear can no longer control your life. You rise above the fear and the emotional attachments to the past and the pasts. You are detaching and creating newness at the same time. It is simultaneous. And yes, it is a progressive process. We are still in linear time for the moment. The clearer you become, the less that time is restrictive.

As your First Chakra becomes clear, something quite extraordinary happens in your Second Chakra. New creative juices, like the elixirs of life, begin to flow. You have new vision, new sight, in your Creative Chakra. You are in charge of your creativity. You *see* you, you know it, you understand it, and you comprehend you are it!

Now everything in your life, your experiences and your relationships to the experiences, are your teaching tools. You *feel* what you choose to embrace or not. You choose how you participate or not. Your creativity is up to you. Good, bad, or indifferent has nothing to do with it. Your creative process changes as you become clearly conscious.

Your vision of your Self is your choice of your Self vision

You totally get it that no one can do anything *to* you or *for* you. How you choose to participate is what makes the difference in all your relationships and even in the relationship you have with your Self.

You are in Self-recognition. You are the one making a difference in your life. You are the person who changes everything. You change what no longer serves you. You keep what does. You keep what you created in the past that you love. And you love it and expand upon it. In clear vision with clarity, you *see* how, what, when, where, and why you create your life. Your Third Eye lights your way. Your Third Eye's purpose is to *see* with clarity. Otherwise, why would you have a Third Eye?

You realize that what and how you create your future is the what and how you determine what "it" is. You don't have to have a future based upon past dysfunctions, behaviors, patterns, or actions. The predictable past/future is not relevant. In this place of new vision, you find the perfection of the void. This is the place of Still Point. When you are quiet, this is the amazing place of creation.

Still Point is the beginning of your creative abilities. Still Point is the beginning of your spiral of creating. The "creating" is whatever your clear idea or clarity of inspiration is. Still Point is the place from which your clear band of intention(s) with the information about your creative ideas are propelled from you with your creative vision into the Non-Duality Universe and Multi-verse.

With the clarity of your vision through your creative Female left side, your message is sent loud and clear. And the Consciousness of the Non-Duality Universe and Multi-verse receive you loud and clear. Your message is received. Now the Non-Duality Universe and Multi-verse, in multi-faceted, joint, co-operative participation, begin to assist you in bringing all the required components together as you now draw all the required elements to you. The people, the contracts/agreements, and all the pieces of the pie are consciously arranged for you.

Please note, you have to **stay out of the outcome**, meaning the results you are looking for, whether it's the place, the people, the money, the partnerships, or the whatever.

"If you are in the outcome, the income can't come in…

You are stuck in the future instead of the moment…

So, where are you?"

-Sherryism

As they coalesce in the perfect timing, all aspects come together. This can only happen – clearly get this – when you are clearly conscious and willing to receive without trying to control anything. By being in charge of your Self, your life, and your creations, all the pieces then come together. This is the implementation aspect of creation and creating. You now are, through your physical body and the wondrous, fearless, powerful Perfect Child Within, in the implementation stage of creation.

As you implement with this Perfect Child Within/Body, you are now required to <u>manifest</u> your creative ideas into physical manifestation. Through the <u>Male</u> right side of your body, physical molecules coalesce into your manifested physical creations. During this process, your computer/brain is in alignment. Your left computer/brain (connected to the right Male side of your body), your right computer/brain (connected to the left Female side of your body), and your Body (your fearless Perfect Child Within) are all operating together.

This is the progressive process of Still Point's clear creative process without the interference of the Duality Programming and all the trauma-dramas which are part of the Duality Programs. Clear creativity is the progressive process of the continuing continuous continuum of the purpose full and purpose filled creative process.

This is Ascension. This is creating with the Godness within you. This is the how it is supposed to be. So, would you rather stay in the confines of Duality or be your Inner Truth? Your choice!!! Either your vision(s) are squelched or your vision(s) are your Non-Duality Realness!

The Clear Progressive Process of Creation

Step 1: Your clear creative idea

Step 2: Your clear visions and intentions sent from your Still Point – *The Beginning*

Step 3: Your clear message is in connection with your Non-Duality Universe and your Multi-verse

Step 4: Your clear components are brought together

Step 5: Your intentions coalesce

Step 6: Your team comes together

Step 7: Your acceptance and receiving

Step 8: Your union: your Female (creativity), your Body/Solar Plexus (Perfect Child Within), your Male (manifesting), and your Heart (most expansive resonance in your body) actualizing your vision into your physical world

Step 9: Creating all the Moments of your time; there are no limits or Judgment, Lack, or Take-Away when you are clear, focused, and directing your creativity consciously

Step 10: Your continuing continuous continuum of creating your creations from a single spiral of intention or unlimited spirals of intentions from your Heart

Step 11: You send out your intentions to the Non-Duality Universe and to the Multi-verse fearlessly unrestricted

Step 12: Your spirals are Multi-Dimensional and create unlimited possibilities and potentials which manifest into actualities, which means you are creating unlimited opportunities without end

Conscious You! Conscious Godness Self...

Non-Emotional Observer (NEO)
Conscious Creator
In Charge of Your Life
Creating Newness
Continuing continuous continuum of Clear Creation

Conscious Creator Godness Self is You!

Creator
Creativity
Creations
Implementer
Manifestor
Actualizer
Continuing continuous continuum of Clear You

With the clarity of your Third Eye, your Perfect Child Within, and your Clear Adult, you acknowledge the Allness within you. You become wondrously vulnerable with life. It has always been taught that vulnerability is a weakness. **Vulnerability is your strength.**

All the walls you have built around you, lifetime after lifetime with every unclear experience after unclear experience, have seemingly held you safe. These illusional walls have held you captive in a fear-filled place. In this closed limited space of vision, you are metaphorically and physically peeking out through an apartment door peephole. This peephole prevents you from *seeing* the whole picture and the whole You.

Your *feelings* and your Truth are walled up in a wailing wall of emotional tears with no Power, no vision, and no *real* participation in life. You are in prison. Imprisoned in a wall of emotions, you are without the facts of *real* insight or vision. You are emotionally held prisoner. You cannot possibly know, understand, or comprehend Who You Are. You are essentially powerless, searching outside of your Self for the answers. You are looking for God in all of the Duality Programs. God is not there.

God is inside of you.

If you cannot see that God is inside of you, you are blind and you cannot see!!!

This illusional bondage is housed in the Duality Fear Programs in your First Chakra. You built the invisible walls from your Second Creative Generative Sexual Chakra because of the fears. **Your Childish Adult Ego had to maintain the walls to pretend to protect you.** Your Perfect Child Within waited, imprisoned in your fears, hidden, while the trauma-dramas swelled around you drawing you in lifetime after lifetime, unclear experience after unclear experience.

As the usual suspect, you are victimized over and over again regardless of the lifetime. The fears cut deep into the Consciousness of your Soul, your Spirit, and your physical body, disenfranchising you by being fragmented and disconnected from your Self.

The fragmentation of your Self is the plan of Duality. Fragmenting you from your Soul and Spirit within your physical body and dis-embodying you from your Perfect Child Within is the way to control and manipulate you. In the Duality Programming, you have to be at war within your Self physically in order to control you spiritually, mentally, financially, and emotionally, as well as physically.

To find your Self, you needed an emissary or go-between for you and God. You were conditioned by Duality's Belief Systems to NOT *see* your Self. Someone or some dogma outside of you would have to save you, to intercede for you, or to make the connection for you to keep you less.

You were conditioned to be less,
think less of your Self,
and to live less

If you are not irritated by now, then you never will be!!! As long as you stay within the confines of these delusional walls, you will be confined to the never-ending Duality trauma-dramas.

Start asking questions. Start questioning your Belief Systems. Start questioning *all* Belief Systems. Start with your Self. When something doesn't *feel* correct or appropriate, then question, question, question! Don't *belief system* anything without doing your homework, your research, and using your Third Eye to give you the insight to *see* beyond the programming.

Your Light is your Knowledge. Knowledge is Light. Embrace the Consciousness of your Third Eye. Use the energy of your Third Eye to direct the Light as you uncover your Truth.

Faith is not Blind!

Faith is trusting your Inner Guidance. Faith is trusting your Godness Self. Faith is NOT trusting your Childish Adult Ego. When you Trust your Childish Adult Ego, you can trust you will be involved in the trauma-dramas. This is a given.

Your Perfect Child Within *sees* and *feels* and is open to be vulnerable with strength and courage. Your Perfect Child Within *plays* with expanded views and enlightened visions for your adult life.

As the walls come down, you *see* the divineness of you and your life, your creativity, your participation, and all you have to offer to others. As you recognize your Clear Consciousness Self, all the blocks begin to tumble down. All the crippling blame-games, the guilties, the less-thans, the why-me's, and any and all of the versions of victimization begin to disintegrate as you disengage. Your Light and your knowledge are your divine equalizer.

Your Perfect Child Within rises to your surface Consciousness, clear and willing for you to participate fully in your life. The key here is "regardless of what is going on outside of you." Your Real Adult Self initiates your life as the Non-Emotional Observer (NEO), the Conscious Creator In Charge of Your Life, Creating Newness with purposes on purpose. You *feel* the alignment of your physical body with the physicality of your Soul's passion for living and your Spirit's energy in motion.

It does not matter at what age you do this. Just make the commitment to your Self to get conscious. Release your Perfect Child Within from the bondage of the Duality Fear Programs. This lifetime is the lifetime to begin. You are healing and you are creating from your core simultaneously.

Don't ask your Self, "How long does it take?" Say to your Self, "I am taking the steps to heal my Self. I am not giving my Power away anymore."

You are integrating and healing Multi-Dimensionally in your time continuum. This Perfect Child Within represents all of the children from all of your lifetimes through all of your experiences.

Consciousness is the key. **The integration of your Multi-Dimensional Self is your empowerment.**

Your Perfect Child Within awakens as you become conscious. Your Third Eye provides the new vision, literally lighting up your Heart Chakra and filling it with the expanded vision of your Clear Conscious Self. No matter whether it is subtle or dramatic, let the connection of your Third Eye's vision lighten your Heart, figuratively and literally.

All that matters is the Consciousness and the energy being emitted from the resonance of your enlightened Heart Chakra.

> The Heart of the Matter
> Is the Matter
> Of the Heart
>
> The Only place
> To start
> Is what Matters
> To the Heart.
>
> *-Wei Chen*
> Ancient Chinese Poet

Give your Self permission to love your Self unconditionally and to accept your Self completely. The union of your

Third Eye and your Heart is the gift of sight and passion rolled into unity. All the old matters of your life and the old lifetimes no longer matter. What matters is that you give your Self permission to heal the pain, the perceptions, and all the dysfunctional hooks to the past.

The Duality Fear Programs are not worth one molecule, one particle, or one cell of your life or your creative abilities to stay engulfed in the turmoil and trauma-dramas of the Third Dimension. They are boring and overrated.

The four chambers of your Heart metaphorically are symbolic of the four directions. Look at all the directions the energy of your Heart has either flowed or has been blocked. Ask your Self, "What *feels* better?" You know the answer.

The Heart's blocked energy manifests illness, disease, and dysfunction. The specific manifestations are heart disease, heart conditions, heart attacks, broken hearts, lung and respiratory issues, and digestive problems. All these diagnoses are the dysfunctional effects of your Heart being affected by the emotional trauma-dramas. Not being loved, not being loveable, and not experiencing Unconditional Love and Total Acceptance are the core of all the Heart Chakra physical conditions of sickness.

Your Heart is sick at Heart
when you don't live consciously through your Heart!

When you think you are not loved or are unworthy of love because of a Belief System in your First Chakra, you create being unloved through your Second Creative Sexual Generative Chakra. And then your Third Chakra with your Perfect Child Within shuts down, your Childish Adult Ego takes over, your Heart is full of Judgment, Lack, and Take-Away. You can't speak your Truth about conscious love, your Third Eye is closed, and there you have it...another experience of being sick at Heart!

You are caught up in the 3D Duality love paradigm of *conditional* love. If you do "this", you will get "this much love" based on what this much love is. Even if the "love" is abusive, your Childish Adult Ego will accept the abuse. You will experience "love" as conditional, manipulative, controlling, and de-powering. You will give your Power away repeatedly. You will continue the search for love outside of you, just as the person or persons you draw to you who are caught up in the same search outside of their Selves.

Everyone is looking for love in the perfect dysfunctional relationships of "fix me, make me whole, validate me, love me no matter what, give me a morsel, it is better than nothing, and something dysfunctional is better than nothing" 3D Duality love paradigm. The abuser/abused, the victim/victimizer, and the controller/controlled are all endorsed to endure this dysfunctional idea of love. Whatever direction you may be going to find love, you are manipulated through this maze of searching for "the love of your life".

First, YOU must *see* with the clarity of your Third Eye that YOU must be the first Love of Your Life

With the clarity of your Perfect Child Within's fearless vision, focusing your Light/knowledge from your Third Eye through your empowered Heart Chakra, you are clearly creating a new foundation for your First Chakra. With a new clarity of Believing in Your Self without Belief Systems (B.S.) impinging limitations on your Creative Chakra, your life changes exponentially. You are indeed In Charge of Your Life. You are indeed empowered. You have indeed opted to Take Back Your Power!

As you do this, you give those in your life the opportunity to love you or not. If they do, fabulous! If they do not…Oh Well!

Whether they love you or not has nothing to do with you. It may have to do with the perceptions, which are not factual, of who they "think" you are supposed to be from the previous Role-playing you did in the past. They will be looking for the "old unconscious you". That is all they have known.

Or, maybe the time has arrived for the end of the old contract. You will *see* whether it is or not. You have the option to continue in the old contract or to write a new agreement. The new agreement may be a more empowered relationship. Or, maybe the time has come to end the contract and move forward.

You are not running this time. You are not running away. You are moving forward consciously. This is the newness! Make a conscious choice for *your* "what's next"!

As your life becomes Heart-centered with clarity of vision, balance becomes more of the norm. Balance is creating through your Female, implementing with your Perfect Child Within (your Body), manifesting through your Male, and actualizing with your Heart.

CREATING NEWNESS

Create
Implement
Manifest
Actualize
…on a continuing continuous continuum of Newness

NO LIMITS!!

Now you can speak your Truth
as you create your Life

From the Heart of the matter to your Throat Chakra, you are empowered to speak your Truth. All the words you speak support you. The people outside of you *feel* your words, whether they agree or not.

You are *clearly* speaking the resonance of you. You are speaking what you represent in life. You are speaking *your* Truth. Make your life as you *see* it, *feel* it, comprehend it, create it, implement it, manifest it, and actualize it. Wordology Is Your Biology. Speak your resonance.

This Is Your Life!

Your life is in full participation. You are living fully. You are the Power and the Power Source.

The Seventh Chakra:

The Crown

Now that you have opened your Third Eye, allow your Self to make the visual connection to your Seventh or Crown Chakra.

Everyone has a soft spot on the top of their head. To evolve beyond the restrictions of the 7 Chakra System, it must be soft, flexible, and relaxed, just like a new baby. Not hard and rigid as it is in a Duality hardhead resonance. Your soft spot actually has a twofold purpose. As you physically relax the soft spot, you allow the fear-based energy to flow up and exit your head/crown and be released. As this occurs, your soft spot widens, expands, and awakens the connection to the Non-Duality Universe and to the Multi-verse. This is a physical action.

As this happens, you are physically allowing your Self to connect to the more expanded Consciousness of your Self. With the opening of your Third Eye, you can allow your Self to *see* beyond the 3D Duality physicality. You are the connector, the connection, and the avenue for connecting to your more expanded awareness. You become aware of your Universal and Multi-Dimensional Self in this current physical body. You are becoming physically unlimited in your vision of your Self.

You do not ever have to be limited in anything. Being miraculous and practical at the same time, you are allowing your Self to connect and integrate through your Crown Chakra and interact and converse with the Non-Duality Universe and Multi-verse. You can now download, upload, channel, be the conduit, or whatever your description is. You determine what you would like to call it. In other words, you are connected. You do not have to look outside of your Self for someone to give you the answers to your questions.

You are the connection. The clearer and more conscious you become, the more consciously you are connected. You provide the avenue to integrate this current physical 7 Chakra body into Allness. At the same time, you are consciously moving beyond the limitations of the 7 Chakra System. This is the progressive process, instead of continuing to process the same old 3D Duality 7 Chakra System of repetitive programming.

You are transforming and ascending your current physical body of Consciousness. Combining the meaning of both words, you are creating your **Transcension**. Duality begins to disappear in your world of reference. Duality has served its purpose for all those lifetimes. This is the Set-Up for what is next!

Before you get to what is next, you must comprehend that at some point in your life, usually more times than not, to escape the trauma-dramas and the Fear Programs, you go out of body and exist somewhere else. When this happens, your physical body is at risk.

The false belief is that when you are out of body, you are connected to your "Higher Consciousness". The Truth is you are NOT connecting at all; you are avoiding your physical Self. Avoidance is not connection. The out-of-body experiences and the Near-Death Experiences are escape clauses in your personal contract under the avoidance section.

The Truth of being alive with your expanded Consciousness and your expanded awareness is that your Godness Self is grounding your 7 Chakras into your physical body through the alignment of your Female's creativity, your Body's Perfect Child Within, and your Male's ability to physically manifest your ideas into this physical world. All aspects of your Self – your Spirit, your Soul, your 7 Chakra System, your mind, and all your physical body's biological systems – are operating in alignment and agreement. You are connected and grounded in the Allness of You. You are a Creative Conscious Being. This is what the Godness within you does: Creates Consciously.

When you are disenfranchised in the 3D Duality Fear Programs, you exist in separation within your Self. You are separated from the Godness within you.

Your Crown Chakra is the avenue to connection. First, however, you must be willing to make the commitment to your Self to be the Non-Emotional Observer (NEO). You must let go of the Self-Judgment, Self-Lack, and Self-Take-Away 3D Duality Programs. You must let go of the attachments to the past(s), no matter what. You must be willing, as the Non-Emotional Observer (NEO), to *see* your part and everyone's part who played out the traumas and the dramas with you. You must be willing to let go of being the victim/victimizer, the abuser/abused, the controller/controlled, and all of the 3D Duality labels.

You must be willing to allow your Self to heal your emotional issues and all the emotional attachments of right and wrong which accompany the situations. You must be willing to accept that you created everything in your life…without being the judge, jury, prosecutor, and defense attorney. You must be willing to stop incarcerating your Self in the 3D Duality jail cell as the prisoner.

There are a lot of musts to do. Only when you are willing to move forward does the progressive process become easier. When you get conscious, it is so much easier to move forward.

Moving beyond the limited 7 Chakra System is the opportunity to expand the resonance of your current physical body of Consciousness. Everything changes. Your DNA template begins to change. You do not have to be locked into your biological 3D Duality DNA clock that ticks away at your life, locking you in your predecessors' DNA box.

You are in charge of your body's Consciousness. You choose the time to activate your personal paradigm shift. As you expand your resonance, you are becoming a collective integrated Consciousness participating in the collective Consciousness of the planet. You are not, however, emotionally hooked into the trauma-dramas. You know without doubt that you are now In Charge of Your Life no matter what is happening on the outside.

From a single, disenfranchised individual caught in the net of the 3D Duality Collective Belief Systems of a particular group, you are now becoming your own personal collective group Consciousness of Allness within you. Your answers are inside of you. As you learn how to ask the correct questions, you get your clear answers at your Cellular Level of Clear Consciousness. You are transcending in this physical body to being Multi-Dimensional, Multi-Faceted, and Multi-Creative. Your validation comes from within you.

Out of 3D Duality, the 7 Chakras, and the limitations to the activation of the Thirteen Chakras, your body of Consciousness changes. You are the Power.

**The Limited Body of Belief Systems
in the Duality 3rd Dimension:**

**The Block Wall –
the Infinity of Duality... Repetition**

Man in the world of history,
is like a seed in the ground
an embryo in the womb.
His full potential is not at all evident here.
No phenomenological analysis of the grain of corn
So also no amount of biology, psychology, sociology, and history
Can reveal to us the true nature of man.

-Paulos Mar Gregorios
Cosmic Man, The Divine Presence

Chapter 7

A PARADIGM SHIFT, THE BREAKTHROUGH

Moving through the Belief Systems of the Block Wall

> "Man is an electromagnetic animal
> and is subject to those forces
> that affect all forms of life existing on Earth.
> Man's electromagnetic system is contained
> within his biophysical makeup
> and affects the total behavior of not only the body…
> also changes in mental activities
> and the electrical biochemical operation of his system."
>
> *-Albert Roy Davis/ Walter C Rawls, Jr.*
> *Magnetism and Its Effects on the Living System*

Your Eighth Chakra, which is above your head above the Crown Chakra, is your connection and connector to the activation of your Thirteen Chakras. The Eighth Chakra, in the old paradigm of 3D Duality, metaphorically and physically represents the sideways figure "8".

This figure "8", the symbol of infinity of the 3D Duality Fear Belief Systems, is the perfect symbol to represent the repeated cycles of Karma, Lessons, and Re-incarnation. You cannot get out of the trap. You are like the gerbil stuck on the wheel. This figure "8" is the spinning wheel of repetitive misfortunes which "spins" you, turning and twisting through the dysfunctional figure "8" nightmare trauma-dramas of Karma, Lessons, and Re-incarnation. You are *destined* and *fated* to hope, wish, wanty, and needy to repeat the cycles.

When you turn the infinity symbol, aligning it from top to bottom, you can see how it aligns with the electromagnetic field of the Earth and your Earth body. The Northern aspect of polarity moves in a clockwise rotation. The Southern Hemisphere moves in a counter-clockwise rotation. In the middle, the two fields come together. This field is dense and taut. This field is known as the Block Wall. Through 3D Duality and its linear time, your Consciousness always encounters both the metaphoric and the actual physicality of this Block Wall.

You are cut in half in your body of Consciousness. The upper and the lower Chakras are blocked from each other. You are conditioned to "live" in either of these hemispheres, disconnected from these areas of Consciousness. You wonder "why" you feel disconnected. This is one very good reason.

The Block Wall holds the energy of the cyclic pattern of fear. There are even phrases such as "I am up against the wall", "I can't break through the wall", "I put up a wall to protect my Self", and "Why are they blocking me out?"

You are sentenced to the limiting 3D Duality Belief Systems by the dynamics of this figure eight, which typifies the cycles of Karma, Lessons, and Re-incarnation. How amazing! As long as this cycle continues, you continue to exist in the Judgment, Lack, and Take-Away Programs, repeating the cycles on an ongoing basis. As long as this cycle of dysfunctional infinity holds you in this pattern of 3D Duality, you will always hit the Wall at one point or another. The Wall is a Belief System of limitation and repetition.

At your body's midpoint is your navel, which is equivalent to the Earth's equator. Funny how you would "think" things would equate at the equator. However, in the body, the only thing that equates is that you are cut in half dealing with all the symptoms which become the diagnoses for illness and disease.

The upper half has conditions of brain/head problems: ears, nose, throat, sinus, shoulders, arms, wrists, hands, fingers, chest, breast, heart, stomach, bones, spine, muscles, etc. And the ramifications of the symptoms eventually are given a label for the physical issue. The lower half of the body has conditions of body problems: digestive, organs, bones, abdomen, intestines, reproductive, spine, legs, ankles, feet, etc. These symptoms are eventually given a label for the physical issue. Of course, the emotional component causing the problems is usually ignored. The problems are only seen as mechanically physical.

The emotional issues are the leading cause of the physical problems. Now you can compound the emotional problems caused by your left computer/brain's disconnection from your body and you wonder why you have problems. You further complicate the issues for your Self and your body when the top half of your body is disconnected from the lower half. You add in further problems and challenges by being disconnected from the knowledge of your 3D Duality 7 Chakra System.

These are all aspects of your human body simultaneously working against itself as you go through life. This is all unconscious, of course. You don't have the full disclosure of how your body works!!! If you know how it all works, why would you get sick or get involved with time-wasting trauma-dramas and unworkable relationships with each other?

At this point in your body at the Block Wall at your navel, the magnetic midpoint where the poles come together is where all the opposing 3D Duality Programs run into each other. Comparatively, in your human body, this electrical equator is where the electrical voltage shifts from positive to negative. At the Wall, there is a 180-degree phase change.

In a sense, it is a two-way highway with both a counter-clockwise and a clockwise spin of the electromagnetic energies. The electromagnetic energies hold the oppositional resonances of the 3D Duality Programs. It's a trap!

At the end of the Wall, a vortex geometrically spirals out perfectly each side or end. As the 3D Duality of the clockwise and the counter-clockwise fields are altered, they no longer are going in opposite directions. They are moving in the same upward direction.

As the spirals of Consciousness and energy move in an upward direction together, the Block Wall is dissolved. The spiral of energy, which previously moved in opposite directions, merge as the Field of the Allness Consciousness. In the Allness Consciousness, the connection is Multi-Dimensional in all directions, fearless and limitless.

The new alignment of the energy fields, clockwise and counter-clockwise in the same direction at the same rate, rises from the soles of your feet up through your entire body. A transformation and transfiguration of your spiritual electromagnetic frequency within your physical body occurs. You are empowered with an electromagnetic field of energy which no longer requires you to maintain a polarity of oppositional Belief Systems with the energy of your Spirit, your Soul, your Perfect Child Within, and the alignment of your Male and Female within you. All aspects of you are integrated and aligned into the Allness of your Consciousness. This alignment activates your new Thirteen Chakra System, and your body transmutes the Block Wall. These changes affect the dynamics of Consciousness on this planet.

Visualize a picture of the Earth, which is analogous to the human body, drawn on a sheet of paper. In the energy flow of the old pattern, the energy moves clockwise above the Earth's equator or the human's navel. Below the equator or the navel, the energy moves counter-clockwise forming a figure "8". This is the 3D Duality infinity symbol. Half is negative and half is positive.

Now fold the picture. The center moves to the bottom and the bottom meets the top. See how the energy flow is altered. In a manner of speaking, what is occurring is you are folding the directions of your energy. At the same time, you are folding time and the dimensions within your physical body.

Your journey through the 3D Duality polarity of oppositional Belief Systems is how you created success and failure in this 3-Dimensional world. Through these opposing forces, you experience and recreate Karma, Lessons, and Re-incarnation.

In the No-Time and the Void, by rising above the conflict of 3D Duality that was programmed into you, you now have the choice to break down the Wall of limitations through Unconditional Love and Total Acceptance of Your Self and transcend. This simply means you are becoming conscious.

You are the One and the Only One who can make this happen by initiating your personal change in Consciousness. You are realizing with *real eyes* that 3D Duality is not the only dimension in town! This is the beginning of integrating in *real*, practical terms that you are a Multi-Dimensional Being in a human body at this point in your journey.

The conflict of 3D Duality is ingrained in your body, your DNA template, and in your biology and physiology through the de-powering, no-progress of conditioning. **Consciousness is the key.** Your discernment between what is your Truth and what are the "trues" of the 3D Duality Programs is the progressive process as you permit your Self to *feel* the difference between these two different aspects of Consciousness. Through your Feeling Center (your Heart and your Solar Plexus Chakras) is where you begin to make the connection and *feel* the difference.

You cannot break through the Wall using your left computer/brain. You cannot think the difference. The emotional thinky-thinky keeps you in the story of the "trues".

It is only through *feeling*, not emotion, from your Heart (which is the most expansive resonance in your body) connected with your Solar Plexus (your Perfect Child Within) in an integrated conscious connection with your liberated Male and your liberated Female that you can break through the Wall of Limitation.

**"Why waste your time thinking out of the box,
when thinking is what put you there in the first place."**

-*Bradford Jones*

The unified Consciousness of these aspects of your Self moving your clear energy through your body is the mechanism that breaks down and dissolves this illusional Wall. You make this change/shift happen physically in your body. You do so by loving your Self unconditionally, accepting your Self completely, and by knowing, without any doubt, you are in charge of your own manifested destiny to get out of this repetitive, cyclical loop of 3D Duality Fear Programs.

Unconditional Love puts the Consciousness Key in your hands! You are the only one who can turn the key and turn your life into the direction of unlimited potentials and possibilities so you can manifest the Realness you require, desire, and deserve.

You are the One! You make the choice. You can choose to nurture your Self with Unconditional Love and Total Acceptance with no conditions. This is all about you!

This is the time to acknowledge your Self and your wealth of experiences in your continuing continuous continuum. How you choose now to continue through your personal continuum is the Fork in Your Road to Take Back Your Power.

You can choose to make the required changes…or…you can go down the 3D Duality Road in your continuing continuous continuum and do all the same Fear Programs over and over again, and have your destiny and fate be Karma, Lessons, and Re-incarnation. Your back is up against the Wall, caught up in the 3D Duality "8" infinity re-cycle bin of your Childish Adult Ego trapped in the survival program running in your left computer/brain.

The moment you choose to initiate consciously and intentionally the activation of your Thirteen Chakras, your body begins to release the density of the 3D Duality Dimension prison. Your "light" body, as the metaphysicians describe it, is set free from the conditions, emotional hooks, and the outcomes from either the past or the repetitious past/future. You now have new and ongoing choices to create multiple futures in the No-Time, which is the space of Consciousness that is not restricted in the time limits of past, present, and future.

Zero Point, metaphorically and physically, is when the hand of the clock is at 12 and you have a choice of going either forward into newness or going back in time and re-living the past. And the Void is the space of creation; the perfect place to start. You are beginning to live your Clear Godness Consciousness of creation, implementation, manifestation, and actualization in your new continuing continuous continuum.

As you make your break through the 3D Duality Wall of repetitive cycles of limitations, you begin to *feel* all of your dimensions of your Self coming together in a unified field of your Clear Consciousness. You are putting your Self together.

Your empowered Clear Consciousness propels your energy through this limited electromagnetic Wall of fear that has prevented you from *feeling*, *seeing*, participating, and accessing the Multi-Dimensional fields of Consciousness that you are. All of these dimensions have always been who you are. The Fear Programs of Judgment, Lack, and Take-Away held you hostage to be less.

As you shift, you are not as affected by the limitations of time – past, present, and future. You are in the moment. The past and the past/future – which are exactly the same – do not affect you in the present as you become the Involved Conscious Evolutionary.

There is no reason to repeat "his"-tory or "her"-story. Repeating the dysfunctional stories is a worthless entanglement of your time. You create your life in each and every moment. You are becoming the Non-Emotional Observer (NEO), the Conscious Creator, In Charge of Your Life, Creating Newness in the Moment of the No-Time No-Space!

Your *Know*-Space/Your *Know*-Time Continuum

**"Time is increments of spaces
in which to have your experiences.**

**How you intend to create in your increments
of spaces in the moment is up to you!"**

-Sherryism

You are not supposed to achieve your Godness Consciousness in 3D Duality Fear Programs

It doesn't matter that the religious programs say, "You will never be worthy, have worth, be valuable, or have value enough to be your Godness Consciousness." You are *supposed* to wait either here or "there", wherever "there" is, to find your Self. You are always struggling to find God outside of You. You are destined to fail. 3D Duality Fear Programs will simply not allow you to succeed to be fully who you are. Why?

You are always in a *temporary permanent* "spin", running to find your Self. Even when the run is into the next lifetime and the next lifetime and the next lifetime, repeating the last lifetime and the last lifetime before that and the lifetime before that, until it's the lifetime after that and the lifetime after that, and so on. Time in 3D Duality never *runs out*. How can you *run out* of time? It is virtually impossible. You can *run out* of a lifetime, whenever that is. However, you can never *run out* of lifetimes. You *run* "back" into the next lifetime, carrying with you all the stuff you have been hanging on to from your previous *runs*. In terms of the trauma-dramas in which you played or had a starring Role, you always had a long-term *run* on your stage of life.

Again, the costumes change, the backdrop changes, the reference to time changes, but there you are on the middle of your stage, more times than not with the same players in all your acts. Sometimes the players take a break, just as you do. You are not always in their scripts, and they are not always in yours.

However, the Profiles are always available to you in your scripts. You know these Profiles so well. Now you know why you have so many of the same relationships! You can't help repeating the same old stuff. The insidious Karma, Lessons, and Re-incarnation Programs are the repetitious, insidious resonances embedded in the Duality energy fields in which you play your Roles and your Behaviors with your Profiles.

The victim/victimizer, abuser/abused, controller/controlled, and all the usual suspects including you play out your unconscious but well-scripted Roles. Until now! There are other choices at last! Oh, to get conscious or not? Now that is a question to ask your Self.

These repeated Duality spin cycles drain you of your vitality, your worth, your value, your creativity, and your ability to live a whole, healthy, wealthy life. Over and over again, you re-cycle 3D Duality. You are forced with NO Self Power to re-create the same stuff with the carrot dangling in front of you. The run for the illusive carrot is that "someday" you will reach the Promised Land. The problem with the Promised Land is that it is nowhere in sight.

Land ahoy, where is it? Land ahoy, where am I? Land ahoy, who am I? Let's see…you could be…the half of your Self now searching for the other half to make you whole. Or, if you run all over the Earth, you will find that "sacred mystery site" to provide you with your answers, especially if it is old or ancient.

You can run all over the Earth looking for that sacred site *outside* of you, when the Truth is that the Truth of You and the sacred site are inside of you. Or, you can wait until you croak, die, or, better yet, transition, and then you will find You. Or, according to your Belief Systems, you may never find You. According to others, when you die, you are whole. If that's true, then why are there Karma, Lessons, and Re-incarnation and re-living the same trauma-dramas?

The opportunity now, on this planet, is to become whole within your Self in your body *before* you die. Or, your Belief System may have convinced you that you can never reach the "big time", or in other words, that you don't have what it takes to be a Master.

By the way, the reason the past was so mysterious for the average "Joes" in the old and ancient times is because they did not read or write. So, they had no other choice but to embrace what was told to them by the external authority figures – religious, political, and the elite. They bought the controller's Belief Systems. Everything in the ancient past appears as mysterious…the mystery schools and the mysteries of the ancient world! Come on, get over it.

The past was mysterious because the majority was not educated. They did not read or write, and without knowledge, they lived in the utmost survival mode. No matter what their circumstances – rich or poor – they were terrified of everything. They were afraid of the gods, nature, the heavens, the omens, and each other. They were afraid of everything. They were confined and restricted by all sorts of limited Belief Systems.

Not much has changed. You are still taught to be afraid of your Self and your own Power. If you are afraid of your Self and your own Power, you are easy to control. Just as before, so it is now. Has anything changed? Technology? Today it is even scarier being controlled!

Traveling to sacred sites is wonderful. It is fun. It is whatever it is to you. The Big Truth is that your sacred site is You. First, you must find the divine within You. Now appreciate how sacred you and your life are. Otherwise, your path is led by someone or something else.

Lead your Self on your own path. Consciousness is the Key to your path. There is no mystery. Turn on the light and your knowledge and you can *see* for your Self the journey along your path is *run* by you. No more *running!*

There are so many caveats in the *run* to find your way, to find you, to find the elusive promise, or to grab the carrot. Ever notice that the answers are always outside of you? Ever notice that someone else always has your answers? Did you ever ask them if they had the answers for their Selves? Hmmmmm…wonder what they would answer?

Even wonder if the *they* don't have the answers either? Even ask, "Why would the *they* have *your* answers?" Ever wonder why the *they* who say they have the answers seem to be as confused as you are? Ever wonder why you can't get a straight answer from the *they?* Always trust the *they?* Never trust your Self?

It is time to begin to trust your Self. Do you believe it is time to begin to ask your Self the questions? If you don't believe it is *your* time to ask the questions, then continue to follow the *their* answers! You will never run out of time or lifetimes.

Each lifetime is full of "theys"
to give you their answers for you

In 3D Duality, the Belief Systems of polarity is the Belief Systems of opposition. Consequently, with the <u>con</u> of <u>sequence</u> in you being in disorder, you are out of sync! You cannot be in order or functioning fully when you are Set-Up to be out of balance through the 3D Belief Systems. As a result, your energy and the use of your energy cannot maintain a full balance of full Consciousness. There has to be the upside and the downside. There has to be the right and wrong, good and bad, and the proverbial clash of the conditioning of Belief Systems opposed to you being fully conscious and living fully. Both your negative and positive poles must be in sync with each other to be fully operational as a fully conscious human being.

All through 3D Duality history, each side claimed God was on their side while they "killed" for the "good" of it. If you were on the "good" side and did the killing, you have the redemption clause in your contract that you can get on the *other* "good" side and be killed the next time. Don't you just love the idea of the "good" side? Now if you were on the "bad" side, you could be the ones killing the "good" guys or gals. Somewhere in the 3D Duality Fear Programs, the good side and the bad side get convoluted.

Do you *feel* you are willing to give up the good and the bad sides? You do it by *feeling* it; you cannot do it by thinking it. *Feeling* is from the Heart, and *thinky-thinking* is the left computer/brain which is unwilling to give up Duality. Isn't it time to move on from this confused paradigm of 3D Duality?

What would the *real* possibilities and potentials be like that take your dreams and make them *real* for you if you are not encumbered by all the limitations and repeated "his" and "her"-stories on this narrow path of Duality? Let's get Conscious. Let's let go of Judgment, Lack, and Take-Away. Let's begin creating consciously. Let's stop the internal and external fighting. The internal conflict makes the external conflict. It is not the other way around.

Who says relationships have to be difficult? No matter what the relationships are – whether personal, professional, community, ethnic, religion, or political – what would happen if all the emotional hooks were severed to the right and wrong of these Duality relationships? What would happen if you and each and every human on this planet said enough is enough! What could happen? Chaos? Maybe yes. Maybe no. There is always a transition time.

Do you have to be vested emotionally in your programming so you cannot *see* the potential of your Self and your creative abilities? There is no script writer in Hollywood or anywhere in the world who could have written your script so amazingly! Yes, you wrote all your traumas and your dramas lifetime after lifetime. Look at the time wasted looking outside of your Self for validation!

It's always based upon the "fix", or the person to make you whole, or the group that would provide answers for you through the long journeys lifetime after lifetime. And then, after all that running, you discover the running was about finding You inside of You. Here you are now, here you were then, and here you will be in the next then. Get the picture? Was all the pain, the suffering, the sorrow, and the fight worth it? If yes, then continue.

If you are willing to let go of the pain, suffering, the sorrow, the fight, the blame, the game, and the opposition, then look inside your Self. You have all the answers. You have all the questions. Now ask the questions correctly to your Self. Not how right or wrong you were or are. Be amazed at your Self. Look now at all the information, all the experiences you have had, and all the relationships you have been in. And now, get in a *real* relationship with your Self.

What if this world got off the Duality Spin Cycle? What would happen? Who knows how creative you and everyone can be if the internal and external wars stopped? Is there really any more reason to war with your Self or anyone else? It is worth wasting your life?

To Be or Not To Be,
Not To Be is Impossible.
To Be is All.

-Wei Chen
Ancient Chinese Poet

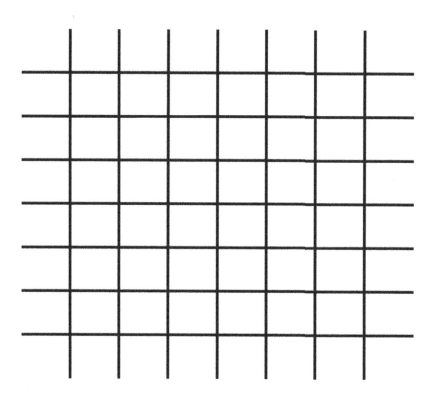

The Thirteen Chakras Open Template
of Unlimited Consciousness and Creativity

The movement of Creative Energy flows in all directions
without restrictions.

Multi-Dimensional Expansion

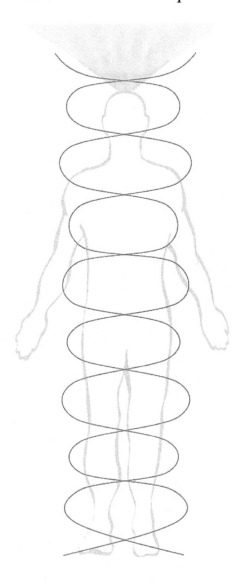

The Activation of the Thirteen Chakras

Synergy and Synchronicity of the New Electromagnetic Fields
and DNA Strands

Chapter 8

THE SHIFT

The Activation of the Thirteen Chakras

**"The twelve faculties of man's divine mind are
symbolized by the twelve disciples of Jesus Christ,
with their origin the One Consciousness
transfigured body."**

Metaphysical Dictionary

**"Angels are the Power hidden
in the faculties and origin of man."**

-Ibn al-Arabi the Murcian
Greatest Master of the Sufi
1165 – 1240 AD

In the Transcension or expanded Multi-Dimensional
awareness of your Consciousness from the 7 Chakras of
Limited Consciousness to the Thirteen Chakras of
Unlimited Consciousness in your physical human body, the
Clear Creative Progressive Process aligns on a pathway of
partnership with many aspects of your Self. During this
progressive process, there is also an alignment and
connection of conscious awareness with the faculties who
represent the twelve divine disciples within you.

The disciples represent the various aspects of you and your
Multi-Dimensions of Consciousness within your human
body. The Christed Consciousness is the alignment of these
aspects of you. When you are in this alignment within you,
you are following the leadership of your own Christed
Consciousness.

The Thirteen Chakras Consciousness is both a metaphoric and physical shift occurring within your human body as you make the change from a very limited view of your Self and your world to being an expansive, multi-faceted person. You begin to become the Christ or Clear Consciousness of your Multi-Dimensional Self. The twelve disciple aspects align within you, connecting to the leadership within you of your Christed Consciousness.

The disciples followed Jesus on the path to Consciousness. As you get connected to all the aspects or Multi-Dimensional facets of you, you are aligning your Self to be led by your Christed Consciousness within you. "You shall do as I do and more." When you stay limited, you shall do more of the same limitations, and no Christed Consciousness is working inside of you, just the same mis-alignment of the Fear Programs of Judgment, Lack, and Take-Away working You.

You have one Path and multi-pathways intersecting along your One Path. Your Path is as narrow as your restricted Belief Systems or as wide as your relationship to your awareness to Believe in Your Self. If your Belief Systems about your Self are narrow, restricted, and fear-based, then your life and your experiences are in direct correlation. If you Believe in Your Self as an unlimited source of powerful creativity and you are In Charge of Your Life, then your path is wide, unlimited, and intersects with multi-pathways along your journey. Narrow is as narrow does. Unlimited is unlimited!

Each pathway intersecting with your Path is the opportunity to experience, to participate, to learn, to grow, and to live life to the fullest. The opportunities on a narrow path are not available because you cannot *see* or *feel* them. Your vision, your physical eyesight, is the same narrowness.

When you are fearful, the thick molecules of fear-based emotions prevent you from *seeing*.

**You can't experience life fully
if you are fear-filled and blind to your Self.**

**Fear is the No Experience, No Participation,
No Fulfillment of the narrow Path.**

Where are YOU choosing to walk?

The twelve 3D Duality astrological signs also represent aspects of your evolution through the 3D Duality aspects of the signs. You can view your path along your astrological chart as your journey through linear time, the same as the Earth's journey as it revolves around the sun through each astrological sign.

Just as in 3D Duality, each sign in which you were born has aspects of oppositional Belief Systems and consequences. You chose the particular astrological sign as another avenue in your journey of multiplicity to gain more insight about your Self along your travels in each lifetime. Whether considered ancient or modern, the Earth as well as you journeyed through the Belief Systems of each astrological sign.

Whatever sign you chose in a particular lifetime has specific information on the how's, when's, where's, and why's you processed the linear frame of time under that sign. Did you *see* all the *signs* along the path you assigned your Self? What was the collective Belief Systems of the linear time frames in which you lived? Master? Slave? Ruler? Ruled? Victim? Victimizer? Don't all the signs look the same? And the envelope, please...the answers always seem to appear the same, whatever Role you played, you played it out through the signs of the times! Now how many times are you willing to do it again and again?

Your journey of Consciousness is analogous to the relationship of the journey of Earth's Consciousness through each astrological sign and frame of time as it moves around the sun. Each sign has a Consciousness, as the frames of linear time do. You have the opportunity to evolve or not through your astrological sign as does the collective of its specific astrological sign. This may not be *your* birth sign, but it is the birth sign of the collective.

For instance, Jesus was born in the collective of the Piscean Age. There is controversy due to Constantine's version of Jesus' birth in December. So, the question remains, what is his official birth sign? People born in the collective of the Age of Aquarius have their own personal birth sign, for example, Aires, Virgo, Cancer, and so on.

If you have a slave mentality Belief System, you create a way to be a slave. Rich or poor has nothing to do with it. You can be enslaved to your *duty* if you are royalty. You can be enslaved to your duty if you are a slave to a master who rules you. Both master and slave are in duty to each other.

This is the way of the 3D Duality Programs. How you participate in the slave/master programs is how you make the journey. "Long live the king or queen" doesn't make a healthy or happy life. Long life usually was meant for the slave aspect of the journey. The king and the emperor are equally enslaved. They just had better housing, food, and servants. The serfs had their children to be *their* slaves.

The astrological signs are all a specific collective Belief System of the time frame with specific resonances. You either resonate to them or not. For example, Jesus, born in the sign of Pisces, is represented by the fish. He also represented the emotional body. The human body is made up of water. The Earth is a water planet. Funny that it is called Earth!

Water represents the emotional body, calm or turbulent. When Jesus rose above the water and walked upon it, he had a 360-degree view. His view was that of the Non-Emotional Observer (NEO). When Peter succumbed to his fears of Judgment, Lack, and Take-Away that he was less than Jesus, he fell into the water. He knew Christ, but he didn't connect to his own Christed Consciousness. When he was fearful, he fell back into the water, hooked into the human emotional attachments to the experience.

All the astrological signs have their metaphoric as well as the physical experience of the collective and the individual experience through the resonances of the signs. Hence, the two sides of the "his"-story and "her"-story of 3D Duality.

Ask your Self,
> **how does your astrological sign affect and influence your Role in life?**

> **Do you have a Belief System that your sign is supposed to act a certain way and then you do?!**
> **Hmmmm......**

In the Shift or experience of moving forward or transcending the 3D Duality emotional body world, you consciously and deliberately expand your energy field. You are physically changing the course of your journey as you become deliberately conscious in the Take Back Your Power progressive process.

You are the connector, the connecting, and the connection as you physically move in all directions through the food chain of Consciousness. You become the inter-link to the Multi-Dimensional levels of Consciousness inside and outside of you.

As you shift out of the limited Belief Systems, your outside world shifts. Everything may change. Relationships, careers, families, and friends, may not look the same to you as before. You begin to *see* without judging the sources or references that these relationships, personal or professional, may not serve you anymore. You may not serve those who are participating with you either.

You may no longer be a match to the lower resonances of participation as before. Your *before* shifts as you shift *forward*. When your inside Consciousness is no longer a resonance match to the old 3D Duality Limited Belief Systems, you no longer resonate outside of you to those constricting limitations. Your participation in your life changes. Your outside life changes.

This doesn't mean you are cutting your friends, family, or career out of your life. The Truth is that you are just not resonating to the valueless, energy-draining inter-actions called dysfunctional relationships anymore. The value of function verses dysfunction has a significant shift. Now, the question to ask your Self is: "What is valuable to me or not?"

As you expand your awareness and transcend limitation, you provide an opportunity for others. As they *see* you in action, they may desire to ask you the "whys" of your change. Or not! As each individual changes one by one to be clearly conscious, the opportunity for the Earth to shift out of 3D Duality occurs. Isn't this what the New Earth is all about? No longer being in fear. No longer participating in the not living, the not creating, and the not pro-creating.

3D Duality is just the re-creation of the same old limited re-cycled Programs of Judgment, Lack, and Take-Away. The more you become the Clear Christed Consciousness, the Earth reaps the benefits of the resonance change. The collective Consciousness of the Earth shifts too. Everyone and everything are connected. The Earth is no different. The Earth is a living being.

The Earth, as a living conscious being, is the place or location in this frame of the time continuum which is providing the place and space for you and everyone who has agreed to participate on this path of discovery. As for the 3D Duality Fear Programs, there is no discovery of anything new in creativity and manifestation. There are only repeated Profiles of experiences.

Ascending above and beyond the fear and the limitations provides the non-emotional place to change. The Earth, like you at your core's purest Christed Consciousness, knows Transcension is Real. You know it…you just have to get past the illogical fear of the "unknown". The "known" is predictable. You should know. You, as well as the Earth, have lived it over and over again. How predictable is the dysfunctional "known"? Very!

The correlation between the expansion of your Consciousness and the expansion of the Consciousness of the Earth itself occurs in a symmetry of the unified field of expanded Consciousness. As you become connected to the Earth, the Earth is aware of your connection. You *feel* the connection. You become the connection. The living Being Earth *feels* the connection.

When you feel life,
it is very difficult to destroy life for no reason

The Earth holds for you and for everyone the energy field in which you travel along your path through the resonance of your Consciousness in the collective into which you were born. Whether the collective Consciousness honors the Earth or not, the Earth prevails.

The idea of the Christed Consciousness, which represents the full potential of the human being, was birthed over 2,000 years ago. What a waste of time waiting to liberate your Self. But not a waste of time for organizations jumping on the bandwagon to convince you that they had the right version of the Christed Consciousness to show you the way!

Hmmmm…is something off here? Wow! Even the Christed Consciousness was turned into a program of controller/controlled, manipulator/manipulated. Of course, like clockwork, more versions of something to war about sprung up faster than the Christed Consciousness could bat an eyelash. Lashed again by the Fear Programs of Judgment, Lack, and Take-Away. The religious whiplash cracked and another form of control reigned. Even the Kingdom of Heaven was unattainable. Heaven on Earth is unthinkable as well.

In this current millennium, the old 3D Duality Grid surrounding the Earth is the trap of the old 7 Chakra System, which is breaking down. The breaking down of this Grid of dysfunctional repetition is happening two-fold. As you and everyone get conscious, the Grid cannot hold its form. However, there are those who are not giving up the control so easily. They are increasing the resonance of fear. They are creating more and more scenarios to hold this old Grid in place. Now is your chance to be free of the Grid. Do not allow this confining, restricted Grid cage to cage you in any longer!

The more Conscious you become,
the less and less fear you hold in your body.

The result is you are not creating from fear.
You are creating from empowerment consciously.

Take full responsibility for your Self. Be responsive in examining the old Fear Programs. Be conscious how they have affected and influenced your life. Your life belongs to you.

You do not belong existing in a Grid cage. You are not a gerbil jumping through hoops, spinning lifetime after lifetime, being controlled for the benefit of the elite, whoever they are.

Ascend! It is the way out of the Grid. Open the door to Clear Consciousness. Get out of the 3D Duality script. Stop existing in the metaphor of The Truman Show. He found his way out. He became the True-man!

The new Grid of Consciousness is not fixed. The new Grid of Consciousness is fluid and flexible as is your unlimited creativity. Be of the expanded Consciousness and not in the old Belief Systems. You have a choice. You have always had a choice. Now the choice is more critical. However, if the traumas and the dramas appeal to you, by all means stay in The Truman Show. Continue to be manipulated by the outside sources – the news media, the stories, the rumors, and the fear mongers.

What goes on outside of you is up to you. Buy it or not! If you "live" from the outside Belief Systems in, your inside is not your Consciousness of Truth. You exist in "their" version of what your outside is according to the 3D Duality Programs. Whoever "they" are, you are not in charge of your life if you give "them" more value than the value you give to your Self.

The Shift from 3D Duality to Multi-Dimensional Realness is a no-brainer. Stay in your left computer/brain and stay in 3D Duality…or move forward consciously. As you connect to those dimensions within your Self, you are connected to the Multi-Dimensions. The match is the result of your resonance.

If you continue in your continuum in the resonance of fear, this life and all of your next 3D Duality lives, you will be guaranteed to match the resonance of fear. Whatever the Fear Program is labeled – not good enough, less than, no good, and all the versions of the Victim/Victimizer Program – you will be in it. This is not living!

"Programs running, dead man walking!"

-Steven Wolf

By consciously releasing your Self with purpose on purpose from the control and manipulation of the Fear Programs, you automatically begin the Shift at your Cellular Level. You have over a trillion cells who are mini "me's" of you. They make the collective of you – your physical, emotional, mental, physiological, anatomical, and biological systems of you. As you align your Self with an expanded resonance of awareness, so will your cells.

In this change, as you make the conscious connection to your body using your left computer/brain to organize information but not to run your life, the intelligence and intellect of your body's cells align with you. You are not fighting your body, and your cells are not fighting to get your attention.

When your cells within your body are having pain, the normal protocol is to medicate your Self. The more you medicate, the easier it is to control you from outside sources. You give your Power Away. You are not in your *right* mind. You are not *listening* to your body. You are following the programs through the lead of your left computer/brain.

Follow your Heart, *listen* to your intuition, and get the facts through medical tests or whatever the protocol you use to get the facts. When you have the facts, you have the Power to clearly make choices. If you stay only in your left computer/brain, you make decisions made for you by outside sources. You always have choices and options. With knowledge and facts, you are empowered to make clear choices.

And now the question is, "Are you willing to expend another minute, day, month, year or 2,000 years of 3D Duality being a Victim of the Fear Programs…or are you willing to change?" Are you willing *or not* to embrace the changes that are required for you to Take Back Your Power? Your life can be up to you *or* you can give your Power away. Your continuing continuous continuum is in your hands.

Your life is in the palms of your hands.

What are you handing your Self?

THE THIRTEEN CHAKRAS

Please review the Thirteen Chakras chart at the end of this chapter. It includes the Zodiac signs, the discipleships, the crystals, the essential oils, and the Consciousness related to each Chakra.

This is the journey of becoming a Real Human, out of the Duality trap of the old 7 Chakra System of re-create, re-create, re-create. The Godness within you comes to Life!

FIRST CHAKRA

FEET: Soul of Your Earth Body-Foundation

As you shift physically, electro-magnetically, and consciously from the Seven to the Thirteen Chakras, the First Chakra to activate is at the bottom of your feet. The metaphor is so evident. When you "heal/heel" your "soul/sole", you begin to stand for your Truth

This First Chakra represents the Soul of your Earth body. This is the foundation of your expanded awareness. The disciple who represents your new stand is Judas. Contrary to popular belief, Judas is not the traitor. He had the courage to take a stand for Jesus as the one who betrayed him. It took incredible courage and bravery to be part of this trauma-drama to play out his Role in the Ascension process for Jesus. Judas was the chosen one and accepted this Role as "betrayer" and performed his Role accordingly.

In the old paradigm of 3D Duality, Judas represents the aspect of you when you betrayed your Self and did not stand for your Truth. He represents when you gave up your Power and stood for something which was not in alignment with your own core Truth. Do not judge your Self for any event, situation, or lifetime. You had no choice but to betray your Self and your Truth. You played both Roles of the two-sided 3D Duality Program. You were both the betrayed and the betrayer.

Now, the only important thing is what you learned about your Self when you gave away your Power. How can you use this information as the Non-Emotional Observer (NEO) to examine the circumstances of the situations and *see* how you participated in the trauma-dramas?

Now connect to the resonance of these events. *See* and *feel* how they resonate to you now. If they still resonate, then you are still emotionally hooked in and holding on to the "right and wrong" of these circumstances. If you *see* the situation(s) as experiences where you learned about your Self and you are now clear you no longer desire to repeat these dysfunctional patterns, then you are on the verge of standing for your Truth no matter what the outside sources say about it.

Stop the judgment of what you or "they" have done. You cannot change the unchangeable past. You require being courageous and brave as Judas was. You must be willing to be vulnerable.

Vulnerability is your strength and not your weakness. Being vulnerable is *seeing* all aspects of the outside world from the "stand" point of standing for your Truth and making choices of how you choose to participate. You do not have to betray your Self or your Truth any longer.

Being vulnerable is letting the Wall down and *seeing* everything outside of you from an empowered place/position inside of you. Physically and metaphorically, *seeing* everything around you and making choices about how you choose to participate is the Take Back Your Power stance. You don't have to be caught off guard or thrown off your feet.

Judas must have loved Jesus unconditionally to do what he did. He did the deed! Now you must love and accept your Self unconditionally to NOT BETRAY your Self anymore. Jesus couldn't kill his Self, so stop killing your Self lifetime after lifetime. Stop killing your Self every day by not living and standing in your Truth.

Initiate Taking Your Stand for Your Self. You change the dynamics of the old paradigm that everyone outside of you is your reflection. This is an old worn out idea. It is "true", in 3D Duality terms, that they are reflections. But the Truth is that they are NOT. Being a reflection of someone else or being a reflection for someone else is keeping you and the others stuck in this old pattern.

If you are being a jerk, is it necessary to draw someone into your life you can label a jerk to validate your belief that you are being a jerk? How ridiculous! Do you know how much valuable time and effort this takes? Plus, it uses up your energy being stuck in the old programming of "reflection". Boring! If you are being a jerk, you know it. You don't have to project your jerkdom on someone else. Otherwise, you have to involve someone else in your jerkdom just to prove to your Self and whoever it is that you are both jerks! See how silly this is? Who made this up? Who cares?

"Life is *not* a reflection of you...it is a projection of you."

- *Sherryism*

The Duality paradigm says that your Life is a reflection of you. There is no substance to a reflection. There is nothing! Beyond Duality you create the projection of YOU through your connection to the Universe and the Multi-verse. The projection of you is POWER. Your projections come from the creative source of you. Your projections are physical and have substance. This is REAL.

Duality is the reflections of realities which have no substance. They are not Real. This is why Duality has no sustainability. That's why things don't last. The cycle is...I have it, I lost it, I have it, I lost it...whether it is money, a relationship, fame, or fortune... Just re-do's of the same thing regardless of the year or century. So, we run from lifetime to lifetime recreating the same thing. Rich, poor, famous, not famous, victim, victimizer, or whatever the Duality Programs in which you are stuck…they just get repeated. Technology may change, but the Duality human, emotionally, physically, mentally, spiritually, and financially, is the same old stuckness.

Pisces, the Twelfth House, is aligned to the First Chakra of this new system of Clear Consciousness. Jesus was born in the Piscean Age. Jesus represents the rising above of the emotional body and the emotional hooks of the 3D Duality Programs of the incessant, non-productive trauma-dramas. His walking on the water, again, represents the rising above the emotions and *seeing* clearly what is going on.

As you expand the resonance of your 3D Duality human body and the Consciousness contained in it, you let go of these emotional hooks which are so dysfunctional and repeatable. Expanding your resonance, especially detaching from the wanty-needy behavioral pattern of being either right or wrong, shifts your ability to create healthier relationships.

The first healthy relationship is with your Self. This relationship requires to be healthy above all else.

Wanty-needy is the lowest-based resonance of relationship, especially when it is involved in the 3D Duality versions of "love". If you don't love your Self unconditionally and even conditionally, you will continue to draw to you, in the Law of Distraction, wanty-needy love "dis-connections" which are not connected consciously, just resonating to dysfunctional "love" attachments.

This resonance is the ultimate victim/victimizer, whether it includes physical violence or not. In this relationship, no one can stand for their Truth. They can't stand each other after the hormones wear off. Both are betrayed by this low-based, wanty-needy *belief systeming*.

The 3D Duality Programs condition you to participate in emotionally-charged fields of energy repeatedly. These fields of energy are called relationships. They program you to be the mirror, and not the person that you are. Like the trickster in a carnival, what gets reflected back to you is that *outside* relationship which defines you as you, instead of You defining You.

In these repeated situations of relationships, you continue to be hooked into non-productive emotionality. You are always thinky-thinking what you are all about according to the *outside* sources. These non-productive emotions are what keep you stuck and locked in the 3D Duality Grid. As you begin to Stand for Your Truth, you begin to free your Self from the confines of the 3D Duality Grid.

In the activation of this First Chakra, you rise above the emotions and you let go of the hooks to the past which cannot be changed. You now can Stand for Your Truth and Stand for Your Self. Your feet are grounded to the Earth. Yet at the same time, your resonance increases and expands.

Your polarity is changing and aligning in a new way. You are aligning to a new field of Consciousness. You are becoming Multi-Dimensional. Healing is happening. The past, where it no longer serves you, has no place for you to stand in the past. Standing in the present moment, feet first, you are becoming your expanded Self.

From your feet to your ankles, You Take a Stand. Your ankles, representing support, which is the same as your wrists, *feel* for the first time *real* support coming from *within* you. You are *feeling* your Power feet first!

The number 1 means new beginnings. This is the new beginning without dragging your feet and dragging the old paradigm of 3D Duality with you.

SECOND CHAKRA

ANKLES: Female/Male Energy Alignment

The Second Chakra to be activated is the ankles. In the old 3D Duality patterns of operation, the ankles represent not having sufficient support, whether it is emotional, mental, physical, spiritual, or financial support. The lack of support is the same issue regardless of how it is labeled.

Lack of support is the 3D Duality Reality which appears Real because of the Lack Program. The Separatism Program is the conditioned Belief System of Lack. Regardless of the non-support issues, keeping you separate from your Self and others is a perfect way to make sure you *think* you are not being supported.

The Realness of support comes from within you when you are clearly conscious that you are In Charge of Your Life. **You are your support.**

The challenge in the resonance of 3D Duality is to align the non-support issues of both the Male and Female aspects of your Self *within* you. Your Male and Female alignment is crucial to *feeling* your own conscious support.

Real support is found inside of you, not outside of you. The reason everyone feels the lack of support is because they have been conditioned to *belief system* that all support comes from outside sources.

You can't love anyone else until you love your Self first. When you love your Self, you will get love. You cannot *feel* or be supported from anyone outside of your Self until you *feel* you are supported by your Self first. This is the how the Law of Attraction works. Otherwise, it is the same old same old Law of Distraction keeping you off balance from your Self.

Resonance attracts resonance. You are either on the same wavelength with your Self and others *or* you are not. This is a no-brainer. When you have no Self-connection, no Self-love, no Self-acceptance, or no Self-support, this is what you receive in your outside world. You get what you send out! You get back what you send out. This is the same thing.

**When you feel support from your Self,
you get supported.**

**When you are afraid you won't have support,
you don't get support.**

When you have Self love, love is returned.

**If your Belief System of supportive love is wanty-needy,
you get wanty-needy dysfunctional love in return
with no support.**

**Yes, be mindful and conscious of what you ask for
when you are asking for support and love.**

You have been trained, conditioned, and taught to be in opposition to your Self and to have the Belief System that you are not supported. Again, whether physical, emotional, mental, spiritual, or financial, you are conditioned and expected to struggle, to exist in fear, and to be fearful of not having something or other that could or would make you *feel* safe, secure, and supported.

Your life throughout your 3D Duality continuum is a Set-Up for you to be constantly striving to find support from someone outside of you. No matter whether you are male or female, the 3D Duality Grid does not have the stability for you to experience Real support. It is impossible. The Male and Female aspects of you are constantly in a battle for control. You are conditioned to be separated from your Self. You are "supported" for it to appear to you that you don't have Real support. An oxymoron for sure!

As a result, you have experienced lives as both the male and female genders throughout your time continuum and remained stuck in the 3D Duality resonance, unable to release your issues. All these experiences are embedded at your Cellular Level as memories, memorizations, and sounds equated with the experiences. You go back and forth with the same issues, no matter whether your gender is male or female.

Your ankles, including their energetic connection to your wrists, are challenged to deal with these non-support issues as a balanced Male and Female Consciousness. Gender has nothing to do with these issues per se.

For the male and female gender, the issues of non-support are all the same. For example: "My husband/my wife does not support me. My father/my mother does not support me. My sister/my brother does not support me. My boss/my friends don't support me." Are you getting the picture? The non-support issues can be as varied as you create them consciously or unconsciously.

The paradigm of 3D Duality does not have the resonance or template in the Grid to support you to let go of these illusional issues. 3D Duality "supports" you to be dysfunctional, separate, alone, and lonely. The Grid, metaphorically, is the continuum of boxes of Duality's

Belief Systems. These boxes of B.S. are piled high and wide, storing the same programmed, limited Belief Systems from lifetime to lifetime.

In the 3D Duality Fear Programs of Judgment, Lack, and Take-Away you are expected to be unconscious.

That's what makes you easily controlled and easily manipulated by Fear!

The dynamics of the physical, emotional, spiritual, mental, and financial 3D Duality Reality set you up to be disconnected from your Self, especially when it comes to the support issues. This dense resonance field makes it difficult for you to connect to all the layers or spaces of Consciousness stored in all the different areas of your body relating to your Male and Female issues.

Every cell, every group of cells, every organ, every system, and every part of your Male and Female aspects of Consciousness are divided. As a human, you are the perfect example of the living proof of divide and conquer. You are divided all the time within your Self. Wonder why you feel so disconnected? 3D Duality is why.

In the concept of "no support", confusion results from the perception of not only your Male and Female aspects of Self, but now you add to the equation your Childish Adult Ego and your Perfect Child Within. They are in a war just as your Male and Female are. Wow…another form of Consciousness divided within you!

Your Childish Adult Ego is your lonely, non-supported survivalist. Your Perfect Child Within awaits your clear conscious connection to your Self. When your Perfect Child Within is silently and unconsciously held in the confining Grid of non-support issues, the division of

Consciousness within you is fragmented. Your Childish Adult Ego has to step up to the plate and endure through another experience or another lifetime of non-support from the outside issues.

Your Perfect Child Within knows you are supported. Your Childish Adult Ego (CAE) has to fight for support and never gets it. When the CAE does get support, as your inner survivalist, he or she knows the support is an illusion – just a temporary, repeated pattern of behavior. "What's the use?" cries the CAE. The Perfect Child Within waits patiently for you to get clearly conscious, in whatever lifetime it is. This is the perfect lifetime.

"The Child is a treasure.

The Childish Adult Ego is the pirate who buries the treasure."

-Sherryism

Please note: Your Childish Adult Ego (CAE) will do anything to survive, even kill you because your CAE knows you have bought into the limitations, suffering, and repetitive trauma-dramas of the Karma, Lessons, and Re-incarnation Programs. The point is…your CAE will force you to return with another scripted version of the same old same old. Death has no meaning for the CAE. The pattern of the survivalist is to suffer, have traumas, be sick, and die without getting conscious. This is the CAE's perfect Role.

Your Perfect Child Within is your implementer of all that you create consciously. Your Perfect Child Within applies the functionality of your Christed Unlimited Consciousness. Its Role is for you to effectively implement your life as a Conscious Creator, minus the trauma-dramas of your Childish Adult Ego. Your Perfect Child Within supports you to live a healthy, prosperous, and fun life.

Emotional and Physical Issues

Look at all of the physical problems occurring in feet and ankles. The physical manifestations of the non-support issues in your feet and ankles include ingrown toenails, bunions, fallen arches, plantar fasciitis, broken bones, "weak" ankles, bone issues, and the list of problems goes on and on. As creative as you can be in the non-support issues is as creative as the physical problems can be in your feet and ankles.

3D Duality cannot provide a continuous energy field to allow for an alignment of your Male, your Female, and your Perfect Child Within. You have to be off balance and in conflict within your Self. To be in synergy and synchronicity with your Self would not work for Duality. You are not supposed to be in sync with your Self.

In the Thirteen Chakra System, your Male and Female Consciousness align energetically as you recognize that **all support comes from within you**. The 7 Chakra System ingrains in you the illusion that support is only provided from outside of you. However, at your clear core, you know this is not the Truth. As soon as you make the required changes to be In Charge of Your Self, the energetics of your Consciousness shift physically, emotionally, mentally, spiritually, and financially inside of you.

You clearly comprehend it is you who determines how you are supported by your Self. At the same time, you clearly understand that you have a choice as to how you receive support from others in your life. There is no longer any reason to hang on to this dense resonance of wanty-needy illusional support. This type of pretend support only further victimizes you. By having a Clear Consciousness that supports you, Real support from outside of you is drawn to you. **It's a resonance match.** You are being supported in a valuable and worthy way because *you know your worth and value.*

This support can now come from family, friends, businesses, professional associates, and whomever. This Clear Consciousness of how, when, where, and why you have support occurs because you are in alignment with your Self. The resonance you send out to draw to you those individuals and groups to support you make the difference now.

As this occurs, those individuals or groups who are not supportive of you won't matter emotionally or physically to you. There are no reasonable reasons to have a dysfunctional match anymore. There is not a reason to draw to you any more of those individuals or groups outside of you who are not supportive. You are not emotionally hooked to either being supported or not being supported in 3D Duality terms. You just know you are. Your Male, Female, and Perfect Child Within are in alignment consciously. This alignment is physical.

Aquarius, the Eleventh House of the Zodiac, represents the Second Chakra. 11 is the Master Number, which represents two symbols both standing in alignment with each other. It is not necessary for your Male and Female aspects to be out of alignment. Each aspect is now working together. Your polarity aligns. Your Male and Female aspects are supportive. The number two represents that alignment.

Aquarius is the pure water bearer, balancing out the emotions and letting go of the illusions of obstacles and opposition to the Male and Female aspects of your Self. You are experiencing the expanded thought form of this air sign. Expanded thought form does not mean thinky-thinky. Thinky-thinky is the programmed left computer/brain with its dysfunctional behavioral patterns.

As your Consciousness becomes more balanced, you *feel* your own support, and the physicality of your ankles become strengthened. You *feel* the difference. You *feel* strong and in your Power. You are detached as you go through the progressive process of becoming your integrated Self. Your Soul is getting involved in your personal physical, spiritual, mental, and financial experience without you taking it personally. This *is* a giant Shift in your Consciousness.

Thaddeus or Jude is the disciple of the newer Second Chakra. His aspect represents the balance and connection of your Spirit with your Female creativity and your Male manifesting aspects in agreement. You are also in alignment and agreement with your Perfect Child Within. Your support is becoming unanimous. You are in agreement to support your Self emotionally, mentally, physically, spiritually, and financially without all the trauma of the drama.

Thaddeus/Jude, a representative of one of your internal faculties, symbolizes the significant release of the Judgment, Lack, and Take-Away Fear Programs embedded at your Cellular Level. After releasing his own fear, he could stand for his own Truth, and he traveled long distances teaching and assisting people to heal.

He had aligned his Self with his own personal Christed Consciousness as a disciple of Jesus. As the Patron Saint of Desperate Causes, he is the one, according to the Metaphysical Bible Dictionary, who asks for assistance when all else fails. This aspect of Thaddeus is an aspect of you. At your more desperate moments, when all else fails, you always find the Truth within your Self.

As this happens, you are initiating the *letting go* of the fear-based, fear-ridden, conditioned thoughts, conditions, ideas, and hidden Belief Systems which are no longer relevant to your life.

Letting go of Belief Systems that no longer serve you is what serves YOU

You can *feel*, as you align your Female creativity and Male manifesting side in accordance with your Perfect Child Within, that you are the support, the supporting, and the supportive aspect founded upon the Consciousness of Self Unconditional Love and Acceptance. You are becoming Allness in the most Real and practical way.

The fear of not being supported is so irrelevant to your life! As you detach, you realize you do have the support. This is the dichotomy of the situation. When you thinky-thinky you don't have support...you don't. When you realize you are the only one who can support you, you send out this band of Consciousness and realize you are supported, first from your Self and then the other supporters show up. They love supporting you.

The ones who have the same non-support issues go along their fearful way. You are no longer a match energetically. They can't drain you. You can't drain them.

You are so over and done with being wanty-needy, which is the most dysfunctional idea of support. You stand for your Truth in alignment with your Self.

The dysfunctional patterns of being alone and lonely are no longer issues. They are the same 3D Duality pattern. You are not alone. You have the support of your Self and of the Non-Duality Universe and the Multi-verse. You are moving forward. Dragging the dysfunctional Self-Separation Program forward is a drag that you are not willing to drag forward. The energy of your Clear Consciousness is ascending and moving up your physical body.

THIRD CHAKRA

KNEES: What You Stand For

Your knees are your Third Chakra. Significantly, in the old 7 Chakra System, the knees represented being "cut off at the knees" and "being brought to your knees" in the resonance of servitude and enslavement. The control and manipulation of you is the focus of the 3D Duality Programs. You cannot resonate to the Consciousness of personal freedom. You cannot resonate to freedom at all.

You are literally "cut off at the knees" and "brought to your knees" as a follower. If you are on your knees in a subservient position, you cannot stand for your Truth. The physical positioning of your body is submissive. You have given up your Power. Your physical and emotional body is conditioned to be in this submissive pose whether you are physically standing up or not! The embedded fear-based Belief Systems override you standing in your Power.

All of you is being consumed to kneel to the outside programs to keep you in the servitude mode. If you can't stand for your Self, you are easily brought to your knees, held down and powerless with your Crown Chakra in this lowly position of servitude. This is the perfect state to control and manipulate you to stay in the Belief System of slavery and subjugation.

Your Crown Chakra, which is your connection to the Non-Duality Universe and the Multi-verse, is disconnected. **You cannot connect when you are afraid.** The repeated delusional ill-reality of Duality is subjugation. You have to conform to the programming. This is the way to fit into a "norm" that doesn't really fit you. Being enslaved is not normal. Being enslaved is abnormal.

Look at all the knee problems manifested physically because people are forced to "live" against their Truth: knee replacements, torn meniscus, arthritis, rheumatoid arthritis, bursitis, inflammation, tendonitis, blunt trauma, and the list goes on. All these physical manifestations, though they are different diagnoses, are all manifested in the knee because they are connected to an emotional issue of being cut off at the knees.

Each individual, according to his or her lifestyle, personal or professional, manifests the "cutting off at the knees" issues in whatever way the physical and emotional knee issue is created. All physical problems, regardless of the diagnosis and regardless of how these problems are created by the individuals in their bodies, relate to an emotional event in their lives. This is the same for you.

Everyone creates a different diagnosis according to their DNA, biology, and their conditioning to these taught Belief Systems from as early as the womb and certainly from early childhood. When you get to the core – to the root of the issue – the emotional connection is right there at the Cellular Memory level where the event occurred in the past.

From the womb to your current age and stage of life, everything is recorded. When you are not conscious of how all of this works, you can't be fully In Charge of Your Life and have your life work for you!

The knees are so significant because of the subservient *bending pose* to be less-than, submissive, and passive. In this submissive pose, a manipulating leader can bring you to your knees and manipulate you and groups of individuals to follow their destructive lead. In this subservient position, giving away your Power through pledged oaths to a cause which is not in alignment with your Spirit or your Heart is much easier to do. This pose is the perfect position to keep you in line to be a follower.

Again, whether you are standing up or kneeling down, when you give away your Power to someone else's Belief System, your body of Clear Consciousness is diminished. You are cut down to follow. The emotional component, encased in a strong wanty-needy to belong to a group, is the perfect avenue to manipulate you or anyone.

At the core of this wanty-needy, cut-off-at-the-knees Belief System is the dysfunctional fear of not being validated. As long as the validation issue is the Belief System that your validation comes from outside of you, bringing you to your knees is much easier.

**You will be easily manipulated if you *think* going along
with destructive group behavioral patterns
gives you the *validation*
your Childish Adult Ego is *craving***

Through the destructive behavior of gossip, prejudice, cults, gangs, or any organization fulfilling the dense resonance of wanty-needy outside validation, the perfect breeding ground for this lowest resonance is created. Those who join in are the perfect candidates for this type of vicious group unconsciousness. The individuals who become members have no value or worth of their own Selves.

Be wise about what groups you join and what they stand for. Otherwise, you will be brought to your knees.

Being brought to your knees by these types of Belief Systems, you sense that you are less. Though these types of groups tell you how great you are, the message is "you are only great as long as you follow their manipulated destructive ways."

At this juncture in the body, being pushed down on your knees and giving away your Power is what happens to you emotionally, mentally, physically, spiritually, and financially. You now belong to *them*! You don't belong to your Self.

You have to ask your Self, "Is this worth my life? Is this worth one molecule, one particle, or one cell of my life and my creative abilities to give my Self away?" This is the proverbial question. This is the question to ask your Self over and over again.

If you have doubts about what you are thinking of jumping into, step back! Follow the lead of your Heart, your *intuitive intelligence*, or your *gut feeling*. Trust your Self. Follow your own Truth and Heart and you will not be brought to your knees in any way, shape, or form. Discern, discern, discern, and discern some more, especially when something or someone does not *feel* correct.

At your knees, there is also the key consideration of the alignment of your Male and Female with your Perfect Child Within. Each side your body has different, sometimes opposing, embedded Belief Systems. This is Duality. It's one side or the other! In your journey of becoming a Clear Conscious Creator, you have to *feel* and *see* what is going on within each side of your body.

Are your Male and Female in alignment with each other? If they are not, then your Perfect Child Within is not in alignment with these two aspects of your Self and your Childish Adult Ego has to stay in the survival mode because of these two opposing forces. **You cannot be in your Power if your Male and Female are in conflict.** Your

Perfect Child Within is forced to stay buried, which is always at your loss when you are always in the Duality survival mode.

Your Female left side is your creativity. Your Male right side is your manifesting side. Whatever issues you have with your knees, whether left or right side, you have embedded in the particular knee the emotional issues causing the physical dysfunctions or problems with your knees.

If you feel disempowered about how you create your life according to your Heart and intuition, then you are brought to your knee on your Female side. If you feel disempowered about how you manifest your life, then you are brought to your knee on the Male side. Physical knee problems are the physical manifestations of your deep-seated emotional issues.

These issues are ingrained with the Judgment, Lack, and Take-Away Programming. **When you think you lack something or some ability, you are literally brought to your knees.** You are judging your Self through the 3D Duality Programs. You then continue to Take-Away from your Self your ability to be a Conscious Creator In Charge of Your Life. This is how you are brought to your knees. Again, whether you are in the bended knee position or not, your body expresses this subservient position as your Belief Systems.

Standing for your Truth does not mean you have to be in opposition to someone else's Belief System or even their Truth. What it means is you are not wanty-needying their validation. You don't have to agree with someone or some group. You don't have to give away your Power when you don't agree with something that doesn't resonate with your Truth. You can stand for your Truth without losing your

Self. This is the inner strength of your own Clear Conscious Strength.

If you are not on someone's or some group's wavelength, then you are not.

You do not have to go to war within your Self or war with them.

Why waste your valuable, creative time investing your Self, your Body, and your life in something NOT worth your time?

Validate Your Self!

Simon is the disciple of the Third Chakra. He is viewed as the typical human with Earthly emotional highs and lows. His ordinary life can be seen as a process, just as in your own life. Part of your journey is to ascend your Consciousness and ground it into your body.

Ascension is NOT death. Otherwise, why do you have to repeat the Karma, Lessons, and Re-incarnation Programs over and over again? Where's the Ascension in the highs and the lows?

Simon represented overcoming fear and bringing his idea into substance. This is what you are here to do. Live your life clearly, and consciously ground your expanded Consciousness throughout your body. This is Ascension.

Here's the Deal!
    Create your life with purpose
    Create your life on purpose
    Create your life for the purpose of:
        Creating
        Implementing
        Manifesting and
        Actualizing your life
        Enjoying the fruits of your life:

Relationships
Family
Friends
Business

Getting clear is the objective. Living in the 3D Duality Programs does not work for you or anyone. When it does "work", you are always waiting for the "shoe to drop", "the ax to fall", or "everything is going so well, it can't last". You get the point.

Capricorn, the Tenth House, represents the authorship of your idea. 10 represents the idea or the number One. One numerically means new beginnings. Your new beginnings begin when you begin to Take Back Your Power from the B.S. Programs.

You become the author of your life. You begin to validate your Self. Yes, it is wonderful when people validate you. YOU MUST VALIDATE YOUR SELF FIRST! You initiate new beginnings in your life each and every day. You must allow your Self and give your Self permission to be the Conscious Creator of your life.

You determine which idea or ideas you choose to focus on by the mere act of making a Clear Conscious Choice. You can also choose to change your choices. You don't have to get stuck in a decision based on other people's opinions of what you should or should not do…and cut your Self off at your knees.

Stand up! Stand up for your Self with kindness and compassion. Your knees become flexible as you become flexible. Your Consciousness and your energy are on the rise.

The number 3 is your Trinity, your Male Manifesting right side, your Female Creative left side, and your Perfect Child Within standing up for your Self. "Trinity", as translated by the Greeks, means superlatively great; in Latin, as happiest; and in Christianity, as the most holy, perfect, and the best. This is the trinity within you, the happiest, superlative Godness of you. Why would you allow your Self to be cut off at your knees and prostrate your Self to someone's limited Belief System?

FOURTH CHAKRA

HIPS and UPPER LEGS:
Passion and Commitment

The disciple Thomas is known as the Doubting Thomas. This is a man who was not willing to believe unless he could *see* it physically. His ultimate test came when Jesus died and was resurrected into an expanded state of Consciousness. When he understood and comprehended that Jesus' death represented the death of the old, fear-based 3D Duality paradigm in the physical body and that his resurrection represented the birth and Conscious Evolution of the Christed Consciousness into the human physical body on this Earth plane, he stopped doubting.

As the representative of the Fourth Chakra, Thomas symbolizes the transition from the constricted to the more expansive Consciousness. This is the Conscious Ascension Progressive Process.

You initiate this progressive process your Self. No one can do it for you. *You* make the connection within your human physical body.

This progressive process is physical. As you evolve consciously, so does your body. You must trust your Self. You must stop doubting your Self. You must stop looking for answers outside of you.

Only when Thomas could *feel* and connect to his Self did he stop doubting his Self and his own ability to be the Clear Consciousness within.

You begin to recognize and accept that the alignment of your physical body of Consciousness, emotionally, mentally, physically, spiritually, and financially, starts with your commitment to your Self. Until then, nothing happens. You continue to doubt your Self.

You must allow your Self to both understand and comprehend that you must trust your own innate, natural abilities of your intuition and be guided by your Heart. Your Heart is where your body houses compassion. You can only *feel* compassion when you are clear of the 3D Duality Programs. Your Heart is the most expansive resonance field in your body. If your body is resonating to fear, which is about Judgment, Lack, and Take-Away, there is no room for it to hold the resonance of compassion.

Compassion is natural to your expanded Consciousness. Compassion is the empathic connection to all life on this planet. Compassion starts with you as soon as you become compassionate to your Self. What emanates from you is what you draw back to you. Compassion is caring, kindness, and consideration. To have it for your Self is to have it for others. Otherwise, you are in opposition to your Self and others.

Your hips and upper legs are the regions of your body embodying the alignment of your Male and Female beginning to take a stand for your Truth. You have the full connection of your feet, both Male and Female together, grounded to the Earth. You have the full support of your Self in your ankles, both Male and Female together in total support of you. You are no longer cut off at the knees. Your Clear Consciousness is aligning and ascending through your body simultaneously.

Your upper legs become strong in this alignment of your Clear Consciousness. Your energy is in an upward movement. Your Male and Female sides are powerfully joining together. You are beginning to stand for your Self and your Truth. Doubt begins to dissipate.

What is the point of doubting your Self? When you doubt your Self, you still have a Belief System that the answers are outside of your Self.

As you are aligning, you are also initiating the balance of this progressive process of creating your life clearly and consciously, and implementing, manifesting, and actualizing all of this through your Self. You are not afraid to step out into the world. As you become clearly conscious and your body aligns, your health and wealth improve. Your entire body is becoming aware of how it all works together. Your body's physical systems, your Chakra Systems, your cells, molecules, and particles, and your Consciousness – all aspects of you – are coming into agreement.

Your physical, emotional, spiritual, mental, and financial alignment, located in your upper legs and hips, is the divine union. Your passionate, creative Female side and your Male action side are now standing up for you, your life, and your creative process on-going.

At this juncture, you cannot be forced out of balance unless you start doubting your Self. Your Male and Female are no longer in opposition to each other. The Male and Female aspects of you cannot be separated again through the 3D Duality Fear Programs. Yes, you can be challenged. You do not have to get involved in the challenges or the trauma-dramas. You have CHOICE!

Your Male and Female are inter-linked and inter-connected as you ascend and integrate your many "levels" or spaces of your Clear Consciousness. Making a passionate commitment to your Self continues your progressive process of consciously evolving. You can *feel* and *see* this progressive process as Transcension, moving up the ladder to Clear Consciousness. You are gaining clarity about your Self, your life, and your purposes.

Please, always be in your expanded mind. The resonance of the 3D Duality world is an extremely dense resonance of fear. This challenge is overwhelming. Always be vigilant how this low-based resonance infects your body. The 3D Duality energy field is heavy, viscous, gelatinous, and gooey. It makes you sick.

If you are not at your optimal health, fully aware of your Self and your body, you are easy to manipulate again and again to give up your Power. You are targeted to continue being infused with Belief Systems which say "your answers are outside of you, don't Believe in Your Self."

You really can't align your Self in 3D Duality. When you do, it is always just temporary. This field of energy cannot support you to be in your own Power.

When you are aligned, with the activity of your energy directed from a clear conscious perspective instead of non-factual perceptions, you begin to *feel* so differently about your Self. No more Doubting Thomases for you. Even if others outside of you – your family, friends, associates, co-workers, whoever – speak the language of doubt, are you willing to give up your Power to them <u>or</u> are you now willing to trust your Self, your Heart, and your intuition?

**Why take the fear-based advice of others
who are not living *your* life?**

This is absurd.

**Now you can see the absurdity of it
when you listened in the past to others
and you missed opportunities.**

You listened to their fears and took them in as your own.

Don't own *their* fears and let go of yours!

Sagittarius, the archer, the Ninth House, corresponding to the Fourth Chakra, projects the ideas of your creativity through the unification of your Clear Consciousness and your aligned energy. Through this alignment, there is no doubt or even risk that your idea or ideas are not worthy of validation. In faith and trust, you are on track. The old patterns are dying away. You are resurrecting your Self out of 3D Duality.

You are becoming the Non-Emotional Observer (NEO). No point in getting caught up again and again in limitations or even getting caught up in someone else's limitations and allowing them to project onto you. You send out your "arrows" with clear messages, particularly the ones that say "I am in Charge of my Life and my creative abilities. I am standing for my Truth with my Male and Female in alignment."

In this Fourth Chakra, you are now choosing to honor your life and your ideas. You get it. You are the Power. You are not buying into the old paradigm that someone else's force is going to force you into something that is not your Truth. You are resurrecting your Self out of the muck of 3D Duality. You are standing up for your Self.

Sagittarius represents the number 9. Numerically, this is the idea of God-Reality in Duality. By completing the old energy of 3D Duality Belief Systems, you "birth" the God-Realness within you. By growing up your Childish Adult Ego and letting go of the survival program, you immediately expand your resonance. No one can make an outside god *real* to you. You are recognizing the Godness within you that connects you to the Clear Godness Consciousness you always have been and always will be.

Your Childish Adult Ego (CAE) has always supported you to survive your scripts from lifetime to lifetime and has always died. So, as you get conscious, the CAE will get upset. It is used to dying, but this time, in getting conscious, "she" or "he" has to grow up in your adult body. It can't die this time and start over and over again. This is why the emotional upset is happening.

Know that you are being and doing your expansion and acceleration of Consciousness perfectly. So, when your Childish Adult Ego gets upset, your body that requires being conscious has to say, "Oh, here we go again. Wake up Childish Adult Ego! I am not going back 'there' or 'anywhere' except here in the moment. So, grow up and stop upsetting us!"

In numerology, number 4 means the basis of all solid objects – the four points construct a solid. Number four also means it is representative of planet Earth and its four elements of Earth, Air, Fire, and Water. You are standing solid on the ground, solid in Believing in Your Self.

FIFTH CHAKRA

REPRODUCTIVE ORGANS: Creativity

The Generative Creative Sexual Chakra is the resource and source of your creativity. The important key in your creative process is to comprehend that what you create and manifest in your life "outside" of your body is generated from your Fifth Chakra.

This Creative Chakra is impacted by your Belief Systems or your Believing in Your Self. *Belief systeming* and Believing in Your Self are *not* the same resonance whatsoever.

When you are fearful in your First Chakra of the old 7 Chakra System, your Second Chakra has no other choice but to create fearful and fear-filled experiences. When you don't have the experience to experience the experience, and you are not consciously aware of how you are creating and manifesting your life, fear embodies the re-cycles of the ups and downs, the dysfunctional trauma-dramas in which you get involved.

Involvement *without* being Clear Consciousness is NOT evolvement.

You cannot expect others to understand you or what you are creating in your life if you don't!

As your new Thirteen Chakra System unfolds, your creativity becomes empowered. You are no longer affected by the concept of Cause and Effect. You are the Effect that is creating your Cause…Be-Cause you are *being* for your *causes* for your life. You are now being Power full and Power filled.

Power is not force. Force is not Power. Force is controlling and manipulating. Power is being In Charge of Your Life. There is a huge difference.

Matthew is the disciple who represents the faculty of your creativity being uplifted through your divine will and divine mind. Your creativity is the gift that can keep on giving to you and to others with whom you are involved. Or, your creativity can be the burden which burdens you with the responsibility of those who are NOT your responsibility.

This refers to responsibility for other adults. When you take on the responsibility for other adults, you are taking away their Power and their creativity. This does not include "asked for" advice. This does include being a busy-body and telling others what they should, could, or would do if it was up to you. This works both ways.

This is the old paradigm of Creative Chakras working against your Self and each other. It is not just butting heads. It is the war of the 3D Duality Creative Chakras dueling it out from the old paradigm First Chakras of control and manipulation.

In the new paradigm of the Thirteen Chakra System, your Creative Chakra is empowering. You know your creativity is your gift in conjunction with your clarity of Consciousness to create through your Female and manifest through your Male all you require, desire, and absolutely deserve to create for your Self.

Being grateful to your Self in everything you create in your life means you are creating clearly without fear and you are devoid of the not-deserving programming of servitude and being less-than. You are expanding beyond the 3D Duality Programs of Judgment, Lack, and Take-Away.

Why would you even consider taking away from your Self an idea or ideas which can bring prosperity, abundance, and affluence to your life? It is no longer reasonable, if it ever was reasonable, to be involved in the limitations and restrictions of those old Belief Systems. You are Believing in Your Self and in your on-going Clear Creative Progressive Process.

Detachment from the emotional restrictions of Lack is a huge step. You are connected to an unlimited Power in your Creative Chakra.

Look at it this way...look at all the events, situations, relationships, traumas, dramas, and wonderful moments...everything in your life that you created. When you expend your energy based upon 3D Duality Belief Systems, you are not living your life to the fullest potential of your Consciousness. Your energy is diminished. You are diminished. Why diminish your Self any longer?

The only requirements and desires are to be absolutely clear about who, what, and where you engage your energy and the focus of your creativity. If something does not serve you, move on!

Stop trying and trying and trying to make the unworkable work!

Standing in the energetic center of your divine will and your divine mind is standing in the core of your Creative Power. You are Power full and Power filled.

Matthew is a tax collector, or someone to be feared. He is in a position of force over others. He is representative of control and manipulation. As the representative of the new Fifth Chakra, Matthew signifies the strength and courage to surrender old ideas and conditions of the 3D Duality Belief

Systems. When you surrender your fear, you are freeing your Self from the taxation on your body of existing in Judgment, Lack, and Take-Away. Stop taxing your Self. Stop punishing your Self.

Surrender is not failure. Surrender is acknowledging that the past no longer serves you and is no longer relevant to your life.

Move on. Don't learn from the lessons. Learn from the experiences and don't repeat the dysfunctional ones. Recognize which Belief Systems create the dysfunctional experiences. Use that information to set your Self free so you can create your life consciously with purpose on purpose and for the purposes for which you came here. Utilizing the gifts of your Clear Creative Sexual Generative Chakra, you choose to generate your creativity clearly through your energy field with intentional focus.

You write the clear scripts, you create the clear contracts or agreements, and you comprehend that YOU are the Clear Conscious Creator of Your Life. There is no needy-wanty to recreate from the old paradigm of 3D Duality unless you like embracing being less.

You are the Conscious Creator
You are the Creativity
You are all the Creations
You are the Implementer
You are the Manifestor
You are the Actualizer

Remember, what you manifest in your life is where you are, consciously or unconsciously. What you manifest into your life is clearly defined by the relationship you have with your Self. At whatever "level", space, or place you are aware about your Self is the "level", space, or place at which you are engaged.

Engage with your Self or not! This new Creative Chakra is the space and place of your divine marriage within your Self. This is the marriage in your sacrum based upon sacredness. Not sacrifice, as the 3D Duality world of marriage is proposed, which is not a proposal supportive of two people let alone the two aspects of your Female and Male inside of you, but it is the proposal of the Self-engagement of war.

Your Female is your Creativity. Your Male is the Manifestor. Working together, loving and accepting your Self unconditionally is the energetic field in which you desire to support your Self creatively. So then, your new Creative Chakra is engaged with your Heart, which is the most expansive resonance field in your human body.

In, through, and with the resonance of your Heart's unlimited capacity of Unconditional Love and Total Acceptance, you create a loving life for your Self. Self love starts with you unconditionally loving and accepting your Self. To create loving relationships outside of you, you must start by loving and accepting your Self inside of you.

Through the Power of Unconditional Love and Total Acceptance, your creativity is infused with Power full and Power filled connections to your outside world. Your prosperity, abundance, and affluence are the direct results of your influence.

When your influence comes from the foundation of Unconditional Self-Love and Total Self-Acceptance in your First and Eighth Chakras, your Creative Sexual Generative Chakra is operating optimally. The relationships in which you engage become stronger and deeper. Your *real* possessions are multiplied. Abundance and prosperity abound for you, not just in terms of money.

Money is the energetic manifestation of your creativity. So is your health, your relationships, your business, your career, and your entire outside life. From the inside out, your outside is created. Self-love is Self-worth. Accept your worthiness. You are worthy. You are valuable. You have value.

Remember when you did create the "good" in your life while still in the 3D Duality Belief Systems, and you could hardly believe it? This is the Set-Up for you to anticipate and wait for the proverbial ax to fall. In 3D Duality, the ax falls. The ax has to interrupt your creative abilities. You are not supposed to be able hold a clear creative process. That's the old paradigm.

As you release the fears ingrained in your old Creative Chakra, you begin to release them. The fears of the past have no relevance at your Cellular Level. There is no worth or value to store fear in your body anywhere.

The number 5 represents wisdom in numerology. Your divine wisdom guides your creativity in synchronicity with your divine mind. The creative process belongs to you. Through this Clear Creative Consciousness, the empowered expression of your energy rises up in your physical body. This Clear Creative Power is created by you.

This amazing Fifth Chakra of creativity is aligned with Scorpio, the Eighth House. The 8 symbolically represents your break through the Block Wall. This fear-based version of infinity impelled you to participate through the controlling and manipulating Belief Systems of 3D Duality throughout your time continuum.

Now, as you ascend your Consciousness, it is becoming clear that it is you who is in charge of your *ship* in relation-*ship* to your Clear Self, this Grid, and the infinity symbol of the re-cycled figure eight. This re-cycled *Marry*-Go-Round gets you NO-where in your continuum except in the same places of Karma, Lessons, and Re-incarnation. This Merry-Go-Round is the perfect dysfunctional ride for your Childish Adult Ego to continually re-live the same programs, regardless of your costumes.

This queasy feeling your Perfect Child Within is providing for you is your *gut feeling* or *intuitive intelligence* telling you to get off the Merry-Go-Round. You are off the re-cycle spin. Are you willing for the next steps to freedom from Duality?

SIXTH CHAKRA

SOLAR PLEXUS: The Child Within, Feeling Center, Balance and Understanding

Your Solar Plexus houses both your **Perfect Child Within** and your personal survivalist, your **Childish Adult Ego**. This Solar Plexus region of your body represents all the ages and stages of your childhoods, including the teenager years throughout your continuum of experiences. Now with the clarity of your expanded Consciousness, you can gain from your experiences without the re-traumatization or re-dramatization re-cycles of the experiences.

Your Childish Adult Ego (CAE) can grow up. Your CAE doesn't have to be your survivalist anymore. Your CAE does not have to exist through the 3D Duality Programs unless YOU get emotionally hooked and jump back into the dysfunctional past and the programs.

You determine whether you lead with the Power of Your Perfect Child Within *or* you force your Childish Adult Ego to run your show.

There is no Power in existing in survival. Empowerment is the gift you give your Self when you are In Charge of Your Life! Living consciously, clearly, and creatively... isn't this the objective of your life?

There is no objectivity in existing in the survival mode, continuing to be a victim and giving away your Power

Your experiences are now your gifts to your Self. You choose how you participate. Your powerful Perfect Child Within is in alignment with the Female and Male aspects of your Self. This is the perfect triangle.

Without judging your Self anymore, you come to understand and comprehend that all of these experiences, even when you were a child, were Self-created to learn about your Self. Now it is time to let go of the lessons and evaluate the experiences.

How can they best serve you now with this valuable information? How can you apply what you have learned? How can this information make a difference in your life now? One way is by not repeating the trauma-dramas. This is a perfect place to start.

Appreciate your Self so you can clearly know, understand, and comprehend how you have handled your experiences, even when you didn't have the experience to experience the experiences. Reflect over all your experiences. No one could have written your script or played through your script as cleverly or as interestingly as you did. Give your Self the credit you deserve.

When you were in the past in those emotional states of fear, you could not *see* the brilliance of your experiences or why you created them. The molecules of emotions prevented you from *seeing* the Truth of the situations. These molecules are physically thick, viscous, and snotty. This makes it difficult for you to *see* or hear anything but the 3D Duality Programming.

As the child who has to bear the brunt of the trauma, the lack of experience keeps you stuck at the age where the trauma happened. In the field of Clear Consciousness in a state of clear awareness, you can now truly appreciate your Self, *see* what *was* going on then, hear how the experiences affected you and your body, and *see* that you don't have to do any of the traumas again.

You are integrating your Self into a Unified Field of Allness with your Male, Female, and Perfect Child Within. The perfection of this Perfect Child Within is your child, no matter the gender, who does not have to be fear-filled anymore.

When you look back and *see* how responsive children are to life in those first years, you *see* that they are excited and they love touching, smelling, tasting, and holding life in their hands. They explore. The 3D Duality Programs of Fear override the children's natural abilities to love and to participate freely in life.

Now embrace your inquisitive, fearless Perfect Child Within. Engage your Explorer without fear. Go out and engage in life. This is why you are here. To engage in the joy of life.

From history's standpoint, children were property. There wasn't a Consciousness of childhood. Whatever place in life a child was born in was exactly where they were when they died. There were exceptions to this rule, of course, however, they were not the 3D Duality "normal". Basically, children were property and were put to work as soon as they were able to work in the fields or in the homes of the privileged or they had to fend for their Selves in any way they could. In many countries, it is still the same way. Exist for the elite. Try and try to be like "them". Wear what they wear and try to be like them.

> **When you "try" to live someone else's life**
> **by their ideas of life,**
> **by their way of projecting their Selves,**
> **or by their standards and rules,**
> **YOU are NOT living *your* life!**

Children are exploited all the time. Their childhoods are stolen away, as well as their lives and their futures. In some of these countries, from the womb, the children are embedded with the Lack Program of survival and forced to accept their life as the way it is. The Take-Away Program begins right from conception because their parents are embedded with the same 3D Duality Program. There is no vision or idea that life can be any different. This paradigm is a Belief System. You do NOT have to accept this B.S. as your own.

Again, remember…until Maria Montessori at the turn of the century in Italy began to work with the poor children and began to define "childhood", there was no concept of "childhood". The Belief System defined children as either property or privilege as a result of their birth. The concept or idea of "childhood" is very recent in the history of the world.

Also, the idea or concept of a "teenager" didn't develop until the late 1940's and the 1950's. By the time a child, male or female, reached age 12 or 13, they were considered young adults, put to work, married off, and were considered at the beginning of manhood and womanhood.

Frank Sinatra and Rock 'n Roll created "teenagers". To the Duality System, "teenagers" represented a new avenue of money. That's the Truth!

When you view paintings of the wealthy, royalty, and the privileged, the children were dressed as adults. Today in some of the Middle Eastern countries, the same as Europe in the past, children, both wealthy and poor, are married at ten, twelve, or fourteen. The marriages were and are still arranged. This is Taking Away the Power of the Female aspect of your Consciousness, which has nothing to do with gender. This is about Clear Consciousness being overridden by the confinement of these rigid and life-stealing Belief Systems.

The Taking of Power from the Female is a travesty because it Takes Away the Power of creativity, intuition, guidance, and inspiration from everyone, including the males. The males are taught to distrust their own creative, empowering Female Consciousness. The males are taught to think of the Female aspects of their Selves as less-than. This is why so much abuse of females is tolerated and accepted in this world. The men, through their actions, are harming their Selves. They are in denial of the most powerful aspect of their Selves. They are literally denying the full spectrum of their own lives. This is pathetic, harmful, and weak!

This Belief System of Self-Hatred of the Female aspect of Self manifests into abuse…sexual, physical, emotional, mental, spiritual, and financial abuse. This happens because of this Self-Hatred and Hatred of the Perfect Child Within. This is tolerated because the 3D Duality Programs do not honor the Perfect Child Within.

Your Perfect Child Within is *your* Power. It's your implementer. The Female aspect of your Perfect Child Within is the Power of your Creativity aligned within the Female side of your body of Consciousness in your Creative Generative Sexual Chakra.

The Male aspect of your Perfect Child Within is your Power to manifest in connection with your Female Creativity. Your Power Source, which is your Perfect Child Within in your Solar Plexus, is the guide for this strategic powerful alliance. Your Perfect Child Within leads the way fearlessly. And in alignment with your Male and Female aspects of your Creative Sexual Generative Chakra, you actualize through your Heart your creativity into life. In connection with your Heart, this alliance adds a fourth aspect of becoming the Godness within you through the actualization from your Heart through your hands.

This perfect alliance is fearless, powerful, and fully conscious. This is how you are meant to be. This is the progressive Ascension of your Clear Creative Progressive Process. Your energy is moving up.

You are not meant to be a survivalist victim going through life powerlessly. That is 3D Duality's Belief System…the B.S. prevention program preventing you from Believing in Your Self and in your abilities to create your life consciously on purpose and with purpose for the purposes of living your life to the fullest of health and prosperity.

Look at the physical problems occurring in your Solar Plexus: digestive issues, stomach, liver, gall bladder, spleen dysfunctions, mid-back problems upper-intestinal issues, rib, diaphragm tightness, kidney, adrenal stresses, and the list can go on with painful results. All these physical issues are the results of emotional issues with deep attachments to the past. The past is creating these problems.

The physical issues are the physical manifestations of the emotional problems from the past affecting your current time frame. The future is the repeat of the past. The present moment is affected, keeping you chained to the past, and you are following the emotional chain right into the repeated future.

Your Solar Plexus is both the Perfect Child Within you and the Childish Adult Ego. Your Solar Plexus represents all the aspects of the Children Within throughout your continuum. Whether you were conscious, cognitive, or not, every one of your childhood experiences is embedded in your Cellular Memory. These experiences can be your greatest gifts *or* your greatest physical and emotional pain.

If you continue to stay stuck in the past and give your Power Away to the dysfunctional experiences, then your teenager, adult, and senior ages and stages of your life continue to be plagued by these experiences. They affect your life and your relationships personally and professionally, which is one and the same.

Without judging your Self anymore, by choosing to be the Non-Emotional Observer (NEO), you begin to heal these experiences. You are witnessing the dysfunctional experiences, not by re-living them but by *seeing* everyone's Role in the situations, including yours. You begin to *see* how afraid the victimizers and perpetrators (the parents, siblings, relatives, teachers, strangers, etc.) were and still are. You begin to *see* that they were victims, too. What they may have done to you is simply carry out their Role with you. However, abuse of any type is NOT acceptable.

As the Non-Emotional Observer (NEO), you now give your Self the gift of physically, emotionally, mentally, and spiritually releasing the Cellular trauma from your body. You *feel* the releases. You experience the releases. You *feel* how much lighter your body becomes. Everything is physical, regardless of the dimension in which you have experienced the dysfunction and abuse.

You *feel* lighter. This is the explanation for the "light body". You have released physical, emotional molecules from your physical body and you physically *feel* lighter. Your body is lighter. Your body is no longer carrying the weight, density, or viscosity associated with the traumatic experience. You are setting your survivalist Childish Adult Ego (CAE) free to grow up.

You are healing the CAE within you throughout your continuum related to this particular physical and emotional issue. You begin to stop the madness of re-living, re-traumatizing, and re-incarnating with the same dysfunctional issues. So, you changed the settings, the times, the clothes, the stages, but in essence it is still the same old same old stuff.

Instead of past-life regressions, you are really connecting to your time continuum and non-emotionally accessing the information. You do not re-experience. You are the Non-Emotional Observer (NEO) using the information to uncover what in fact happened. Sticking to the facts, instead of conjecture, empowers you. Conjecture is emotional, has no facts, and is extremely dysfunctional.

**Healing the *Childish Adult Ego*
throughout your Time Continuum is becoming
Allness with All your Clear *Perfect Children Within* You
from all your lifetimes**

James, a half brother of Jesus, at first did not believe in Jesus or his teachings. He was influenced by the opinions of others. There is no doubt about it. Everyone has done the same by giving their personal Power and freedom away to someone, some doctrine, or some Belief System that does not resonate with personal Truth. Why? To get accepted outside of their Selves at the cost of sacrificing their own Truth. James, it is said, thought Jesus was out of his mind.

Are you any different than James if you give away your Power to a collective doctrine that doesn't agree with your Truth?

Are you any different if you give in to what is unacceptable to you?

Are you out of your Divine Mind?

Is your Head up your First Chakra of the old system of Belief Systems?

After Jesus' resurrection, James became a believer in his own Christed Consciousness that he *felt* within through his Heart. Is it not time to resurrect your own Truth and stop following the B.S. Programs that go against your own Truth?

James is the aspect of your faculty in your expanded Consciousness which represents your expanded awareness or your expanded ability to discern between the "true" of the old B.S. Programs and your own *real* Truth. The old paradigm of your Childish Adult Ego's survivalist behaviors is no longer relevant and only serves to hold you stuck in the dysfunctional past, the dysfunctional Belief Systems, and the dysfunctional behaviors.

Your Childish Adult Ego (CAE) begins to grow and to grow up simultaneously. Your CAE doesn't have to search for the outside validation. You already know this Truth:

"I am the only one who can validate me.

For those outside of me who validate me, I thank them. And for those who don't…. OH WELL!!!"

Through your own discernment of your expanded awareness, you are connected to your Self, the Non-Duality Universe, and the Multi-verse. You empower You. This is another giant step to Take Back Your Power.

You are aligning your Self emotionally, mentally, physically, spiritually, and financially. This is all about becoming a Conscious Creator from the standpoint of the Non-Emotional Observer (NEO). Your Perfect Child Within comes to life. Your Perfect Child Within, your Female, and your Male are connected in a powerful Trinity.

With your Perfect Child Within, you *see* life with new eyes. You definitely realize with *real eyes* that always and forever you have all the abilities to live your life to the fullest. Survival, poverty, victimization, less-than, etc. are all symptoms of the 3D Duality Programs. They are symptoms. They are not YOU!

There are no longer dysfunctional demands from the outside that you have to take in or take on. Guilt, shame, blame, shoulda's, woulda's, and coulda's are so NOT relevant to your life. These paradigms are too draining, too debilitating, and too exhausting to carry around in your body.

Abandonment and rejection are so not applicable anymore. They are energy-draining, illness-creating, life-consuming Belief Systems.

You cannot change the past; it was one second ago. You can change the future, and it is one second from now, by not dragging a dysfunctional past forward.

Dysfunctional means "it," whatever the "it" is, is not working. Why hang on to the "it" or the "its" that have no meaning to you as a Conscious Creator?

**Hanging on to physical and emotional pain
is dysfunction at the worst level of Belief Systems
of being controlled and manipulated
by a Past that is so over!**

As a Clear Conscious Creator with your Perfect Child Within, your past experiences become a resource within your Cellular Memory to draw upon your experiences and to discern how all your experiences, situations, and conditions occurred. There is no reason to blame your Self or to have any shame or guilt. You did the best you could with what you knew and didn't know. Through the 3D Duality Belief Systems, you could not know much. You are not allowed to know your Self. You are programmed to run the Programs of Judgment, Lack, and Take-Away.

Now is the time to STOP the programs. Now is the time to allow your Self to be your Truth. There is a discernment progressive process as you begin to allow your Self to know your Self. The Solar Plexus is a place of empowerment to retrieve your Self Power.

You begin to comprehend that every adult of you, whether male or female, participated in the best and worst of ways. They are the same. Stop measuring! Each of your adult experiences throughout your continuum were influenced and affected continuously by your survivalist Childish Adult Ego, programmed to survive and programmed to repeat the dysfunctions throughout each lifetime. You were conditioned and taught to not believe in your Self. You were expected to give away your Power.

*Giving Away Your Power
prevents you from Believing in Your Self*

The Consciousness of your Perfect Child Within <u>or</u> of your Childish Adult Ego is integral to your creativity and behavior in all your adult lifetimes. Intellectually, you may *think* your Child, through his or her ages and stages of childhood, does not influence or affect your life as you psychologically process your child's experiences and fears through the logic of your left computer/brain. However, you can intellectualize and logicalize all you wanty-needy, but you cannot heal your emotional and physical issues through your left computer/brain. You prevent your Perfect Child Within, your Childish Adult Ego, and your Adult Self from ever connecting within you. **Your left computer/brain just runs the programs.**

Your Real intellect and intelligence are in your body. Your Cellular Memory, Cellular Memorization, and your Cellular Sound give you the answers to your experiences. Your answers provide the information. When you are clearly conscious, you discern what to keep and what to release.

Not every experience, situation or condition was "bad". You have an unending supply of experiences you can draw upon and use as a base of information that does, in fact, serve you.

"Information" is in-form-at-ion, which means you have the information or the resources at your ion or Cellular Level of Consciousness that you can use. Keep what serves you and dump the rest. Stop taking up space in your physical body with ineffective and dysfunctional information which is no longer applicable to a clear, creative, and prosperous life.

Exist in the 3D Duality Programs
or
Create your life Consciously!

Your left computer/brain is a complex computer controlled by your Childish Adult Ego (CAE). You are programmed to survive and *not* to live life to the fullest. Your CAE knows the programs. Your Perfect Child Within waits patiently for you to grow up and get clear.

When you step up to the plate and stop craving and eating the food of Consciousness that makes you sick, then your Childish Adult can stop running the food of Consciousness programs that make you sick and fear-filled, and you can stop manifesting ineffective behavioral patterns. Stop validating the invalidation of your Self. Stop the B.S.!

Stop and consider...
if you are experiencing your loss of Power,
then stop giving away your Power
and you won't have these losses of Power experiences
throughout your life!

Through your Cellular Memory, you can unlock your history without re-experiencing the trauma-dramas. Your history is the source of your participation.

Keep the fear <u>or</u> focus on being clear. You have *choices* to make. Stop making your Childish Adult make *decisions* that Take Away Your Power.

As the Clear Conscious Adult, you move beyond the illusional criteria upon which your actions, behaviors, and participations were unconsciously based. You no longer separate your Adult Self from your Perfect Child Within. In your expanded Consciousness, you recognize and accept that your Childish Adult Ego has been your best teacher throughout your continuous continuum. Now your Adult is the student discovering and learning from your Clear Perfect Child Within how to be fearless. You are integrating the most powerful resource you have, your wondrous Clear Perfect Child Within.

You comprehend what is correct for you to live the life you require, desire, and deserve. You realize that **every event in your life is Self-created**. How powerful is this! You choose what honors you or not. You choose. If you are not satisfied with what you choose, then choose something else. You do not have to be stuck. You came here for the experiences.

Your fearless Perfect Child Within is an active participant in the creative process of your Female and the manifesting process of your Male. Through this partnership of participation, you create a balance in your life. You no longer have to hold the restricted energy field of a wounded child inside of you who is accompanied by illness. Your Childish Adult is healed and grows up. Your Perfect Child Within is empowered and, in turn, fearlessly empowers you.

Libra is the Seventh House representing the Scales of Balance. The significance of this aspect is the balance of your Perfect Child Within and your Female and your Male in a harmonious relationship. There is no requirement to go back through the old 7 Chakra System of 3D Duality and re-traumatize your Self. The re-cycle bin is obsolete.

You now comprehend that your Body of Clear Consciousness is your intelligence which supports you to move forward without dragging the dysfunctional past with you. You are the intelligence. You are your intelligent Truth. You can no longer be manipulated by the 3D Duality Programming. You determine how you participate in life. You are *feeling*, not thinky-thinking or rehashing the fear-filled programs. Your Perfect Child Within is your Christed Consciousness, your connection to your Godness Self.

In numerology, 6 represents balance. The Female and the Male, the yin and the yang, are balanced within a circle. The circle embodies the embryo, the connection between your Female, your Male, and your Perfect Child Within.

Your energy moves up your physical body and your Body of Clear Consciousness. You are physically ascending, rising above the emotional 3D Duality Body of Fear-filled Duality Programming. Your Perfect Child Within is your champion.

SEVENTH CHAKRA

DIAPHRAGM: Information Assimilation (Food of Consciousness)

The diaphragm is the site within you which inspired your body with your Prana or expanded breath of Consciousness. This more expanded breath supports you, your lungs, and your respiratory system to breathe Prana throughout your body. You literally are breathing life into *your* creativity, implementing *your* creations, and giving breath to *your* manifestations. You give the breath of life, breathing life into *your* life. This divine breath of yours energizes your imagination and creativity.

This breath has an expanded resonance. There is no fear for you to breathe into life. You don't have to hold your breath or breathe shallowly anymore, waiting for something to happen. You are in charge of what happens. You have the full range of breathing throughout your body, bringing life-filling breath to your cells, molecules, and particles to the sub-atomic level of you. You are giving the breath of life to your Self.

The disciple Nathanael/Bartholomew signifies your divine imagination inspired with the breath of your expanded

Consciousness. Jesus called him "an Israelite indeed, in whom is no guile". In this descriptive, Jesus depicts Nathanael/Bartholomew as being trustworthy.

When trust is an issue you have, not only can you NOT trust your Self, you cannot trust others. This trust issue is deeply ingrained in the cells of your body consciously and unconsciously. This trust issue affects you emotionally, mentally, physically, spiritually, and financially.

If you can't trust, you have no foundation upon which you can breathe into life. You hold your breath. You breathe shallowly and your body is affected by the physical lack of oxygen. You can't trust and you cannot breathe into your own life. You suffer the consequences that life is untrustworthy and you have no worth or value. Unworthiness and being valueless takes your breath away.

How can you inspire your Self in this state? There is little to no Self-inspiration. There is no Self-motivation if you do not have the breath to inspire your creativity. No breath, no life! Your life is being sucked out of you. You are giving your Power away.

The lack-of-trust-in-your-Self issue triggers the Take-Away Program. You Take-Away from your Self your imagination and your creative abilities because you are holding on to a Belief System that says "you cannot trust your Self". You make your Self sick.

Resulting *physical* issues caused from the Lack of Self-Trust *emotional* issues are breathing problems such as pneumonia, pulmonary problems, lack of proper oxygen levels in your body, weakness, shortness of breath, etc. Your lungs don't function properly. You are not breathing into life to your fullest capacity. You are fear-based.

You *think* your life is being sucked out of you by someone or some issue. You are allowing your Self to be victimized. When you cannot find the victimizer, you victimize your Self. The Lack Program is running at full capacity and Taking Away your inspired creativity as the result. No breath, no life!

As you connect deeply inside of your Self and accept that the one and only person you must trust is your Self, your breathing from and through your diaphragm infuses your divine breath into each cell of your body. Your cells are inspired to release their knowledge of you from your deepest levels of Clear Consciousness.

In these clear levels of information are your history and experiences beyond your 3D Duality Programs of Judgment, Lack, and Take-Away. These levels or spaces of Clear Consciousness in your time continuum can inspire you to know and acknowledge that you have, indeed, experienced and participated in these multiple dimensions of your Self and in these realms of Consciousness where you are the Master. **You are a Master, you just forgot your Mastery.** You gave your Self up to the 3D Duality Programming.

In the creative process, whether it is through Clear Consciousness or through the 3D Duality Programs, you breathe your manifestations into life. In order for your manifestations to become your physical reality in 3D Duality, you first imagine it, write it and/or speak it. Then the physical process begins. The question is…are you clearly conscious in your creative process <u>or</u> are you stuck in the limitations of creation in the 3D Duality dysfunctional re-cycle process?

The level or space of Consciousness in which you participate is the level or space in which you manifest your life. **Consciousness is the key to everything.** Clear Consciousness is the key to the clarity of everything. Clear Consciousness is the key to clear creativity, clear implementation, and clear manifestation. Breathing clear, conscious breath into this progressive process is the clarity of being a Clear Conscious Creator. When you breathe clearly and consciously into your life, you have clarity. There is no ambiguity. You are no longer holding your breath, waiting to exhale. You breathe into life instead of Duality taking your breath away.

As you breathe the resonance of your divine breath into *your* life, you shift the movement of your energy field of your Consciousness from within you to your outwardly manifested life. The level of your Consciousness determines how your energy field is utilized. If you are clear, you create clarity in your life. If you are fearful, you create fear in your life.

As you clearly expand your Consciousness from fear-based limitations to openness, your breath of Consciousness simultaneously expands. You are more open and more flexible. You are willing to step into life. The breath of your Clear Consciousness is an expanded band of energy flowing outward. You *feel* it.

For those who are more of an energetic and conscious match to your resonance, they can *feel* it also. As this expanded field of Consciousness flows from you through your aura or electromagnetic field, your inspired breath is *felt* by others who match *your* resonance.

As a Master who is now remembering your Mastery, the essence of your empowerment breathes the example of Mastery to others. The words you speak, the thoughts you have, and the concepts inspired by your imagination become Real. What you are doing is manifesting your creativity by breathing these into life to actualize into your outside world.

> **Outside in**
> > **the Changes bring…**
> > > **Duality**
> > **Changes Real**
> > > **from the Inside out**
> > > **bring Life**

In the breath or field of Consciousness of a Master, there is no place for a resonance of 3D Duality and all the emotional garbage that goes along with opposition. Fear is neither a concept nor Real. There is no requirement to speak a sound or word through your breath which resonates fear regardless of the language.

The field of your expanded Consciousness is not in any realm, dimension, or place outside of you. This divine breath is in a deep level of your conscious being. Infusing your expanded Consciousness into your creativity generates your creations into the physicality of your world.

You are being the Conscious Creator, the Creativity, and the Creation.

How and what you breathe into your life can inspire your continued creativity and your manifestations. Or, if you continue to participate in the 3D Duality Programs, you will at some point or another allow your Power to be taken away and have your energy drained out of you by some outside source.

The illnesses related to breathing issues are not just physical. There are emotional issues attached to a past Cellular Experience stored in your unconsciousness which manifest in your body as though your breath and life is being sucked out of you. You are not breathing into life to your fullest capacity. These illnesses are your body's physical manifestations created from the fears of not being able to fully breathe physically, emotionally, mentally, spiritually, and financially.

Breathing from your expanded Consciousness brings you to an expanded energy field from the Mastery Consciousness within you. A Master is not affected by the outside or by the illusion of fear. A Master is not concerned with being a cause or an effect. A Master is.

Virgo is the Sixth House, which represents the purity of your imagination that is breathed into life through your expanded Consciousness. In simple terms, the purity is Virginal. This simply means…without the contaminating breath of fear.

7 numerically represents completeness. When you breathe empowerment clearly into your manifested creation, you create, implement, and then manifest a specific creation and then begin again. This is the creative, progressive, continuing process. Your creative abilities are unlimited!

Clearly breathe into your life and your energy ascends and your life is clear. Breathe from your diaphragm, fill your lungs, and exhale your empowering breath into your life.

EIGHTH CHAKRA

HEART: Feeling Center

The disciple John symbolizes the Heart Chakra. He was the only Apostle present at the Crucifixion. Jesus entrusted the love and protection of His beloved mother to John. He is also known as the one Jesus loved.

Baptism symbolizes the releasing, the letting go, of the old Belief Systems of not being connected to your Christed Consciousness or to the Godness Self within your physical Self.

The baptism process symbolism is the cleansing of the past and the preparation for newness in your life.

Through the Heart Chakra, the Belief Systems of the Fear Programs of Judgment, Lack, and Take-Away are purged from within you. The purpose of this purging is to open your Heart to Unconditional Love and Total Self-Acceptance and to connect to the Allness of you and your entire body.

Always remember, the Heart Chakra is the most expansive resonance in your body. As you embrace the resonance of **Total and Complete Acceptance of your Self**, the Shift in the resonance within you is even far more impacting and transformational than Unconditional Love.

When your Heart is full of fear, then your Heart's most expansive field is encased in a very low resonance. And the resonance of Unconditional Love and Total Acceptance cannot live. It's out of the question. The wanty-needy "love" resonance is what gets emitted and hooked into your dysfunctional relationships, whether considered romantic, family, or friendship.

John is representative of your personal faculty of your inner core Truth that resides in the resonance of Unconditional Love and Total Acceptance. Underneath 3D Duality's disappointments, frustrations, anger, sadness, and sorrow of the Fear Programs is this natural resonance of Unconditional Love and Total Self-Acceptance.

This is the root of everyone's search to find a match. This is the origin of everyone's pursuit to find the perfect *soul mate,* to find the "one" who will fulfill your Heart. The perfect one, in all your searches, is finding your Self in your own Heart. You are the first soul mate for your Self. You have to connect to your own Heart first.

When you search and expect your Heart connections outside of you to be connected through the resonance of Duality, all the issues of disappointment, sadness, emptiness, and despair will manifest in your search. In Duality, love connections are supposed to have trauma-dramas. This is expected.

The concept of John as the faculty of Unconditional Love and Total Acceptance is the embodiment of your Spiritual Truth guided by the divine intellect and intelligence of this expanded resonance of your Heart. This is the physical embodiment of you in the purest form of your body's physicality. Your Heart is where it is at!!!

As you align your Heart with your Solar Plexus, the representative of your Perfect Child Within, this area of your body is your personal Feeling Center. When you connect to your *feelings*, you are connected from your Heart and your Solar Plexus with your Self.

When something does not *feel* correct in your Heart or in the pit of your stomach, your *gut feeling*, then don't do it. Until you have more information, more facts, more data, do not go against what you *feel*. Remember always…fear is lack of information. You must get all the facts, all the information.

When you go against your Heart and *gut feeling*, when you go against your Feeling Center, you know intuitively you are making an emotional decision. You are NOT making a Clear Conscious Choice.

Emotional decisions lack empowerment. They have no clarity or substance. Emotional decisions are just that...emotional. Emotional decisions are connected to some past issue in some experience where you gave your Power away. Emotional decisions do NOT support you. Emotional decisions support the wanty-needys of others at your expense.

When you express your Self through your *feelings*, you are strong. You have conviction about your Truth no matter what is happening in the circumstances surrounding you. You don't have to buy into emotionally-charged events that Take Away Your Power.

You know intuitively and physically when you put your Heart into something. You feel good, you feel great.... you *feel!* When you put your emotions into something, you have that sense of uncertainty. **When you trust your Heart, when you trust your Solar Plexus, when you trust your Feeling Center, you are trusting your Self.**

The energy of your Feeling Center has an unlimited capacity to experience the essence of your creative abilities. As you create from your Heart, your Creative Chakra expands your abilities to create consciously. You energize your Self from your Feeling Center.

In 3D Duality terms, there are no descriptive adjectives that define this unlimited capacity for living your life through your Heart and standing in your Truth by creating and manifesting from that Truth. 3D Duality language is limited by perceptions, illusions, and attachments to the Fear Programs of Judgment, Lack, and Take-Away.

Where you put your energy, based upon the resonance of your Consciousness, is where you are. The restrictions and confinements of 3D Duality's limited capacity is the perfect field to continue to re-create the same patterns and behaviors in the same old same old ways. Newness cannot be created from 3D Duality. Different backdrops, different costumes, different weapons, but nonetheless, the conditions are the same.

The challenge is to consciously open your Heart. The 3D Duality density of the thick, viscous resonance of fear is the ultimate challenge for your Heart and your Solar Plexus, which is your Feeling Center. The fact is…it is a challenge for your human body in general. Compound this density with an entire collective Consciousness around the world ingrained with the Fear of Take-Away, and the intensity of the collective becomes heavier.

Is the challenge worth it? Yes! The changes must happen from the inside out. Regardless of the Belief System, everyone desires the same things…someone to love, to be loved, to have a productive, healthy life, supportive relationships, a job, a home, and a community to share in. This deserves to be the Realness, and not the dream.

Through your Heart is the only place to start. **What matters to the Heart is all that matters.** To create the physical embodiment, the physical matter or manifestation of the world you absolutely require, desire, and deserve can only start in your Heart! You must believe in your Self. You must believe you have the ability, even when the outside world says, "you don't have what it takes, you never get a break, you can't do it, and you don't deserve it." These are all just limited Belief Systems. Purge them from your Heart. They are too low of a resonance to sustain in your Heart.

The Clear Consciousness of your Heart in the Thirteen Chakra System is the Unlimited Consciousness of the Allness of You and of your connection to the Allness of the Non-Duality Universe and Multi-verse. This field of Allness

Consciousness does not delineate differences as opposition. This field of Consciousness *honors* the differences and the uniqueness of everyone and everything. It does NOT buy into the separation that 3D Duality perpetuates.

Your Heart Chakra of Unconditional Love, Total Acceptance, and Truth is not only the conduit for you to live and create from the vast realms of your Self, this is also the way for you to connect and link to the expansive realms of Consciousness in other dimensions without fear. Though these dimensions are different, they are not separate from you.

The dimensions have never been separate from you. There is no veil. The "veil" is the 3D Duality of Fear!

The resonance band of your Heart Chakra is both a transmitter and a receiver of Unconditional Love and Total Acceptance. You transmit the energy from within you. Remember, you also transmit the energy of fear if that is the resonance you are holding in your Heart and your body. Your bands of Consciousness are how you connect to the outside world. From your inside, your bands go out!

As the transmitter of Unconditional Love and Total Acceptance, you attract more Unconditional Love and Total Acceptance into your life. People around you *feel* the difference. They may not know how to describe what they are *feeling* from you, but they know there is a difference. Animals know it too. They know it before humans do.

As this open, clear, conscious transmitter, you connect easily with the other dimensions of your choice. You connect to expansive levels of Consciousness because you are that. As the transmitter connector, you become the conscious receiver. You connect to angels, guides, soul groups, and other beings outside of the Earth plane.

You don't have to worry or be concerned about connecting to lower, fear-based beings or energies. You do not match their low resonance. Any lower energies or beings would be afraid of you. Now how's that for being powerful without being controlling?!!

This also works for humans. You won't attract lower levels of fear-based humans. Now that's a plus! You simply cannot resonate to them. They cannot resonate to you. There is no match.

You cannot Unconditionally Love some being, entity, or person who cannot receive this resonance. They are not a resonance match. So, don't waste your time trying to make something work that simply does not match! It may not be the time for that person, being, or entity to connect and receive Unconditional Love.

Stop pressuring your Self that you have to love everyone and everything in Unconditional Love. You can be the resonance of Unconditional Love in your life. Just comprehend that some people or groups cannot accept this resonance. Again, there is no match. This is okay!

In your Heart and Solar Plexus, which is your Feeling Center, you are connected in Allness with your Self as the Creator, the Creativity, all the Creations in your life…every event, every situation, everyone. You are also connected as the Implementer and Manifestor of your life.

You are in Charge. You are in your Power. In this resonance, there is no use wasting your valuable time making excuses to deny Who You Are. You are the perfect person in the perfect body you chose in this lifetime.

In this alignment of Consciousness, your Female, guided by your innate and inherent intuition, supports your Perfect

Child Within to implement your creativity and inspire your Male to manifest into your physical world the inspired inventions and ideas of your creativity. The connection and the interaction of your Female, of your Perfect Child Within, and of your Male begin to flow from your clear unlimited Consciousness to manifest all your creativity through your continuing continuous continuum. You are living and creating through the resonance, intelligence, and intellect of your practical, divine Feeling Center.

The bands of conscious communication tell the world you are on track with life. You are the writer, producer, and director of your life. Your stage and stages of life are determined by you. You are not caught up in the limited Belief System that you came here to do just one thing, or to have one purpose, or to have a limited life. You are Multi-Dimensional. You can begin to live Multi-Dimensionally. You do not have to be trapped in the B.S. of 3D Duality.

In 3D Duality, the physicality of the human body in this old paradigm is Male. Consider these words: his-story, hym-ns, he-al, he-art, he-il, he-aven, he-ll. This is not male-bashing.

Through the left computer/brain connected to the Male right side of your body, you manifest the same old same old because your left computer/brain is hardwired to keep the 3D Duality Fear Programs running over and over again. You are conditioned, taught, and programmed to stay in your left computer/brain. You are conditioned to stay out of your Heart.

Once you open your Heart consciously, you are not easily controlled by the programs or by whatever party is running those programs to keep you from being in your own personal Power. This is just how it works. Stay out of your Heart and stay in your head and the controlling parties, through their limiting Belief Systems, will keep you under control. Wow, what a system!!

As long as you stay hardwired in your left computer/brain, your life is hard. The purpose of your physical body is to physically manifest your creativity into the physicality of your life. Otherwise, what would be the point of having a body? If you hold limited Belief Systems and only exist through your left computer/brain and your Male right side, then you can only re-create repeatedly the patterns that are hardwired in your left computer/brain. Your right brain, directly connected to your Female left side, cannot create newness.

You are destined to be a left-brainer, constantly re-creating patterns and behaviors hardwired in your neuronets, re-acting emotionally. Caught up in repetitious patterns, the challenge is in connecting both sides of your brain and both sides of your body. Your Male and Female sides are in opposition to each other. This is the 3D Duality Programs running you, your life, and your lifetimes, trapped in the silly infinity loop of Karma, Lessons, and Re-incarnation.

The connection of each side of your brain connects when you connect and live in your Heart. Always remember, your Heart is the most expansive resonance field in your body. Your brain, especially when you are only using the left computer/brain, cannot match the resonance of your Heart.

Stay out of your head…
Let your Heart lead the way!

Look at it from the standpoint that your Heart, especially in the 13 Chakra System, is your Real brain. Your left computer/brain is the perfect tool to organize information and to send clear signals to your body through your nervous system *when* you are clearly conscious and In Charge of Your Life.

In the 3D Duality Programming, your Male and Female are separated from each other, holding oppositional patterns of behaviors. In this oppositional resonance field, it is difficult to live in your Heart when the left computer/brain is keeping the separation program running within your body. To sustain a compatible harmony is the challenge.

In the 13 Chakra System, your Heart and Solar Plexus (your Feeling Center) connected with your Male and Female and your Perfect Child Within provide you with the resonance to sustain this powerful Allness in your physical human body. This is definitely something to work toward. Truly this is a no-brainer!

The number 8 in numerology is seen as the elevation or Transcension into your expanded awareness of Consciousness. This 8 symbolizes the eternal and spiral motions of cycles. 8 is significant. You either break through the Eight Block Wall into your expanded Galactic Consciousness or you hang on to the old 7 Chakra System of 3D Duality limitations. You have a choice.

8 is 4 doubled. 4 is practical, sensible, and reliable about money and the management of money. Double 4 into 8 and you have the capacity in your expanded Consciousness to create, implement, and manifest these traits in your life without the Fear of Judgment, Lack, and Take-Away. 8 is a significant step to Take Back Your Power, break through the Eight Block Wall, and live the life you so readily deserve.

You deserve healthy, emotional, mental, physical, spiritual, and financial stability without the threat of any of this being taken away from you

Leo, the Fifth House, signifies the ruler of fire and passion. When you have passion and compassion in your 13 Chakra System, there are no obstacles to your creativity or your abilities to manifest what is in your Heart. Where you direct the Clear Consciousness of your Heart's passion, you create from your Truth. **Your Truth is always in your Heart.** Your Heart is your powerful center of life.

Five numerically embodies wisdom. With the wisdom of your intuition and the creative alignment of your Male, Female, and Perfect Child Within passionately and compassionately embracing life with Total Acceptance and Unconditional Love, you live your Truth. You continue to ascend your Consciousness without the fear of restrictions and limitations.

This is not a dream or an illusion. You are creating your Realness for your Self, for your life, and for your world. You never have to be an illusional version of your Self ever again. Simply, you don't have to pretend who you are and who you are not!

NINTH CHAKRA

NERVOUS SYSTEM: Conscious Integration

The Ninth Chakra is your nervous system and your spinal column. These systems metaphorically embody the Tree of Life within you.

Your nervous system is your messaging system. Your historical information is imprinted on each disk in your spinal column and is collectively known as your Akashic Records. This is your entire his-tories or her-stories throughout your personal time continuum.

These records are not floating around out there somewhere in the ethers inaccessible to you. They are not in some etheric library waiting for you to someday attain the magical password or code to get into this previously mysterious library. There is no one outside of you who has the "passcode". There is no one who can deem you ready for your own Akashic Records. There is no one who is "above" you who will lead you to these Records. All this information is inside of you. The Akashic Records are stored in your spinal column. This is another source of your Cellular records, aka Cellular Memory.

How exceptional is the metaphor and physicality of it all? Your "spin-al" column has the "spin" of "all" your experiences recorded! Now you have the choice not to be your own "spin doctor". Now is the moment to stop putting your emotional body's spin on everything. Now you can choose to be the Non-Emotional Observer (NEO) and observe all of your experiences. Your incredible body so amazingly recorded all your experiences to provide you with the greatest opportunities.

Your opportunities are to *see* all your experiences, not as good, bad or indifferent, but as the records of your immense creativity. You created every experience in your life and your lifetimes. You are so amazing. You did all of this for the experiences. You did it to learn about your Self.

You had all of these experiences through all of the parts you played throughout your continuing continuous continuum to learn. What a hoot! All the suffering, sacrifice, tragedies, and victimizations were and are about getting conscious within your Self. You really didn't have to go through all of this. Yet you did.

Now ask your Self, "Is it time to stop these endless cycles of trauma-dramas and giving my Power away?" Only you can answer this question. You can now apply what you have learned, move up the food chain of Consciousness, and stop repeating and re-cycling the same old his-tories and her-stories of the past.

It's definitely time to create newness. How can you ever know what newness you are capable of creating if you continue to use your creativity to re-create the same oldness, the same Profiles of your Self, and the same Profiles of the players in your life and lifetimes? Is the answer and answers getting clearer to you...or not?

This is all about the Conscious Integration of Your Self

Throughout your systems (physical, emotional, mental, spiritual, and financial) your body receives information on a daily basis, whether you are consciously aware of it or not. Whether you are processing this information through your Childish Adult Ego or through your expansive Self is dependent upon where you are emotionally and consciously in your time continuum.

The more emotional you are, the less you are aware of your body and what your body is taking in. The more clearly conscious you are, the less you allow your body, your life, and your own personal creative process to get trapped into the emotional trauma-dramas, especially when they are some else's crap.

A good question to ask your Self every day is, "Am I just unconsciously processing the same old same old or am I clearly and consciously progressively processing and filtering out what has no relevance to my life and what brings me down into the 3D Duality muck?"

When you are in a cycle of repeated behaviors and actions, regardless of your linear age, you are still processing the experience and the information from an age or stage in your life in which you are emotionally, mentally, physically, spiritually, and financially stuck. In releasing your Self from this particular place and time of these re-cycled behaviors and actions, you realize with *real eyes* that you are required to rise above this re-cycled pattern and to let go of the emotional attachment of the "right" and "wrong" of it.

Now you can *see* it as facts. Whether you like or hate what happened, you are rising above it...

As the Non-Emotional Observer (NEO)...

Detaching from the repeated cycle...
Seeing all the players, including your own Role...
Letting go of all of it at your Cellular Level of
Consciousness...

Because you can't change the past...
Moving forward in your life...
You can change your future...
The past is one second ago...

YOUR FUTURE IS ONE SECOND FROM NOW!

This is the time to...
Non-emotionally evaluate your information...
Discern what this information is all about...
and what this information means to you in this
lifetime...
and how all your information has affected and
influenced you...
and what you choose to keep and what you choose
to dump from your Cellular Level...
and when are you willing to stop the judgment of all
of your experiences?

Stop beating your Self up!!!

As you ascend and expand your awareness in this physical 3D body, you physically, mentally, spiritually, and financially rise above the dull resonance of 3D Duality. Your body begins to change. You are becoming in charge of your body.

The resonance of your nervous system and spinal column become calmer. You become more detached from the emotions which previously clouded the messages you were sending through to your body. As you detach from the emotional hooks to your past experiences and situations, you become calmer. Your cells are thrilled. Your left computer/brain calms also.

In this state of calmness, you can *feel*, *see*, and evaluate the messages as pure information. You can choose what information you take into your body. You can now clearly choose what you experience in your body. You choose how you interact in your life through your body.

Your left computer/brain is not controlling your life, continually running the 3D Duality B.S. Programs. The intelligence and intellect of your body is in charge. Trust your intuition as the guide it is.

Your nervous system is the conduit in which the resonance of your expanded Consciousness assists you in evaluating and discerning the Truth of your participation in your experiences. How you experience your experiences is crucial to the resonance of your Clear Consciousness <u>or</u> your clouded emotional resonance.

Resonance attracts resonance.

Emotional trauma-drama resonances attract emotional trauma-drama resonances.

Low-based resonances attract low-based resonances.

Nothing happens by chance.
You choose your chances…consciously aware or not!

Your experiences are your experiences. Your messages are the messages you choose to convey to your body. Your actions and behaviors are the messages you choose to convey to the world outside of you. The resonance of your Consciousness is who you are, what you do, how you present your Self to you and to your outside world, and how you resonate to life.

The more expanded your awareness, the more expanded the resonance of your Consciousness, the calmer your nervous system becomes, and the clearer the messages that are sent to your body, your cells, your molecules, and your particles to the sub-atomic core of your being. From the inside calmness to the outside, your world becomes calmer.

There no longer is the emotional necessity to process the current emotional upheavals of life, which are not *your* issues, through *your* nervous system. And you do not have to process any of the emotional issues of the past in your current circumstances. You simply do not have to buy into any of the physically and emotionally draining situations. Your once unconscious behavior patterns and actions become conscious to you. You are in clear awareness. This is the Realness of Consciousness!

As your conscious awareness expands, the messages, once thought to be so relevant or viable to the old patterns of trauma-dramas, are no longer worth it to your sanity and well-being. Just the same old song, same old patterns, and same old trauma-dramas hooking you into the dysfunctional sameness of oldness!

Since your Consciousness and the movement of your energy are no longer embroiled or hooked into the dense resonance of limiting Belief Systems, you are consciously aware of everything you are doing. You are not only accessing the expanded resonances of Consciousness outside of you on this planet and in this Universe, you are now open to connecting to the Multi-verse fearlessly.

Your nervous system is functioning at an expanded resonance above the 3D Duality fears. Your calmer, more stable nervous system is becoming increasingly intuitive. You are now *feeling* the expansive realms of resonances throughout your entire physical body of Consciousness. Your nervous system is becoming in tune with the Multi-verse. At last! You are really becoming the multiplicity of your Self. No room for fear. No room for limitations. No room for the exhausting, draining trauma-dramas. You are more productive and more creative, and you are creating within you "the more" of you.

As Jesus said... *"You shall do as I do and more."*

Hello... the more is here!

Wake up and respond!

In your spinal column, you can access your Akashic Records, your his-tories and her-stories. Without the fears or stress of the emotional issues in your tissues at your Cellular Level, you now can access your his-stories and her-stories in your personal time continuum from a factual "just is" perspective. They no longer are perceptions which are the receptions and deceptions of your conceptions. Now you are getting the facts. You are the Non-Emotional Observer (NEO) getting the facts.

Your Akashic Records provide you with the historical and sometimes hysterical accounts of your lifetimes, not only on Earth but from other dimensions and realms as well. Remember, whether you were or are conscious of your

Multi-Dimensional Self or not, you have always been this. Forgetting Who You Are has been the fear dynamics of this 3D Duality illusional reality. You are conditioned to forget your Self and exist in the repetitive cycles of Karma, Lessons, and Re-incarnation tarnation of your Self.

In your expanded Consciousness, you connect to your records and recordings. In these records are your experiences as the Master. You were the Master and you are the Master. On planet Earth, you have also been programmed to be the slave. Master or slave, they experience the same control and manipulation resonances. Are you done with the master/slave resonance? A master can be as enslaved in the programming as the slave. They are flipped sides of the same band. It's time to move beyond this debilitating resonance.

You do not have to be fearful of your Self or be afraid of these incredible creative experiences you recorded so adeptly in your Akashic Records. Your body records because your body records. It's as simple as this! When you are clearly willing to access the records, you can access them. If you say you are not ready or you discount your Self or are afraid of your Self, then you stop your Self from accessing any and all of the information that you have stored in your body. It is your *willingness* that counts. If you are not willing, you will never be ready.

Your Cellular Memory provides you with the recorded information of your experiences. Always remember…fear is lack of information. With clear information, there is no necessity to be fearful.

You have the Power to move beyond 3D Duality. Or, you have the force to force your Self to stay trapped in the 3D Duality Programs. You determine everything. When you determine the perfect time is to get connected to your Self simply depends on the clarity of the resonance of your Consciousness. Either you are clearly connected to your Self or not! Clear Consciousness is clear awareness. Fear-based Consciousness is not clear.

You are the source and resource. Your expanded Consciousness illuminates your information. Light is information.

When you are enlightened, this simply means you have the information required to make an illuminated choice. You *feel* the information is correct and worth keeping. Or, you thinky-thinky in your left computer/brain that it is worth the physical and emotional efforts to hang on to this irrelevant, dysfunctional information. The physical release of the information comes when you choose to physically release these emotional, dense, thick, icky molecules of emotions glued to the cells in your entire body. Or, you think you have to keep them and re-live the trauma-dramas.

Connecting to your historical information is easy. When you *feel* you require knowing about your Self, choose a particular area of your spinal column or a specific disc and direct your Consciousness to the selected area. Allow your Self to receive the information. **It is this simple.**

This is your information. Use it to get the answers and the explanations for your experiences throughout your time continuum. In your more expanded awareness, you can choose to keep the information or release it. You stop taking up space in your body with irrelevant information.

This Ninth Chakra, the nervous system, is the activation of your conscious integration within your physical body. The more expanded your resonance, the easier it is to access your Cellular Memory. **The more Cellular Memories to which you connect, the easier it is for you to know,**

understand, and comprehend your Self. What a concept! It is not worth having a nervous breakdown and making your Self sick. The more you know about your Self, the more powerful you are.

During this integrative, progressive process, the strength of your Truth is *felt* throughout your entire body. Your cells are joyful and healing simultaneously. You FEEL! Your nervous system is empowered to communicate the messages of your Truth to every cell in your body without the Fear, the Belief Systems, or the energy of Judgment, Lack, and Take-Away.

You absolutely have the strength and the courage of your Truth to stand for your Self, by your Self, and with your Self. You are empowered with your "nerves of Truth". Your body emanates a Consciousness of strength. This strength is not to be confused with your Childish Adult Ego's idea of strength in control and manipulation accompanied by the emotional and physical pain of the 3D Duality Programs.

There is no *real* strength in control and manipulation, only emotionally painful experiences within dysfunctional relationships with your Self and others. There is no strength in pain as your Childish Adult Ego would have you think. Spiritual strength has no requirement for endurance. You just are strength because you are your Truth.

James, the disciple of the Ninth Chakra, was the half-brother of Jesus. He was the first of the twelve disciples whose life ended as a martyr. The lesson in his life and death is that he had the spiritual strength to stand for his Truth. This does not mean standing for your Truth requires you to die physically as a martyr. This represents the old Belief System that when you stand for your Truth you have to sacrifice your life. What a B.S. Program is this!

James represents the strength which is inexhaustible when you are your Truth. This is the strength which emanates from the conscious integration within your physical body and your clear mind.

Your clear mind is not in your brain. Your clear mind is your expanded awareness without fear. Everything is in order. You can label it divine order. The Truth is…everything can be considered divine…even tragedy. You choose what is divine to you, whether it's the trauma-drama or being clearly In Charge of Your Life.

Cancer, the Fourth House, represents the water electrically charged with your expanded Consciousness in your Ninth Chakra, your nervous system. Numerically it is a 4, metaphorically representing your Now. The Now is your dimensional field of Consciousness of the No-Time and the No-Space. You are in the perfect Moment and Moments of your life. In this field of Consciousness, you are clearly detached from the emotional issues and agendas of the past.

As this clear, detached observer, you *see* through the illusions of the emotional 3D Duality delusional reality. You *see* through the nightmare. You have risen above the dense resonances which have hooked you to your past experiences when you were not clear to *see* them as learning events throughout your continuum. There is no reason to doubt your Self. There is no reason to be weak or fragile. There is every reason to be strong and courageous. You know your Truth. You are stronger and more courageous. You are the Non-Emotional Observer (NEO), detached from the trauma-dramas, speaking your Truth naturally.

In numerology, 9 is humanitarian, intuitive, independent, generous, and compassionate. 9 is also the number of completeness. This is the end of the human gestation period as well as the precedent for new beginnings. This is the number of initiation.

You are initiating your Self through the clear messages you are sending through your nervous system to your entire body of Consciousness. More expanded mental and spiritual achievements are occurring, inspiring your Self and others. You are moving into the leadership of your Self. With clear information from within, you are clearer in the information you are experiencing through your behaviors and actions.

TENTH CHAKRA

THROAT: Communication

Wow, if there ever was an issue in any place or space in your body, the issues in the Throat Chakra say it all! When you can't speak your words out loud, the words get stuck in your Throat.

Speaking your Truth, regardless of your language of origin in any lifetime, you are programmed to hold back your Truth and your intuitive guidance. The programs state… "say the right thing", "don't say anything at all", "keep your mouth shut", "speak when spoken to", etc.! All the blah, blah, blahs that *infect* your abilities to speak up, speak out, and speak for your Self.

Right off the bat, the throat issues are cancer, tonsillitis, nodules, thyroid, adenoid problems, chronic sore throats, swollen glands, and the list goes on. You don't have to wonder anymore why you have Throat Chakra issues. These issues are a continuing continuous continuum of having to hold back your own Truth in favor of the current limiting Belief Systems, whatever century, eon, or time frame.

The edict of the controlling and manipulating Belief Systems is to keep you from speaking your Truth, regardless of the time frame. They are just under different guises. "Children are to be seen and not heard", "what do you know", "your opinion has no value", "keep your mouth shut", "don't say anything", "you don't know what you are talking about", etc. These are just examples. The list can go on and on just like your time continuum.

Speaking the TRUTH is the challenge of this lifetime, as a matter of fact, in any lifetime. The controlling fear of speaking your Truth is overwhelming, especially when the worst-case scenario is getting hung, imprisoned, and death. The physicality of not speaking your Truth is a *death* like the metaphor of sucking down and swallowing your Truth. Follow the leaders or follow your Self to death for speaking your Truth!

Keep your mouth shut at all costs or it will cost you embarrassment, punishment, abandonment, devaluement... all the *"-ments"* that prevent you from being and speaking your own Truth and cause you to give up your Power over and over again. Then illness occurs, related to the Throat Chakra, or the explosion happens.

The explosions are the angry, hurt-filled behaviors that create abusive patterns affecting the physical, emotional, mental, spiritual, and financial Consciousness of those involved. You can either be the explosive abuser or the partner (personal or professional) who is then the experiencer of the angry, pent-up explosion that is blasted your way.

You become either the victim or the victimizer, which in turn places you on both sides of these Roles. The venom spewed through the Throat is sickening and makes you sick. Whether you are the spewer of a venomous Belief System or you are the one being spewed upon by a venomous Belief System, everyone is affected by this dense resonance as it "negatively", in Duality terms, impacts your body and the bodies of everyone involved in the situation. No one can get clear or communicate clearly. Only the victim/victimizer behavioral patterns prevail.

When you cannot speak your Truth, your body physically and emotionally is diminished. When you are spewing words which are de-powering, you are de-powered. When this dense language resonance is directed at others, everyone involved in the situation is affected, including you. Everyone loses their Power.

Look at the physical issues which occur when you are suppressed from speaking your Truth: throat cancer, chronic sore throats, thyroid problems, glandular issues, problems swallowing, tongue cancer, etc. This is all because you had to shut up and not be heard. Disease happens because you are programmed to get sick. When you can't speak your Truth from your Heart, you are being programmed with cancerous Belief Systems that stick in your throat.

Philip is the disciple who represents the Throat Chakra. He demonstrated his Power through his speaking the spiritual word. As an evangelist and Bishop, he founded the Church of Glastonbury in Britain to teach the word of High Consciousness. Through the Throat Chakra, your words either empower you or take away your Power.

Philip represents the Power and the strength of your words when you are speaking from a resonance of your more expanded, more aware Consciousness. He symbolizes the Power or the vital expression of your words, language, and vocabulary that you use. Your expanded Wordology Is Your Biology language carries the more expanded resonance, which resonates with your Truth. You are not speaking the 3D Duality Programs of Judgment, Lack, and Take-Away. You are speaking your Truth.

The physicality and the physical tones from within your body now emanate at a more expanded expression through the language of your Heart Consciousness. You are not speaking from the dense resonance of the old 7 Chakra System's First Chakra of repeated trauma-dramas. You don't have time to waste spinning around in the re-cycle bin of your left computer/brain, leading you around with your head/crown buried up your old First Chakra. You don't have time to waste your valuable creativity stuck in the old 3D Duality victim language.

The sounds and tones of your Wordology Is Your Biology have shifted. You are more in tune to your Self and your Truth. The "trues" of the old programming are not relevant to a productive life. The talk of Lessons, Karma, and Re-incarnation tarnation is repetitive, time-consuming, creativity-busting, squanderous, energy-draining, and a non-productive waste of your life.

Being harmonious within your Self is the objective. To be more harmonious, you have to speak the language, words, and vocabulary which support a harmonious resonance from within your body. Harmony begins inside you. To maintain harmony, no matter what is going on "outside" of you, you must maintain the resonance of harmony within your Self. Yes…it is difficult at times.

The more you live in your Truth…
The more you speak your Truth…

The more your life is your Truth!
No Matter What!!!

Now it becomes easier. Life becomes easier because you are having Truth full and Truth filled conversations. This is a huge difference from the covert, manipulative, controlling, judgmentally repetitive 3D Duality words, language, and vocabulary. Comprehending this, is there any other choice than to move up the food chain of Consciousness? Isn't this transcending from one paradigm to another?

Living in your more expanded Consciousness, in the more luscious resonance of being in your Power, you automatically speak the language of inspiration to your Self and empower your Self. In turn, you inspire others who choose to be inspired.

There will be those who do not have a clue what you are saying or speaking. Oh well. You are expanding *your* resonance so that *you* get clear. Your job is not to be clear *to* or *for* others. They are on their journey. However, by being a role model, you will inspire. Start with your Self.

You *feel* an extreme difference when you speak the language or words from the old programming which sabotage, degrade, and violate you. Your body is repulsed by this resonance. Your body no longer resonates to this type of Self-debasing talk. Your body also does not tolerate being spoken to in a manner that does not serve you and does not support you to live a healthy, prosperous life.

This new Wordology Is Your Biology is the resonance which supports you to be inspired, creative, and unlimited as the Non-Emotional Observer (NEO) and the Conscious Creator who is excited to Create Newness in your life. Go for it!

You are not stuck in the old paradigm of ridiculous language such as "you made your bed so now you have to lie in it", "this is your lot in life", "this is the best/worst you can do", "you are not smart enough", and "you have to accept your life this way". All this garbage language requires to be released from your Cellular Memory. Dump it out permanently from your cells, your molecules, and your particles to the sub-atomic level, and your entire body and life!

There is a new language in your life. As you speak your Truth without any opposition within your Self, you are standing firmly and balanced in your life. You are speaking your Truth, Creating with your Female, Implementing with your Perfect Child Within, and Manifesting through your Male the physicality of your Truth. You are doing all the steps of the progressive process originating from your expanded state of awareness. You are in your Power. No More B.S.!

Your words are the sounds of the inner resonance of your personal music. You are resonating harmoniously from within you. As you allow the clear thoughts of your expanded Consciousness to evolve every day, your words, language, and vocabulary evolve. You don't have time to talk trash about your Self or anyone. Too time consuming! The energy of your creativity is enhanced from a more expanded place of productivity. Your productivity is not hampered by Self-inflicted sabotage anymore. Hooray for this!

When you speak the language from this expanded resonance, you manifest an expanded level of Consciousness into your life. You are attracting more support, more love, and more of everything. This is about the more. You are actualizing what you require, desire, and deserve. No More Wanty-Needy language. No More Wanty-Needy relationships!

You know what you require in your life and for your relationships. Expect to get what you ask for. You did before. Only you were completely unconscious that what you were getting was totally created by you. Remember, the old programming says, "Everything that happens to you happens because of someone else or something else." There is absolutely NO Power in that old conversation.

> **"If what you say is what you create…**
> **Why the heck did you say that to your Self?"**
>
> *-Sherryism*

Now you are in a clear conversation with your Self. What you say is what you create is what you manifest is what you say is what you create is what you manifest on a continuing continuous continuum. Be clear about what you say.

One of the best aspects of speaking your Truth is the way you attract newness to you. As you speak your Truth, you are not limiting your Self anymore. You can *feel* opportunities you may have missed in the past because you were in your left computer/brain instead of your Heart. When you speak your Truth from your Heart and your Feeling Center, the resonance from which you are heard is expansive and amplified. You attract more conscious people to you. You attract more support because your sound is more attractive. Your language is more attractive. Your Wordology Is Your Biology is more eye and ear-catching. You are a tractor beam.

From the perspective of the Multi-verse, you are also attractive. Who knows what wondrous dimensions you will attract to your Self? Be open. When you are living in your Truth, operating from a resonance of expanded awareness and Consciousness, there are no viable reasons to be fearful or fear-filled. The Multi-verse is unlimited. So are you.

Give your Self the opportunities to connect to other like-minded dimensions and realms. Be it that there are other realms and dimensions, whether they are called angels, guides, or beings, why not open up a conversation? Trust your Heart. If it *feels* correct for you, then speak up and speak out. You have everything to gain. More knowledge, more connection, and more fun. Why not?!

The Tenth Chakra is Gemini, the communicator in the Third House. Gemini, the sign of the twins, portrays speaking your Truth with the balance of your Female and your Male who are no longer in conflict within your Self. They each know their Roles.

Your Female speaks your Creativity. Your Male speaks the physical Manifestation or Actualization of your creative abilities. You, your Female, and your Male are in the language of connection *with* your Perfect Child Within, who implements your creativity and your creations. This Trinity within you speaks harmoniously in the connectedness of Allness. No longer are the three aspects disjointed and disconnected from each other within you.

You are the Triad of your Truth. You are speaking from and through your Heart with a voice unified through the conscious integration of your Truth full and Truth filled Wordology Is Your Biology. Strong and empowered, you have the choice and the voice to speak your Truth no matter what. Your tones, sounds, words, language, and vocabulary are uplifting and life-changing through this tremendous resonance of your New Consciousness.

The number 10 represents perfection, completion, and fulfillment. 10 in the Kabbalah is the same as Malkuth or

Kingdom in the Tree of Life. Speaking your Truth is the spoken resonance of your Heaven on Earth, both metaphorically and physically. 10 is exceptional Power. When you speak your Truth, you are exceptionally Power full and Power filled. You are an inspiring, exceptional individual and the leader of your Self. You have your Voice!

ELEVENTH CHAKRA

THE THIRD EYE: The Vision Center

When you have an idea or a concept of something you would like to create for your Self, what if you can't *see* the vision of your idea? What if your vision is similar to the statement, "it is on the tip of my tongue, but I can't remember what I would like to say"? Could it also be possible that you have an idea but you can't quite *see*, can't quite put your finger on it, or can't quite *see* the whole picture of your creative idea?

This could be the blockage which is the underlying current of those 3D Duality bands of fear in which you are entangled. The noisy, silent roar of your Childish Adult Ego's voice screams, "You can't do it. You can't even see it, so why bother talking about it?" You simply don't have what it takes to *see* for your Self what you are capable of creating. You can only *see* the downside. There is no upside. If there is, it can only be temporary. Therefore, what is the point in *seeing* a vision of a better way for you?

Your vision is not sustainable. Something has to go wrong, be wrong, or simply your vision is wrong for you. Other people's ideas of what is perfect for you are much more acceptable to your Childish Adult Ego (CAE). Besides, this gives credibility and validation to your CAE who loves to sabotage you. After all, sabotage is the best Role your CAE knows how to play to keep you in check.

Your Childish Adult Ego must follow the 3D Duality rules to prevent you from accomplishing your vision. If you can't *see*, you are encouraged to only see what others tell you to see, whether you *feel* good about it or not. 3D Duality expects your wins to be temporary. 3D Duality expects your vision for you and your life to be limited. This is the way of limitations and limited insight.

Here's the rub. "You have to see it to believe it." That's impossible. To create your vision, you have to *see* inside your Self first. You can't *see* outside of your Self. Otherwise, you are looking at someone else's idea or creative concept.

The expanded awareness of your Consciousness believes in YOU. Your Childish Adult Ego *belief systems* the limitation of your sight and insight! Here is where the rubber hits the road. Believing instead of *belief systeming* is the way to keep your road open. Believing instead of *belief systeming* is the forward movement of your energy based on the expansive Consciousness of your Female, Male, and Perfect Child Within.

Within insightfulness, you can *see* the full spectrum of how you can create, implement, and manifest the actualization of your full-sighted insight. You can *see* what you are creating by *feeling* the connection from the inside of you to the outside world in which you actualize your creativity. In other words...your insight, vision, and sight are not blocked by limitation. Unlimited vision begets unlimitedness. No hang-ups and no blockages. These versions of limitation are irrelevant and extreme wastes of your time, effort, and actualizations.

The more you allow your Self to use your unlimited vision, the more you realize with *real eyes* what a waste of your Self-expression it is to continue to experience limitations! Your Vision Center provides you with the visual substance to *see* the possibilities and potentials of your unlimited creative abilities before you manifest them into your Realness.

The possibilities and potentials are no longer hanging out in the ethers as a dream. The visions of your possibilities and potentials are assembled into the practical applications to construct your manifested actualities. Yes, actualities! Multi-Dimensionality is many actualities. You are not stuck in limitation anymore.

3D Duality is a limitation of creativity. Therefore, 3D Duality is a very narrow band of a limited reality. When you get right down to it, 3D Duality is only a repetition of the sameness. Though the circumstances "appear" different, the only differences in the trauma-dramas are the stages, the costumes, the lighting, and the Roles. The trauma-dramas are essentially the same with only different reference points of time.

Your Vision Center, pulsating in tune with the more expanded resonance of your Consciousness, produces visual special effects. You are affecting the effects that are occurring in your life.

You are the happening making the happening happen.
You clearly see your Self as the Conscious Creator.

You clearly see your Visions
as the futures you are creating consciously.

Remember...
the future is one second from your Present Time!

You have many futures living Multi-Dimensionally!

In the density of the 3D Duality resonance, how could you *see* the vision of your possibilities and potentials? The density does not allow or provide the space to hold any vision of the Vision Center for an extended period of time. The density of 3D Duality limits the range of your visions.

When your intuition, or your *gut feeling*, is connected to your vision and inter-linked to your Creative Chakra, practical miracles happen. Your creativity has the visual effects emanating from your Truth and your passion. Your creative process is progressive. Your creativity can *see* no boundaries or blocks. Visual unlimitedness!

Andrew is the disciple of your Vision Center. Through this aspect of your Self, Andrew represents your expanded, Multi-Dimensional sight and insight. He brought his brother Simon to know Jesus as the representative of the Christed Consciousness's unlimited sight and insight.

Andrew depicts the aspect of you which provides you with your natural ability to *see* the potentials and possibilities of your future. Andrew is the aspect of you which provides the opportunity for you to *see* your future which is in the current moment being created by you.

How? Your Christed Consciousness is your unrestricted clarity, providing you with this extraordinary tool for unlimited insight and sight. What you *see* inside your Self is the dream which can indeed become Real. You must trust your insight. With focused clarity, you choose how you create, implement, manifest, and actualize your life. No limitations, only Multi-Dimensional experiences for you to experience, to learn, to grow, and to be amazed by your Self.

Your intuition gives stability to your visions. Your Heart provides the *feeling* to comprehend that you are creating from your Truth. Trusting what you are *seeing* from within your Self is the Believing of "seeing is believing". You cannot *see* something outside of your Self first. You *see* it first *inside* of you, trusting your Heart and your intuition, and then the vision begins to come into view. From these unlimited ideas, you are now unleashing into your world from the inside of you to the outside of you.

Your Vision Center shows you that without a doubt you have the potential to create, implement, manifest, and actualize at your most expanded resonances in Multi-Dimensional ways. So, allow your Self to *see* that Multi-Dimensional Realness is your unlimited opportunity to express your Self and your creative ideas. Limiting your Self is so 3D Duality boring.

You are no longer locked or bound by fear. You are fearless. Your Vision has no room to hold the resonance of limited sight or insight. You are creating clearly. You are *seeing* and creating consciously. You don't have to go into an altered state. The practical side of being conscious is that you are participating in your life, grounded, open, and Multi-Dimensional all at once.

Taurus the Bull is the sign of strength in the physical realm. The Bull is the Second House of the Zodiac. 2 numerically symbolizes the alignment of your physical strength with the strength and courage of your expanded awareness and Consciousness which is a *sighted* platform from which your Vision Center operates with clarity. You can *see* for your Self through your expanded vision of life that nothing can be taken from you or negated by some limited Belief System outside of you. You absolutely trust your Self, your Vision Center, and your Heart. Everything is falling into place without you falling down repeatedly.

You are the Vision. You are the source of your Strength. Now you can comprehend that what you *see* is your Truth. You can *see* your Truth because your Vision Center is in operation.

Numerically, 11 is the idealistic visionary, inspired and inspiring others as a teacher of Self and others. Visionaries are courageous and insightful using their skills to assist others. 11 is a Master Number. Visionary intuition goes beyond the thinky-thinky of the left computer/brain. Being the Master of your Vision Center shifts, expands, and develops the scope of what you *see* for your Self, what you *see* for your life, and how you choose to participate. You *see* your worth and value. You are aligning in the Vision Center of your Mastery.

TWELFTH CHAKRA

PITUITARY: Activation

The Twelfth Chakra is an important step in the activation of your Thirteen Chakras in your physical Earth body. This Twelfth Chakra establishes the resonance of your Consciousness to new heights within your physical Earth body. This is Ascension, grounded and open without any fears or trauma-dramas. In this resonance is your Pituitary.

Your Pituitary gland is your Master Gland. When it is not functioning correctly, all sorts of physical problems occur which are emotionally-based. The Pituitary Gland is connected to your thyroid, adrenal glands, your ovaries and testes. How interesting. When you can't speak your Truth, your thyroid is affected. When you are stressed, your adrenals are affected because you cannot assimilate or eliminate the physically challenging emotionality being programmed into you. Your ovaries and testes are part of your reproductive system. You don't like what you are producing.

There are other ramifications when your Pituitary Gland is out of balance emotionally in your physical body. Illness happens, not by chance, but by the emotional hooks to physically challenging issues. Dissolve your emotional hooks to the past!

The 3D Duality fear-driven resonance has no place in the practical Transcension of your Self, your Consciousness, or your beingness. Letting go of this dense resonance is truly being on this Earth without being stuck in the re-cycled muck of 3D Duality. As you ascend and transcend 3D Duality, you are simply resonating at new heights.

You are not on the same wavelength of the fear-mongers. Fear is a waste of your time, your creativity, your ability to implement your life as you choose, and your focus on manifesting what you require, desire, and absolutely deserve. Life-draining, energy-sucking relationships are a waste of your life and your time.

Here is where you activate the resonance of Self-Trust and Self-Faith. Peter is the disciple representative of this expanded resonance. Peter radiates the Faith and Trust Consciousness. In his journey to his own more expanded Consciousness, Peter tested his own faith, just as you test your Self.

Here's a great practical mantra: **No More Tests!** You are graduating. Here's why tests are simply a waste of your life, time, energy, and your Consciousness. The Universe, God, Source, or whatever your name, label, or identification for your connection to God is, does NOT test you.

You set up the tests for your Self. *You* test your own Self-Faith and your own Self-Trust. These tests are your Self-Activated Set-Ups. Most of the time, these Set-Ups in 3D Duality Reality are, simply put, re-cycled time continuum versions of the same tests.

At this stage of the game, tests are no longer required. You are too clear to bother with tests. Besides, what is the point of the tests? You passed! Move forward.

Peter, after Jesus' arrest, denied knowing him three times. How convenient. How many times have you denied your Self, your abilities, and your creativity? Tons of times! What a waste! Don't deny your Self your Christed Consciousness because of the 3D Duality Programs of Fear.

You deny your Self a healthy, prosperous life because in the past you thought you did not deserve the best. Get on with your Transcension. Move up and out of the confinements of 3D Duality. Now is the time to let go of the dense, limited realities.

Metaphorically and in Duality's reality, Peter, denying Christ and his own Christed Consciousness of the Godness within his Self, later repented his denial of Jesus and the denial of his own Self. He did not trust or have faith in his Self. When he restored his faith in his own Self, he trusted his Self. He became a leader and spokesperson of the disciples.

It's time for you to step up to the plate. Literally, change the menu of the B.S. Food of Consciousness of 3D Duality. Begin by dining on the supportive, unconditionally loving Food of Consciousness which is nurturing and provides you with the physical, emotional, mental, spiritual, and financial nutrients to have a healthy, prosperous life. Anything else is not acceptable. Don't eat the crap anymore! You don't have to no matter who is dishing it out.

Becoming your own clear leader and the leader in charge of all the aspects of the discipleships within your Self, you know you are faithful to you in your expanded Consciousness. You trust your Self. No one can pull you down or off kilter. Fear is irrelevant. Self-Creativity is so relevant for you and your life.

The lesson or experience here for Peter, as well as for you, is that Faith and Trust are not something found outside of your Self. Faith and Trust are inside of you. Trust your wisdom, trust your experience, and trust that 3D Duality is not on your side. Trust and Faith are natural and inherent attributes to you as a Soul.

If something doesn't *feel* correct to you, do not do it. Trust your intuitive Soul. Your Soul knows. Your left computer/brain does not know anything except the 3D Duality Programs. This is a no-brainer.

At this stage of your resonance, you are on your Soul's journey. You are no longer limited by your Childish Adult Ego's version of life. Your Soul is physically, emotionally, mentally, spiritually, and financially involved with you. Hip Hip Hooray! Don't you *feel* it is about time and timing in your continuum?

Did you *think* your Soul was waiting around for you to get through the Karma, Lessons, and Re-incarnation tarnation stuff? Did you *think* your Soul was waiting for you to eventually wake up?

Do you *feel* it is time to wake up and taste life? Your Soul is very patient all the while you are acting out the victim/patient Roles over and over again. "Hello", says your Soul. Timing is everything. Is this current lifetime *the* time?

Step up and be your own leader. Trust and have faith in your Self. Easier said than done? Only if you *think* life is hard, is life hard. If you *feel* life is easy, it is. Remember, what happens outside of you beyond your life is what happens. However, what happens in your life is what *you* make happen. There is no happening in your life unless you make it happen or you choose to jump into something or some circumstance that may or may not be for you. You have to choose where you jump in or not.

You must have faith and trust in your Self. Faith and trust begin with you. Faith and trust are not a permanent aspect of the 3D Duality Programs. You may *temporarily* trust and have faith in your Self. Always remember…3D Duality is the re-cycle bin of fear. You can escape for a few moments in time, but the lure of the trauma-dramas draws you back into the stuff.

"Fixing" someone else is impossible. Just the idea of a fix is predicated on the Belief System that fixing is only temporary, a stop gap until the dam breaks again. Then you are right back into the same mess, whether it's this lifetime or in the next one.

This Faith Consciousness along with the Trust factor signifies your receptivity and your Self-permission to accept the Truth that Godness is *within* you. You are Godness in this connection. You are not *A* God! God is and never has been outside of *you*. Your Power is the Godness *within* for practical applications to your life. Practical applications are the focus and direction of your Consciousness using your Self-generated energy to create, implement, and manifest your requirements, desires, and comprehending you deserve this. The life you create is the life you create.

You and the Godness within you operate in practical terms or not! You have the choice to Take Your Back Power, live your life in Your Power, and be Power full. This does not mean controlling and manipulating. The Godness Connection from within you to the physical manifestation of your world outside of you is not just having a conversation with God. It is using your Godness tool in your everyday life. This is the Godness of you in action for life and living.

Godness is the resonance of your Consciousness in your unlimited capacity to love and accept unconditionally. Again and again, Unconditional means NO Conditions. This begins inside of you as you take ownership of trusting and having faith in your Self, regardless of the old, tired, played-out 3D Duality Programs.

Faith is resonating and comprehending Total Acceptance and Unconditional Love in every cell, molecule, particle, from the macro to the micro of your Self in the Non-Duality Universe and Multi-verse of your Self. You cannot hold the resonance of fear when you ARE BEING the resonance of Total Acceptance, Unconditional Love, and Unconditional Faith for your Self. The Godness or the resonance of the essence of God within you activates through your Pituitary Gland as you accept your Self as a God Being.

The expression of the oppositional 3D Duality Reality of the old, tired, worn-out 7 Chakra System does not have a hold on you anymore. This is the practical growing progressive process. This is Transcension, Ascension, becoming Clear Consciousness in your physical Earth body. This is being fully grounded and open, and not floating around outside of your Self, hoping, wishing, wanty-needying, and expecting things to be different, stuck in the old programming.

Expectation of change is absurd when you stay in the old 7 Chakra System. The only "growth" is temporary insights without practical applications. So there is no growth. Stop talking *to* God. Be the Godness within you. Follow your Heart with Total Acceptance and Unconditional Love. Create the changes you are inspired to change.

If you like the trauma-dramas, then stay in them. If you choose to shift and create the life you love to experience instead of the trauma-dramas, then by all means, make the commitment to be the Godness within you. You already know what happens when you choose the old, worn-out 3D Duality system. Take Back Your Power or not!

You have the knowledge, the experience, and the faculties within you. The twelve disciples represent the aspects of your Self as your faculties. Create your Heaven on Earth…a much better life than a living hell!

Stop crucifying your Self over and over again. This accomplishes nothing except pain and more pain, sacrifice, and suffering. This definitely is an old program.

Sacrifice and suffering never helped you or anyone. Real support comes through beneficial action that honors you and the ones you are assisting. If helping comes in the form of enabling, then the only result is victimization. Both the victim and the victimizer are victimized, just on different sides of the same victim band.

The old, worn-out 7 Chakra System is tired, dysfunctional, and supports wanty-needy repetitive cycles of trauma-dramas with the commercials in between for respites and temporary reprieves. Nothing really changes. The 7 Chakra 3D Duality System is the same old stories.

This is what raising your Consciousness, expanding your resonance, and creating your life through the Godness within you is all about. Do you believe you came here to this Earth to suffer over and over again? No, you did not! You just got caught up in the 3D Duality Programs like everyone else. Now you can free your Self or not! You have the choice to Take Back Your Power or continue to give it away.

You are the one who chooses to connect and inter-link to the Multi-Dimensional levels, spaces, and places of your Consciousness. Trust your Self. Have faith in your Self. Believe in Your Self. It is not that difficult unless you *think* you are not worthy. Let that B.S. Program go. You have nothing to lose by letting go of 3D Duality. Your gain is your Self, your life, and your clear ability to use all your faculties within you.

The First House in the astrological cycle is Aries. Aries represents the number 1 metaphorically. This is analogous to an idea originating from your creativity. In this expanded resonance of Consciousness, in the alignment with your Multi-Dimensional Self, you comprehend, you "get it", that you are not only the Creator, the Creativity, and the Creation of your life and your experiences, you are the Originator of the idea.

Each new idea emanating from the passion of your Truth and your Heart deserves to be manifested and actualized in your life. Each day is a new beginning in which a place, a space, and a time are provided for you to bring your new ideas to life in your physical world. In the expanded resonance of your creativity, you are not attached to it from a perception of past and future. You are in the moment with your creative process.

This is the genesis progressive process working within. Producing your creation into your *outside* world begins with one idea about your Self and what you would love to implement and manifest. Perhaps the idea is about something you desire to have for your Self or an idea of a relationship you require and desire to have in your life. Whatever the idea is, the idea begins with the clarity and focus of your Godness Consciousness. There can be no emotional or physical hooks to the past. You are creating newness in a new field of Consciousness. Trust and have faith in your Self. You can do it!

YOU can create your life fearlessly. The whole purpose of ascending, which is expanding your Consciousness, is recognizing and taking actions that any and all ideas about your Self is *your* journey of Self-Creation. This is the practical application of becoming and being conscious and living consciously. This is Co-Creating with the Godness Consciousness within you through your physical Earth body. Go forth and create consciously. Have fun.

Numerically, number 12 is the number 3, your Trinity, raised to the expanded levels, spaces, and places of your Consciousness. You have the experience, the courage, and the wisdom to rely upon your Self. You trust and have faith in your Self. You share with others in a much different resonance. You are caring without enabling. 12 is the Self-Trinity of You. It is the marriage of your Female and your Male inside of you with the union of your Perfect Child Within.

You are the detached, grounded Non-Emotional Observer (NEO), Conscious Creator In Charge of Your Life. You comprehend that You are the Creativity in charge of all your Creations, all your situations, your experiences, and everything that happens in your life. Now you comprehend in trust and faith that you are the implementer and the manifestor of your life. Your Heaven on Earth is up to you.

THIRTEENTH CHAKRA

THE CROWN: Ascension/Unlimited

The Thirteenth Chakra represents the use of your energy based upon the resonance of your physical Christed Consciousness within you. You are ascending beyond the fear-based paradigm of 3D Duality and the Programs of Judgment, Lack, and Take-Away. The emotional hooks to these Programs have no value to you. They are simply an aspect of the 7 Chakra System, the activities of the re-cycled, dualistic programming and resultant re-cycled events of your 3D Duality time continuum. You simply don't have any more time, space, or place to waste as you create your life consciously. You are fully responsible and responsive to the life you are creating, implementing, and manifesting as your actualized life.

Your Christed Consciousness is the embodiment of your physical Earth body which has ascended above the fear-filled, dense resonance of Duality. Duality is not worth your time, efforts, focus, or direction, unless you are still hanging on to it.

You have broken through the Grid of Duality. Just like Truman when he escaped through the door in The Truman Show movie, he saw the programming, the left computer/brain which is running everyone's life. Everyone is hooked onto the trauma-dramas, the soap operas, the manipulation and control of "living" through other people's lives.

No one in 3D Duality is living free. You *were* programmed to exist as someone else's idea of who you are or should be. Now you are not caught up in the gridlock anymore. Free at last, free at last! You don't have to suffer or die to be free. There is no freedom in death. Death is only another trip through the re-cycle bin of 3D Duality, back again to do "it" over! Boring.

You can open your Crown and you can connect. You do not have to be afraid anymore. No boogey man is going to get you for connecting beyond this reality. Don't close your Crown. Wear it proudly as the Master of your life, your body, and your Realness.

As you activate your connection to the Non-Duality Universe and Multi-verse grounded in your Earth body, you let go of the limitations. The limitations are not worthy of you. You have broken through the Grid of re-cycled patterns, behaviors, and actions which have kept you stuck and boxed in the Grid. Your new opportunities are gridless. No more boxes piled in all directions keeping you "boxed in".

Not only are you letting go of limitations, you are letting of the emotional hooks to your past, whatever the time frame. The past becomes a reference point only, not a point in your continuum to be re-lived, especially if it did not serve you. You can be hung, imprisoned, maimed, lamed, blamed, stuck in the yuck, and do it over again for lifetimes. Or, you can take the opportunities in your hands and move on. Transcension and Ascension are the practical applications of the Godness within you. It's the essence of co-creating with the Godness within you.

Experience your Feeling Center. This is the time. Experience your Female Creativity, the Implementation of your Perfect Child Within, and the Manifestation of your

Male...all working in unison with each other. Otherwise, why would we have a system of Transcension or Ascension? Stop talky talking and get into action.

Limitation is crazy. Wherever you are in the script right now, take a step back. Be the Non-Emotional Observer (NEO). *See* what does not serve you, including the dysfunctional relationships. When you free your Self, you can assist the other person or persons to free their Selves. If it happens, it happens. If it doesn't, then it doesn't.

You are the Master of your Universe and Multi-verse. There is no Master outside of you. Step up to your Mastery. Get over your 3 Duality Programs, unless you love the pain and not being able to *feel*. If you embrace being disconnected with your Self, then be disconnected. If you do embrace the pain and repetition, then hang on to the past and the programs. You do have choices. Or, you can choose your Self and NOT choose the 3D Duality Programs anymore. Everything is up to you.

Ask your Self the questions for which you require answers. Have the conversation with the Godness within you. Embrace your Self-Truth. Trust your Self-Truth. Have Self-Faith in your clear Christed Conscious Self. Your Self-Trust is the best discipleship. Your Self-Truth is always in alignment with your more expanded Self-Awareness.

The clarity of Consciousness resonating to your Christed Consciousness is what puts you above it all. You are the connection, the connecting, and the connected to the Non-Duality Universe and Multi-verse. Put these dimensions to work for you. After all, you have been employed by 3D Duality for eons.

This is the perfect time, place, and space to consciously evolve. Synchronicity is what connection is all about.

Perfect timing, perfect place, and perfect space of Consciousness begin with you. Involved Conscious Evolution! You are in Allness with all aspects of your Self, here, there, and everywhere. You are Multi-Dimensional.

Now on this journey, you can explore, be inventive, be open, embrace, and allow. Fearless is the way forward in all directions. Now it is no longer the limited "so above so below". Now your life is in all directions – up, down, forward, and diagonal. You are Multi-Faceted and Multi-Dimensional. No requirement for the "up" to be good and the "down" to be bad. As the Commander of your ship and the Master of your life, you are using your clear Mastery to make your life happen. You are being the Christed Consciousness within you.

In the stages of opening the energy vortices or connections of your Thirteen Chakras, the point is to align your more expanded Consciousness and awareness throughout your entire physical body...connecting, inter-linking, and integrating all the levels, spaces, and places of your Consciousness. Play, explore, discover. There is no rush. You have lots of time. You have your whole-time continuum ahead of you, especially *this* lifetime. Begin now. Multi-Dimensionality gives you so many choices and options.

**There is no reasonable reason to be stuck in the past
or even to get stuck in your future**

You are Multi-Dimensional. Your creativity is Multi-Dimensional. Your life is Multi-Dimensional. Comprehend that you are becoming Who You Are. You are no longer stuck in the trues of 3D Duality. You are your Truth. Be flexible as you step into this new journey. Fearless is the way.

As you serve and honor your Self as Allness with the Godness Consciousness within you, you honor and serve, without sacrifice and suffering, those with whom you participate in life. You can choose to participate with different realms and dimensions without fear. You are fearless because you are In Charge of Your Life and you are connected to the Godness of your Self. You are in your Power.

The Thirteenth Chakra is the connection of your unlimited Christed Consciousness to wherever you choose to go. As in Star Trek, perhaps now you'll choose to go to places you have never gone before. When you were stuck in 3D Duality, you probably thought that "this" was all there was. There is so much more.

You have many futures to create from your clear *Now*, no longer limited in timelines of linear time. You have the potentials and possibilities which you can actualize as manifested actualities. Again – *actualities* – because you are not limited to one reality as 3D Duality is. Your opportunities are unlimited and boundless.

Start creating newness. Give your Self some linear time as you shift out of 3D Duality into your connection with the Non-Duality Universe and Multi-verse, while being totally grounded, open, and connected.

You are aligning with different resonances. Give your Self some time to adjust. Enjoy your progressive process. Your physical body is ascending above the resonance of 3D Duality. You don't have to resonate to Duality anymore. Be your Truth and utilize your physical Earth body as your amazing tool to be connected Multi-Dimensionally. Go for unlimitedness. Create new experiences and allow these experiences to unfold.

Numerically, 13 equals 4. 4 is the dimension beyond the resonance of limitation. You now have the benefit of not being limited by time and space. Therefore, in very practical terms, the No-Time and No-Space concept becomes Real. No limitations by either space or time. You are connected.

All the dimensions are within you. Each dimension has its own resonance. Again, **inside of you are all the dimensions**. You make the connection when you resonate with a dimension *inside* of you. You can connect with any dimension that resonates with you. If something does not *feel* correct for you, do not connect. Be discerning. This is no different than connecting to a relationship, a group, or a Belief System.

If something does not resonate with you, then do not do anything until you have more information. Fear is always Lack of Information. After you get more information and it still does not *feel* correct for you, then no matter what the situation or relationship is, it is not correct for you. Move on. Don't try, like in the old 3D Duality Programs, to make something that does not work try and work. This is simply a waste of your valuable time and effort!

Use your efforts to be conscious. Learn and apply what you learn to your life. No lessons, please. Learn for knowledge's sake. Or for Pete's sake, you will be re-learning those "valuable" lessons.

Believe and trust your intuition. This is your best guide and guidance. Apply what you are learning from the Non-Duality Universe and Multi-verse. Don't ever limit your Self again. You are the Godness within you. You are the actualized Christed Consciousness. At last, your Multi-Dimensional time has come. Hello Godness!

Chakra	Zodiac	Disciple	Body	Energy	Essential Oil	Crystal
13	Transcension	Godness Within	Crown	Christed Consciousness	Myrrh	Azeztulite
12	Aries 1st House	Peter	Pituitary	Activation	Tuberose	Charoite
11	Taurus 2nd House	Andrew	Third Eye	Vision Center	Frankincense	Tanzanite
10	Gemini 3rd House	Philip	Throat	Communication	Yarrow	Celestite
9	Cancer 4th House	James	Nervous System	Conscious Integration	Basil Nepal	Amethyst
8	Leo 5th House	John	Heart	Feeling Center	Rose Moroccan	Emerald
7	Virgo 6th House	Nathanael Bartholomew	Diaphragm	Information Assimilation	Eucalyptus Radiata	Yellow Fluorite
6	Libra 7th House	James	Solar Plexus	Balance and Understanding	Boronia	Citrine
5	Scorpio 8th House	Matthew	Reproductive Organs	Creativity	Jasmine	Carnelian
4	Sagittarius 9th House	Thomas	Hips and Upper Legs	Passion and Commitment	Vetyver	Sunstone (natural)
3	Capricorn 10th House	Simon	Knees	What You Stand For	Patchouli	Danburite
2	Aquarius 11th House	Thaddaeus	Ankles	Female/Male Energy Alignment	Helichrysum	Kunzite
1	Pisces 12th House	Judas	Feet	Soul of Your Earth Body Foundation	Spikenard	Rhodocrosite

The Inheritance: The New Thirteen Multi-Dimensional Galactic Human Chakra System

Your transcended physical body of the Allness Consciousness of your Multi-Dimensional Being, completely integrated and aligned in your new field of electromagnetic energy, lives through the divine law of your discipleship of Total Acceptance for instant manifestation of your creative seed/idea.

The Thirteen Chakras

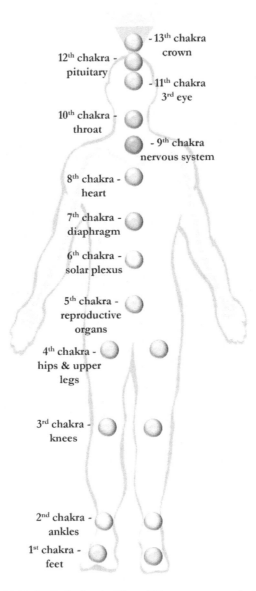

12th chakra - pituitary

- 13th chakra crown

- 11th chakra 3rd eye

10th chakra - throat

- 9th chakra nervous system

8th chakra - heart

7th chakra - diaphragm

6th chakra - solar plexus

5th chakra - reproductive organs

4th chakra - hips & upper legs

3rd chakra - knees

2nd chakra - ankles

1st chakra - feet

The Shift in Polarity in Your Electromagnetic Field:
A Unified Field of Consciousness

You can download the color version showing the 13 Chakra colors at:
www.SherryAnshara.com/Thirteen-Chakras

Chapter 9

YOUR DISCS OF KNOWLEDGE, YOUR AKASHIC RECORDS

Accessing Your Records, Your History and Herstory, Your Self

"Your Akashic Records are your personal encyclopedia recordings of you in your continuing continuous continuum of times in Duality's *spin* of *all* imprinted in your *spin-al* column... Stop spinning!"

-Sherry Anshara

A unique and practical methodology in your personal healing journey is to access the information stored throughout the cells of your body, which is your Cellular Memory and your Cellular Memorization. **Cellular Memory** is the recorded history or herstory throughout your personal time continuum. **Cellular Memorization** is the more current or current lifetimes.

For example, you could NOT have Cellular Memory of being a Mormon in the 16th Century. This does not fit a correct timeline. Therefore, Cellular Memorization is the recorded information from a more current Belief System in your time continuum.

Remember, **all Belief Systems are meant to control and manipulate you**. If you resonate to being controlled and manipulated, then you will be controlled and manipulated whether you admit it or not. This is just a fact. You will even justify a Belief System so that you are not *wronging* your Self. At this juncture in the book, you may be beyond this "right and wrong" issue, and you may be sticking to the facts.

By accessing your Cellular information, you can expect both physical and emotional releases. To reiterate, everything about you is physical, regardless of the dimensions in which you are connected. By connecting to your Akashic Records, it is typically not as emotional as accessing the Cellular information in your cells, although this is not a rule of thumb.

Connecting to your Akashic Records is metaphorically and physically akin to opening the Encyclopedia Britannica of You. As you access this information, usually you become more excited, less emotional, and more intrigued with the experiences, the timelines, the people involved, and your involvement in the situations.

As to the idea of "Is your glass half empty or half full?", the question to ask is, "What is your glass half full *of*?" If it is the same old 3D Duality Programming, then empty the glass and fill it with what you choose.

What does not serve you, release it, dump it, let it go, delete it, get rid of it! Again, the releases are usually not as emotionally charged as when you are releasing old issues from your Heart, Chest, Solar Plexus, etc. You are by now not as emotionally attached, since you are in your progressive process to being clearly conscious of your Self.

By accessing these Akashic Records, you are also giving your Self the opportunities to more clearly discern and select the information and resonances you desire and require to keep and expand upon. These experiences are your valuable tools which serve to support you.

Your Akashic Records are uniquely stored and encoded in each of the discs of your spinal column. Look at the word "spinal". The recordings are metaphorically and physically the Spin-of-All your experiences. So, when you put the emotional spin on some experiences, for example as a victim, the spin you see is that you are the victim no matter what the circumstances. However, if you are the detached Non-Emotional Observer (NEO), you now can *see* your participation, others' participation, the situation, the circumstances, and the timeline. You can let it all go and stop hanging on to past histories or herstories that are out of date and have no relevance to your life now.

The benefits of your Akashic Records are to find the purpose and the purposes of your lifetimes. This is no longer the Lessons, Karma, and Re-incarnation tarnation approach. It is simply what you did learn from the experiences, what are the facts, and what can you do now to either learn from the past experiences, let it go, or love the experience, keep and expand upon it. You did not always have "bad" experiences. You did live some great lives. Glean the information, discern the information, and then ascertain what is valuable and what is not.

Accessing your Akashic Records, your personal library, your personal encyclopedia, supports you to remember Who You Are, what you have been, how you experienced your lifetimes, and what you can bring to this lifetime that is valuable to keep or not.

There is nothing outside of you which has been created into your physical world that you did not choose. Of course, you weren't always conscious. You were caught in the gridlock or the loop of 3D Duality. This no longer has to apply to you.

In the past, through your collective Consciousness, your DNA, your Biology, and the conditioning of the Belief Systems, you were influenced to be less than Who You Are. You were influenced to fit in and to give up Your Power. Every space and time of your Beingness was inundated with limited Belief Systems. Whether rich or poor, 3D Duality is a gridlocked trap of being less, being a victim, and being controlled. There is always someone richer or poorer than you. Go figure! Your body of Consciousness has always been continually bombarded by this dense resonance of the Fear Programs. 3D Duality made you resonate to illness. **Illness is the resonance of 3D Duality.**

Most of your times, you are overwhelmed by 3D Duality. Though there are times of insightfulness, intuitive hits, and glimpses beyond, they are guaranteed not to last. If in the past you attempted to live your Truth, you were harmed or killed. Those times are so over!

This is why this book is being written. To explain to you how the 3D Duality System works *you*. *You* don't work *it*. You are embedded and imprinted with this resonance. Now you no longer have to resonate with it. The best aspect of this challenge is that you are the one in the driver's seat. You are the one In Charge of Your Life.

Always, your creativity was influenced by limitations. You were indoctrinated to the limited Belief Systems. You were indoctrinated to dance to 3D Duality's resonance. This is no longer viable unless you continue to agree to have limitations be viable for you. It's always up to you.

Look at the physical spinal issues. Broken back, fractured discs, crushed discs, fused discs, and bulging discs are the physical issues linked to the emotional issues. Consider when discs are removed. What viable information is being destroyed so you won't know what is going on in your continuum? Consider even deeper what you are ignoring or denying. Illness comes at a price that is exorbitant to the value of your life and lifestyle.

Here is how you access the information in your spinal column. Focus your Consciousness and awareness to a particular disc. Ask your Self, "What does it look like inside of it?"

Don't rush…you do this consciously. Don't go into an altered state. If you go into an altered state, you will NOT get clear information.

Whatever your description is – dark, cloudy, tight, constricted, etc. – focus on your description and consider it a space, a place, or a room. In this space or room, all the windows and doors are wide open and you cannot be stuck in there. Get in the "room". Ask your Self, "How old am I in the room? Is it this lifetime or another?"

Ask clear questions. The clearer and more direct the questions you ask your body, the clearer are the answers. You are requiring your body, as the Non-Emotional Observer (NEO), to get to the facts, to *see* what the experience is showing you, to keep what serves, and to release the rest. There is no sense hanging on to stuff that is not viable to a healthy, prosperous, creative life. Lessons, Karma, and Re-incarnation tarnation are so over!

Make the commitment to your Self. Be Total Acceptance and Unconditional Love to your Self. Be accepting of all your lifetimes and experiences. You did the best and worst you could with what you knew and did not know. It was mostly what you didn't know that caused the havoc. Be open to your Self.

You cannot change the past.
    The past is one second ago.
        You can change your future.
            The future is one second from now.

How you create in this moment creates all the futures in one second from each of your moments. Make your life count to you.

For those outside of you who support you in becoming fully conscious, thank them. For those who don't...Oh Well! They are still waiting to become their Selves.

Be your Self now and into all the nows of your futures. Don't hesitate.

What, where, and how you focus
your Consciousness
is Your Life

Chapter 10

WORDOLOGY IS YOUR BIOLOGY

**"What you say makes your day,
and what you say can make or break someone else's day."**

-Sherryism

Every word said to you and all the words you have spoken to your Self or to others throughout your time continuum are embedded and stored in your body. You are virtually a walking, talking dictionary of experiences gleaned through language, vocabulary, and words.

Your Cellular Memory is embedded with imprinted information from the second the sperm hits the egg and you are conceived. Much of the information imprinted and stored in your body has a direct connection to your parents. Some of the 3D Duality Programs influencing and affecting you and your life are derived from your parents.

Of course, in the contract you made with them, you wrote their Belief Systems into your script. What you like about your parents, you have cleared. What you don't like about your parents is what you are here to learn about your Self.

Your parents are vehicles for you to discover your Self when you are willing to detach from your emotional hooks and *see* that they are the perfect hosts for you to get through the old 3D Duality Programs. They were the primer for you.

Consider that all the words you speak on a daily basis come from the 3D Duality Programming. English has more "negative" words than "positive" words. What does that tell you about the programming? You have been taught and conditioned to remember the "bad" experiences. This is the re-living of traumatization. Believe it or not, you did have some great experiences. But you have been programmed to only thinky-thinky about the bad. Isn't that what Reality TV is all about? The negative, the bad, and the ugly!

How do the words, language, and vocabulary you speak affect and influence you in your daily life? How do the words you use affect you, your health, and how do they influence others? Does your vocabulary support you to have a great life? Is your vocabulary really yours, or is it simply a version of someone else's idea of you? Are you defined by someone else's version of you? These are pertinent questions to ask your Self.

Your words are the molecules and particles of your resonance. Your words are the sounds of your Consciousness. Your words emit the molecules and particles, no matter whether you can *see* or *feel* them or not, into your outside physical world. From the inside out, your outside world is created and manifested.

From your language, vocabulary, and words, the energy of your actions and behaviors are manifested into your actualized life. Your words set into motion what you manifest, even if the words are never spoken out loud.

Silent, withheld words can be louder than spoken words. The unspoken carry much more intensity. The reality of your life can be unproductive when this happens. When you swallow back your Truth, you internalize a huge amount of suppressed energy. You will eventually get sick and cause harm to your body.

Words are not "right" or "wrong". They are, however, either supportive of you or not. When your thinky-thinky, non-productive language is rolling around in your computer/brain and then is spoken out loud, the difficulties of living in a balanced manner are beyond challenging. You become drained and victimized by your Self. Life does not flow.

When you use language, vocabulary, and words coming from the resonance of your Heart, your life begins to resonate more clearly, more productively, and more joyously. This is not pie in the sky. This is how it works. *Your* Wordology Is Your Biology makes all the difference in *your* world.

Each day, millions, billions, trillions, and beyond that number of words are spoken around the world. The resonance of the words spoken affect not only you, but everyone and everything on this planet. The more the resonance of non-support and non-productivity is spoken, the more that non-supportive, non-productive resonance is produced. Be aware of how you take in and speak out *your* Wordology Is Your Biology.

What you say is how you live

Although you may not hear every spoken word, your body records and remembers the language. How you process the information is how you experience your life. Your body can reveal so much to you. Listen to your body.

Consider all the words, the different languages, and the different meanings you have spoken or not spoken throughout your time continuum. Your languages influenced your life. Good, bad, or indifferent is not the issue. The issue is…how did you allow the *Wordology* that *is* embedded in *your Biology* as your Cellular Memory affect you, your health, wealth, and life?

At whatever level of Consciousness these words became stored inside of you, they are embedded there. Sometimes you are unknowingly influenced, which can then affect your behaviors and actions. This just happens. The more conscious you are of your Self, your body, and the effects and affects and infects of the 3D Duality Fear Programs, the more aware you become of what words, language, and vocabulary to keep or release.

If there are words inappropriately affecting and influencing you, it is time to purge them out of your body from your Cellular Level of Consciousness. What no longer is of service to you no longer requires being stored in your body.

The more aware you are of words and how they can affect you, your health, wealth, and your life, the less emotional you become. Your emotional body and the emotional hooks to the past are not relevant to a happy, healthy life or lifestyle.

The Self-language you use every day says a lot about where you are and where you are going and from where you came. If the words don't serve you, it is time to let the Self-defeating language go.

As an exercise, write down the words you use when you talk about your Self. Are they supportive and affirming? Or, do the words you speak about your Self make you less?

When you speak your Self-language, what is the Self-message? When you speak about others who are in your life, what do your words say? If you speak "negatively", in Duality's terms, about others who you engage in your life, who are you really speaking about? Isn't it about you?

Who you judge is your Self. Ask your Self, "Why do I have people in my life that I speak so Duality-based negatively about?" You will be amazed at the answers you get from your Self-Talk.

Carefully consider the words, language, and vocabulary you use when you speak about your Self, your family, your friends, your co-workers, your associates, and particularly to the children in your life. The children don't even have to be yours. How do you impact those children?

You can make a difference in your own life by making a difference in others' lives. The difference is in your resonance as you express and speak, whether silently or out loud. More times than not, the silent words are more impacting than the spoken ones. Remember this, especially when you are silently berating your Self.

Now…make two separate lists. On one list, write down all the words, phrases, and sentences that support you. On the other list, write down the words, phrases, and sentences that make you feel less or not supported.

Then, ask your Self, "Who said these words to me?"

Where do you *feel* these words in your body? Where did you internalize them? Is there a correlation to illness or dis-ease in your body? All words are physical and impact the physicality of your body.

Here's another exercise to do:

Change:
Need(y) to ***Require***
Want(y) to ***Desire***

And know without doubt
YOU *Deserve* to have a great life.

Wanty-Needy is a very low-based resonance of 3D Duality's emotional hook for "love". **Wanty-needy is desperate for validation**, especially in 3D Duality's dynamics of love. Wanty-Needy is the Country Western song of dysfunctional love.

Require is pro-active. **Require** is defining. Wanty-Needy is wishy-washy.

Desire is the conscious art of siring or birthing your life. **Desire** is to birth what you **require**.

Deserve is of service to Self without being Selfish. When you absolutely know without doubt you **deserve** a great life, you have released the emotional hooks to the Self-Sacrifice, Suffering, and Martyr Programs. There is no joy or creativity as a Self-Sacrificing, Suffering Martyr, unless you love existing as a victim.

Remember, it is what you require, desire, and deserve. Wanty-Needy sucks!

Change your Consciousness, change your life. Change your words, change your world! Wordology Is Your Biology!

Chapter 11

PROFILES, BEHAVIORS, AND ROLES

**"The Label, the Profile inside of you,
has held you in confinement and in a repetitive loop."**

-Sherry Anshara

From the beginning of your life you are assigned a Profile which is infused with Behaviors and you become a Role. This is a formula of Duality to keep you from your own Power, which in turn affects and infects the way you process through your life's journey in a limited box, packaged under an assigned label to make sure you follow the Grid or matrix patterns of Karma, Lessons, and Re-incarnation.

This formula is a re-cycle bin of activity which can include this lifetime of repetitive involvements of relationships, both personal and professional, or your continuum of start-ups and do-overs again and again. It really doesn't matter the time, date, place, decade, century and/or gender. What matters is you have the embedded Belief Systems, the B.S. Duality Programs, keeping you stuck in the repetitive figure eight loop of infinity…

You slide from one side of this repetitive loop to another. Where the loops meet in the changing point could be described as a place of "death" or as a place of seeming change of venue in your current lifetime. Yet, the prognosis is the same. You are caught in a loop of repeated Profiles, Behaviors, and Roles. Time really has nothing to do with it.

Although it falsely and confusingly appears that time is the equation of the repeated loop, time is not the loop. Time is Duality's measurement of how you process your life or lives to supposedly have lessons, learn from them, and then move on. The Truth is you really don't move on or move forward. This loop is endless. When you are stuck in the Duality loop of Karma, Lessons, and Re-incarnation, nothing really changes for you.

Duality does not resonate to change. Duality only resonates to the repeated loop of infinity. Although Duality has an infinite number of scenes, backdrops, places, events, costumes/clothes, calendars, and ages and stages of life, the **Duality Programs are filled with the sameness of Profiles, Behaviors, and Roles.**

Well, how does this all work? It works you, that is how it works. You are embedded with all these limitations with the idea that you are supposed to struggle through life, you are supposed to sacrifice, get points to get to heaven, lose points to go to hell, and always be continually *wrong* about something. Who could get anything *right* in Duality? Oh, for sure there are moments when life appears to be working. Then an accident, an event, or a circumstance appears out of nowhere! Hmmm!

Where you are in the "nowhere" is the point where the loop begins to slide down into the emotional abyss of *wrong* from that part of the loop where you had been *right!* Remember, if it is so good, it can't be true or real.

Chapter 12

THEMES

**"If you would like the outside theme of your life to change,
then you have to change the theme
of what is going on inside of you…**

Is it really *your* theme park?"

-Sherry Anshara

In the 3rd Dimensional Duality Fear Programs of Judgment, Lack, and Take-Away, the figure eight infinity symbol is the perfect symbology for Karma, Lessons, and Re-incarnation of the re-do's! The dysfunctional perfection of this symbol of infinity is the repetitive traps you experience through this lifetime and other lifetimes in your continuum. As long as you stay trapped and emotionally hooked, you will continue to participate in this re-cycle bin of Profiles, Behaviors, and Roles in which you are caught.

In the Duality programs of *right* and *wrong* you can never achieve the conscious balance in your life or lives while caught up in the repeated cycles of Karma, Lessons, and Re-incarnation. When you are clearly conscious, you already comprehend that what you project out, you get back. When you are clearly conscious, there is no point or points to getting involved with the same old same old lessons or to re-incarnate them in this lifetime. When you clear these re-do programs, you do not have to repeat them in your next re-incarnations. This is what Ascension is…ascending your expansive, Non-Duality Consciousness to utilize your energy in creative, productive, and illuminating ways in *this* lifetime.

Ascension is actually physically grounding your expansive, Non-Duality Consciousness throughout your entire body. You don't have to keep dying in the pretense that you will ascend. How many deaths does it take to get "it", the "it" being Ascension? How's that program of Ascension working for you? Not so well! You keep coming back, ending up in the same old place. It's time to stop the Duality madness. You can do it!

Karma, Lessons, and Re-incarnation are actually the same Themes on your spreadsheet, disguised under different labels that result in the same dysfunctional Behaviors playing out your Roles with the same Profiles you have repeatedly drawn into your life and lives. There is the idea that you can come back with the same people, although in different Roles and genders. Great idea!

However, what if one or more of these individuals with whom you have participated in other lifetimes opt out? Now what? Well, what happens when a person does opt out of your life? You simply attract the Profile with which you resonate. If you resonate to dysfunction, the resultant Profiles and your Behavior are dysfunctional. Remember, resonance attracts resonance, whether it's Clear Consciousness *or* limited Belief Systems (the B.S. Programs).

Comprehend this... *You* write *your* script. And comprehend that not every lifetime will the same people return with you. They may avoid being cast in your current script. The Profile, however, is a different thing. The Profiles are what you know in Duality regardless of the time(s). Until you choose to opt out of Duality and get clearly conscious, you will get stuck. It is a Duality thing!

When you begin to Take Back Your Power, you absolutely *get it* that YOU are the one who cancels your Profiles, your Behaviors, and your Roles as you ascend your Self beyond the limitations and repetitions of the Duality Programs.

The moral to the Duality stories of the repetitive trauma-dramas is that you *see* objectively that Duality is a spreadsheet of Themes. The underlying Theme is, of course, FEAR.

Fear drives the Duality Themes. Fear propels you in Duality. Fear is the way of the Duality world. You are supposed to be afraid of your own Power. You are programmed to be afraid of success. It is never a fear of failure, although you can use failure as the *excuse* to not be success full or success filled.

Fear is the element of all the Themes. Let go of the Themes of Karma, Lessons, and Re-incarnation. Get out of the Fear-based Duality Theme Park. It is not fun.

The Themes:

Abandonment
Abused/Abuser
Disabling Enabler
Dismissed
Don't Fit In
Dysfunctional Labels
Dysfunctional Responsibilities
Entitlement
Have/Have-Not
Invisible
Judgment
Limited
Longing/Alone
Lot in Life
Non-Validation
Not Good Enough
Not Speaking Your Truth
Sabotage
Sacrifice/Suffering
Separation
Servitude/Slavery

Victim/Victimizer
etc., etc., etc.

and the Duality list of Themes goes on and on.

You can *see* how the Themes of Duality disempower you. They are constructed to keep you trapped in the Fear Programs. When you are emotionally stuck, you actually cannot *see* your way out of the trauma-dramas. Your eyesight is cloudy and you become blinded by the molecules of emotions that are physical, snotty, gelatinous, thick, icky, and sticky…you are getting the point.

When you clear these molecules of emotion, you actually *see* clearer. As you become the Non-Emotional Observer (NEO), you recognize how these Themes of Fear have affected and influenced your life in the most non-productive ways.

The Ways:

dysfunctional relationships
stress/illness
money issues
success issues
addictions
pretending
stuck in the past and/or future
fill in *your* blank_____

So, as you make the choice to be conscious, to embrace the release of Duality, and to activate your 13 Chakras, you exit the Duality Theme Park. You are in your Power and your life belongs to you.

Chapter 13

SELFISH, SELFLESS, OR CENTERED IN SELF?

"As long as you make someone or something outside of you more, you will always be LESS!"

-Sherryism

Have you ever been told to get centered and grounded or to be conscious of where you are, what you are doing, and what is happening in your life? Yet, how often do you get off-kilter or feel off balance and go out of body without being aware of it? You might have struggled through the day, the week, the month, and even the year.... for years!

Without judging your Self in any way, there are days when "stuff" happens and knocks you out of balance. Perhaps life is not happening the way you thought it was supposed to happen, and you get emotional and upset. Sometimes you can take "it", and sometimes you simply cannot. Your relationships may become stressful, and your business, job, or career can seem to be challenging without being fulfilling. Yes, it happens.

So, you find a way to cope. It can be by going out of body, getting sick, or escaping in some way... and sometimes that way is death!

The coping mechanism that you and your body have to contend with roars to your body's surface with behavior which can be described and judged from the outside as being Selfish, Self-centered, and only caring about you. Really, this is not the Truth. This coping behavior propels you into becoming the "survivor", and with all your energy you survive all the chaos.

Many times, this non-productive behavior pattern is repeated over and over again and becomes your way of life. It can make you sick. Survival issues can get expressed in your tissues as depression, anxiety, fibromyalgia, digestive problems, and the list goes on.

Being in the survival mode even once is caustic and energy-draining. Besides your health, the emotional survival resonance can affect and infect your wealth. When you are sick, isn't it a challenge to work? And your relationships become unhealthy and non-productive.

In this state of being overwhelmed, you can appear Selfish and egotistical. Remember, it is all about survival. The "survival of the fittest" mode is re-active and non-responsive to living in healthy and productive ways.

Sometimes, in order to survive another facet of this seemingly Selfish behavior, it turns into a Selfless pattern through Self-guilt, Self-shame, and Self-blame. So, in order to counteract being called Selfish or egotistically Self-absorbed or Self-centered, you may flip the switch and take the deeper dive of survival behavior into Self-sacrifice. You become Self-less.

What is Self-less? It is becoming a survivalist invisible Self. You are less! You begin to sacrifice your life for the so-called good of others.

This is *not* about assisting and being supportive of others. This is about sacrificing your life as the non-entity person who absorbs the problems and issues of others in your life. Their lives become more important than yours. You become, again and again, LESS… while those around you are MORE!

The more you give into this sacrifice mode, the more you become less. Your life revolves around someone else outside of you, no matter whether this relationship is beneficial to you or not. You seek validation for your "good work" without real concern for your Self. You are invisible to your Self and invisible even to those for whom you are sacrificing your life. They expect you to be less because you make your Self less.

**"How you are treated
is how you give people permission to treat you!"**

-Sherryism

Being Selfish and Self-Less does not support you, your life, your relationships, or anything about your life to be healthy in any way. They are both about sacrificing your Self in one way or another. **Selfish is pushing people away in your life. Self-Less is diminishing your Self with people in your life.** In both cases, it is sacrificing your Self!

What is Centered in Self? Centered in Self is being balanced, focused, directed, and clear about you. You are not hooked emotionally to any past experiences, situations, or events. **You are completely in the moment.** You realize with "real eyes" that you are the Conscious Creator of your life and of all your experiences. Being Centered in Self is neither Selfish nor Self-Less in any aspects of your life.

**"Knowing at my deepest knowing,
I cannot change the past.**

**The past is one second ago,
and the future is one second from now.**

**And I change my future by not dragging my past forward
where it no longer serves me."**

- Sherryism

Here is the point… Being Centered in Self is being Power Full and Power Filled!

FORCE is the Selfish You trying, trying, and trying to force someone to see it your way.

Self-Less is you giving up your Power to someone else, some group, and/or some way that forces you to be or do something that does not serve you. You give in to be LESS for "them", whomever he, she, or they are!

Being Centered in Self is YOU determining how *your* life is every moment in every day in a kind, loving way. Being Centered in Self is Heart-based.

Remember…your Heart is your most expansive resonance in your body. Being Centered in your Heart-based Self, you become UNLIMITED in how you create, participate, and how you are involved in your life.

Being Centered in Self is creating and having loving relationships without the traumas and the dramas. Being Centered in Self supports both your personal and professional life to be FULL filled.

Being Centered in Your Self is YOU completely comprehending that you are the Creator of your own life.

In this stance, people know where you stand. This does not mean you are hard or inflexible. It means that you are loving, flexible, accepting, and involved in all that you are being and doing. Your beingness naturally creates your doingness!

When you are Centered in Self, there are no reasons to have regret, guilt, or shame about anything.

**"You did the best and worst you could
with what you knew and didn't know.**

And it is mostly what you didn't know at that time.

Don't hold on to the past!"

- Sherryism

Being Centered in Self is freeing. In this state of beingness, you are being authentic. You never have to explain your Self, and you know who you are.

Is this a process? Of course, Rome was not built in a day, but it got built. And remember, it also got destroyed many times because of the Selfishness and Self-Lessness of whomever!

Being Centered in Self is a progressive process of learning about your Self minus the judgment. As you recognize how you are participating in life, you can now choose how you participate or not, without *wronging* or judging anyone else. You are living and creating in your own TRUTH!

What is your Truth? Your Truth is guided by your Heart. It is how you *feel*. It is not what you thinky-thinky of your Selfish and Self-Less ways, which are based on always surviving and sacrificing your Self.

Being Centered in Self is never having to repeat any relationship, situation, or event ever again that never did serve you. Being Centered in Self is definitely being in charge of your life! You do NOT have to explain or excuse your Self as to how or why you created your life to anyone. Why? Because you are Heart-centered…first for your Self and then for others! You are ALIVE, no longer surviving.

Each moment, each day, each week, each month, and each year belong to you. They provide you with opportunities to experience life as you create the experiences you are choosing to experience in your life. This is being Centered in Self... in full purposes, in full participation in every way... personally and professionally.

Embrace your Centeredness. Embrace your Purposes. Embrace your Fullness of Life...Centered in your Self Beingness!

Chapter 14

BELOW NO MORE!

"Changes come from the inside when you let go of the outside."

-Sherryism

Have you ever considered the idea of the word BELOW? Through all the religious, metaphysical, governmental, military, educational, corporate, professional, and personal/family paradigms, there is this word that defines a pecking order or placement of an individual or a group. You are taught that god, the angels, the avatars, the masters, the leaders, and even aliens are above you and that you are below.

Look carefully at this word, BELOW. *Feel* carefully how the impact of this word affects and influences you on a daily basis or even in your time continuum. Even if you are royalty, a king or queen or leader of a country, there is always the Godhead above you! You are always programmed or taught to "look up" and for you to BE-LOW someone, or that something outside of you knows more, is smarter, wiser, and better than you. You are never shown how to go inside your Self to connect to the Godness within you.

According to Duality's Belief Systems, if you consider your Self first, you are viewed as Selfish because you "should" be Selfless. This B.S. sets you up to be LESS. This does NOT make any sense.

When the plane is going down, the pilot says, "Take the oxygen first so you can assist others." This is not Selfish.

This is the empowerment of being Centered in your own Self, empowered to empower others to live!

When you are Centered in Self, you are in connection with your own Self first, and you are then able to connect with others. This is service, not sacrifice. This is the resonance of everyone being connected together. By being Centered in Self, you are truly of service to all, without judgment, for you are projecting the **resonance of connectedness**.

So, how could anyone be less, including you? When you connect to your Self beyond the less-than programming of Duality by first being the Non-Emotional Observer (NEO) and detaching from the emotional/physical hooks of the past trauma-dramas, you begin to look and *feel* inside of you. Inside of you is where you find the Godness within that connects you to the Allness of you and everyone and everything. You never have to BE-LOW again.

Embrace YOUR GREATNESS!

Chapter 15

CHILDREN OF THE SHIFT

"Newness is a state of being."

-Sherry Anshara

The reason I am so passionate and committed about what I do is because of the Millennials and all the New Generations to come. I am creating a legacy for you and for them and for everyone who chooses to live free and unlimited and NOT restricted by the Duality Belief Systems…the B.S. Fear Programs…ever again!

The "New Kids on the Block" are the children of the Shift out of Duality. These brilliant Souls in human form are the future from this moment going forward in the Non-Duality time continuum. This is freedom. The children of the Shift are creating this freedom courageously and bravely.

When you stay in the 3D Duality Belief Systems, then the future is the same as the past...recreate, recreate, recreate war, prejudice, and even hatred.

The old paradigm of 3D Duality does not fit the Consciousness and energetic matrix of these new children. They are challenged by the 3D Duality Belief Systems for they cannot live fully and vibrantly in this dense resonance. This is why the medical and educational systems are drugging them into a false compliance.

These children are different. You bet they are. They are here to teach us so much. Yet, if they are drugged, stuffed with chemicals, and stuffed with the old paradigm of Judgment, Lack, and Take-Away, they will not be able to share their new brilliance. Nor will they be able to share what they know beyond this paradigm of limitation.

You can call these children all the labels…crystal, indigo, or rainbow. These are just labels and tags. Don't label these children. Don't tag them with limitations.

Let's recognize that they are more conscious and that they are the teachers who have come to support the people of this planet to get conscious. They are not here to be probed, studied, or examined for your pleasure or scientific research. They are here to participate with all of us to raise the resonance on this planet.

Perhaps in the metaphoric sense, they are the Christed Consciousness who bring the 1000 years of light. Let's not screw these kids up with our programs. Enough of 3D Duality!

When they are drugged, slugged, and forced into the 3D Duality box of illusions that all the previous generations have existed through, it won't work for them. The high rate of suicide and illness is what they are creating to leave this resonance of limitation, control, and manipulation. They take one look at this B.S. and say, "I am out of here."

Duality is the resonance of opposition

This is the time to give Clear Consciousness an opportunity. This is our opportunity. Listen to these children. Let's stop ingraining them with out-dated information. They are ahead of the 3D Duality Game. Don't push them onto a game board that bores them to death, literally and figuratively.

Adults, Wake Up! These children are more aware, more connected, and have so much more to teach us.

Be the guide, whether as a parent, an educator, a relative, or a stranger. Don't be afraid to let your own limited Belief Systems go, no matter what your background is...religious, political, ethnic, race, color, or creed. These are just the 3D Duality identifications. These programs are not who you are. They are definitely not who these new children are.

Embrace the newness these children bring to this planet. Embrace getting conscious your Self!

These children are the newness! They are the everyday connection to the Quantum Field. They are vibrating and resonating to new heights of Consciousness. These children are the gift that keeps on giving if you and everyone provide the environment for them to be who they are.

3D Duality does not provide an environment for them to express their creativity. 3D Duality is only for the few and the privileged, not for the masses to excel. The masses are the individuals who did not achieve their individuality. The masses have to fit into the 3D Duality box.

These children don't fit and they never will fit. Their Consciousness is the light that leads the way out of the box for everyone!

If you are blessed with one of these children in your life, support them to be who they are. Don't hand them over to the systems that will only box them in, limit them, and attempt to make them over in the image of 3D Duality.

If ever there is a time on this planet or in this Universe and Multi-verse to get conscious and rise above the limitations of this old 7 Chakra System, the time is now. Don't put them in boxes physically and metaphorically just to satisfy your Childish Adult Ego. Don't make them over. Don't work them over to fit into a paradigm that doesn't even fit this planet anymore or this limited Universe for that matter.

**"In Duality, there are boxes and labels.
They are all realities.**

**In Truth, there are no boxes or labels…
You are REAL."**

-Sherryism

Open the Duality boxes, let these children out, erase the labels, let them breathe, and *listen* to them. Listen with your Heart and with your whole body.

These children resonate with the Truth. They have a lot to share. Who knows what marvels of technology, what new ideas, what creative ways they have to create a better place to live?

Are you willing to get out of your own 3D Duality box and embrace the Shift of Consciousness on this planet from 3D Duality limitation to unlimitedness? Potentials and possibilities mean nothing until you implement and then manifest them. So, let's together create, implement, manifest, and actualize a New Earth. Let the New Children of the Shift lead the way. Let's guide them, embrace them, and support them. Never put them into the Duality boxes of limitations. Everyone deserves better than that!

The time is becoming for all of us to live Multi-versally and Multi-Dimensionally. Thank you, New Kids on the Block!

A Message to Today's Generation

by Aspen Cline

a 12-year-old "New Kid on the Block"

You have a choice
Happy or sad
Choose how you feel
Will you later feel the same as you did
About the choice you made

What will your day turn into
Which option will you choose
Glad or gloomy
The choice is up to you

You chose to be sad
Now you resemble someone
Someone not like you
But remember when things aren't the same
The only person who made that choice was you

You chose to be happy
You are the best you
Smiles and laughs are shared
But you let a single word get to you
You let it pull you back in

Sadness once again fills your body
You again aren't you
You chose to let it bother you
Please explain why
Why did you choose to let it affect you

Learn to laugh it off
Learn to take a joke
Don't let the other get to you

Because their happiness is a hoax

They don't know what to do
They keep it all in
Slowly emotion seeps out
Turning into unnecessary anger

It's them who are the fools
But please
Don't let your brain be your bully
Telling you lies
It doesn't matter how you look
You should be comfortable in your own body

Chapter 16

WHAT IS THE POINT OF HEALING?

**"If you are searching for your Self, the search is over.
Look inside, not outside of you.
That's how you initiate healing."**

-Sherry Anshara

In Duality, you are always healing something, whatever that something is. An illness, a disease, an addiction, a relationship, a boo-boo, and the list goes on… There are so many ideas, methods, processes, books, rituals, and experts on how to heal something or other in your body or your life. There are so many things to heal in the Duality human body that it is impossible to be completely healed. This sets you up for the re-creation process.

What does this mean? It means there is always something in your body and in your life that you have to heal in Duality. Even death does not stop the healing process because you have to come back in another body, dragging your Duality Cellular Memory along with you as "baggage" from *other* lifetimes. You are continuously continuing to "work" on something, which is not a 9-5 job. You even say, "I am a work in progress."

Now consider this, in Duality, with the idea of healing, where is the progress? Duality is a process. It's a repeatable process. So, where's the progress?

Whether you stub your toe, cut your finger, get sick from something, or become terminally ill, each genre must have a healing modality to go along with it. Whether it's a band-aid, a chemical, a product, or cutting something out of you, in Duality, healing always has an aftermath. The aftermath is always SURVIVAL.

Where is the health and thriving in survival? There isn't anything optimal in survival. In survival, there can also be the factor of re-creating the illness, i.e. cancer, addiction, repeated dysfunctional relationships, or whatever, in this lifetime or from another time frame.

There are so many caveats to healing, and all the caveats come from external sources. The best resource for healing anything is YOU. After all, you created it in the first place. Remember, you are the one who wrote the script. So, you have prequels and you have sequels.

In Duality, the Belief System is that healing must take a long time and you must suffer and you must age. This is total B.S.! What happens if you don't suffer? You won't have a story to tell?!!

The more you stay stuck in the story, the more difficult your challenge is to heal. What you are doing every time you tell and re-tell the story of illness, dysfunction, or suffering is keeping your Self stuck in the resonance of your story and stuck in the resonance of your illness. Do you ever wonder why it's a challenge to heal? Stop wondering.

> **"Nonsense is the absence of sense.**
> **This is Duality…No sense!"**
>
> *-Sherryism*

Healing can never take place through the brain. **Self-healing must begin with YOU connecting to your body.**

For example, pain is the body's attempt to get your attention. And what is the protocol? Ignore the pain, cover up the pain, go unconscious about the pain, and look for something outside of your Self to release the pain.

The body can't speak through words. It speaks through pain. When you connect to the pain and *listen* through your Heart, your body can tell you what is going on. The pain in your body is the manifestation in whatever form the illness is. **The pain is the voice at the origination point of the physical and emotional trauma. When you ignore the pain, you are ignoring your Self.**

So, connect to the origination point of your pain. Your body knows. Place your Self in the position of the Non-Emotional Observer, no matter what your age or stage is, and observe the dynamics being played out in that time frame and *see* your Self and anyone else involved.

At this point of your observation, from a past time that can never be changed, you realize with *real-eyes* that no matter what happened unconsciously, you created the experience or experiences. Without judgment, blame, shame, or guilt, or any emotional attachment, you are giving your Self the opportunity to physically and emotionally remove and release the trauma and the drama from your body.

In metaphysics, it's called the light body; in medicine, it could be determined as an origination point of healing; in functional medicine, it could be called psycho-neuroimmunology. In everyday life, it could be called "something happened" that made you better.

The Truth is you have begun to Take Back Your Power. By recognizing and accepting you cannot change the past, you have changed your present moment. Healing at your Cellular, Molecular, Particle, and Sub-Atomic Levels has begun. You changed the origination point of the trauma-drama, the illness, the dysfunction, the addiction, the abuse, or whatever the label is into a current moment of Taking Back Your Power. You are beginning the progressive process of healing your Self for Real. Healing does NOT have to take a long time.

It's so interesting when people say, healing means, "I got it". Got what? *It* can be a contraction in Duality for "I tried but *it* didn't work."

In Non-Duality, the *IT*, without the confines and boxes of Duality, is your **Inner Truth**. When you got *IT* and you are clear, you got connected to your **Inner Truth**. And your Truth sets you free. When you connect to your **Inner Truth**, you can connect at your deepest core to your Cellular information, which is *in-form-at-your ion* or Cellular Level of Consciousness.

Examples of the Duality emotional physical core of the issues of illness, disease, and dysfunction include:

- **Addiction** is seeking validation; it's desperation for connectedness
- **Anxiety** is unrealistic expectations
- **Arthritis** is rigid Belief Systems
- **Asthma** is can't breathe into life
- **Back aches**
  Lower back – 1st Chakra limited Belief Systems
  Mid back – Solar Plexus victim
  Upper back – broken Heart
- **Cancer** is eating your Self up alive
- **Chronic fatigue** is sick and tired of being sick and tired
- **Chronic pain** is life is painful
- **Depression** is deepest disappointment
- **Diabetes** is life is sour

- **Fibromyalgia** is rigid Belief Systems everywhere in your body
- **Headaches/Migraines** are a 1st Chakra issue of Belief Systems, your head is up your 1st Chakra or someone else's 1st Chakra
- **Irritable Bowel Syndrome** is I.B.S. my Self
- **Knee issues** are cut off at the knees
- **Neck/throat/thyroid issues** are not speaking your Truth
- **Spine injuries** are Akashic Record time continuum issues
- **Numbness** is can't *feel*, no connection to your body
- And the list goes on…

**Pulling your head out of your 1st Chakra
is the first step in *seeing* how limited
the Belief System Programs are**

The band of "sickness vs. healing" is Duality. You can't heal unless you're sick! So, can healing be a Duality con job? Without sickness, there can be no genre of healing.

Heal your Body, your Self, and your Life of Duality by **Taking Back Your Power**…and **Becoming YOU**…in this lifetime…or Not!

Beyond Duality…there is no reason to heal anything.

Chapter 17

BECOMING A REAL HUMAN

Wow... Aren't we human already? Hmmm... So, what does it really mean to be a Real Human?

Do Real Humans...

> Kill each other? – *We came here to live our lives creatively and productively.*

> Abuse each other? – *We came here to love and accept each other unconditionally.*

> Abuse animals? – *Animals are sentient beings who came here to live out their lives.*

> Abuse children? – *This is not normal; it is an aberration of Duality!*

> Abuse the planet? – *How many people comprehend this Earth is Alive?*

What do all of these behaviors have in common? They do NOT honor life! These behaviors are NOT "humane". Not blaming, shaming, or judging anyone...these are the facts of what can happen when the Duality Fear Programs of Judgment, Lack and Take-Away separate all humans from each other. This is what happens when *you* separate *your* Self from *your* Self from the inside out. The Duality Programs of Fear are insidious and impact and infect everyone from the Cellular Level within the human body.

Your CLEAR Cellular Memory resonates to LIFE...and to REAL connections through Total Acceptance and Unconditional Love.

This is not at all a woo-woo concept that exists up in the ethers through out-of-body experiences. Becoming a REAL Human means to rise above Duality's density, conflict, and war, which are not viable for life on this planet. You free your Self from Duality's force from *your* Cellular Level.

You are a Sovereign Being! You have sovereignty within your Self and you are sovereign over your own life. There is no reason or reasons to be controlled and manipulated by any limited Belief System any longer. Duality's pain, suffering, and sacrifice programs are endless in their variations. However, at the core, it is the same resonance that does NOT honor your life or any form of life.

Duality is Survival

It is NOT Life

The REAL Human Being honors his or her own life *first*, and then honors all forms of life on this planet, including the planet itself. So, could becoming a REAL Human be the meaning of creating Heaven on Earth? For sure! To become a REAL Galactic Human is for everyone to take back his and her Power from all the forms of Duality's repetitious recycle bin of dead existence.

Becoming a REAL Human is to experience the fullness of Life through Heartness, Allness, and Connectedness.

THIS IS THE MOMENT. Be willing. Be the one person who makes the difference in your own life as you *shift* your resonance into TAKING BACK YOUR POWER. You then naturally and influentially radiate the newness resonance of the Freed REAL Human within you. From your inside out, Duality Program-FREE, you create, implement, manifest, and actualize the GODNESS Who You Are.

From your individual Me-Power, joined with the collective Me-Power of everyone, together we become REAL Humans. This is ALLNESS... the Multi-Dimensional ALLNESS of Clear Consciousness. ALLNESS honors LIFE. Duality's Separation Programs destroy life to recycle it again and again.

Ascension for the REAL Human is to ascend in this Human Body which you have chosen in this lifetime. To become a REAL Human is a Clear Conscious CHOICE.

You do not have to "get a life". You ARE Life. Honor *everything* about YOU. And then make the choice! Your life is in the palms of your hands.

As you make your clear choice to exit the Fear Programs of Duality, you are the resonance which productively and honorably resonates to others as a Paradigm Shifter.

You are the resonance of the **Involved Conscious Evolutionary Revolutionary**. Your resonance of becoming a REAL HUMAN lights the way for others to connect to their REALNESS.

Remember... Light is information, and fear is simply lack of information.

Congratulations!

You are becoming You...

"Your Authentic Self is...
LIFE itself."

Sherry Anshara

TESTIMONIALS

"I first heard of Sherry Anshara in the summer of 2013, from a friend who had done one of her workshops, which profoundly shifted her relationship to life. Subsequently, I had a chance to do a workshop with her in the fall of 2014, when I was in Phoenix after an Integrative Cancer Symposium that I had helped to organize there. I brought along a group of 5 physicians (and 1 veterinarian) without really knowing what to expect. The workshop was profound for all concerned, as we learned how to view ourselves and the events that were unfolding in our lives from the viewpoint of the 'non-emotional observer', as well as to become aware of, and begin to manipulate subtle energies in and around each other's bodies, as well as those in the 'ordinary' reality around us, which with Sherry's guidance, proved to be an extraordinary reality that we just hadn't fully noticed before.

"I have had occasion to be the beneficiary of Sherry's 'hands on' energy healing work several times, and though this wasn't new to me, she certainly is the most gifted healer I have experienced in my life. Having dealt with chronic headaches off and on for much of my adult life, the worst of which being triggered by caffeine withdrawal, I found that I could stay at Sherry's home for 3-5 days and abruptly stop caffeine, without experiencing any headache whatsoever, with Sherry giving me energy healing sessions several times a day. I have also seen her create truly amazing resolutions of an entire spectrum of human suffering, across the entire spectrum of human ages, from young children to very elderly individuals. Often she has gone to hospitals when friends were critically ill, and changed seemingly hopeless prognoses for recovery, without taking any credit for it.

"Though it's likely that no one else will ever be as good at Anshara Method healing as Sherry is, it is clear that it is a teachable skill, and quite a few people who have studied with her have become very proficient at it. A unique blend of psychotherapy, teaching, and energy medicine, Sherry's teachings are valuable to all for use in their everyday life, for work with clients, and to medical and other health professionals, both at a personal and professional level."

Dwight McKee, MD, CNS, ABIHM

"Sherry has assisted over 500 of my patients with various physical health issues including stress, anxiety, depression, pain and digestive disorders. Her workshops are unique because not only can you get to the root cause quickly but long-standing issues can often be resolved when other modalities have failed."

Anup Kanodia, MD/MPH

"Sherry Anshara has written a number of excellent books, two of which are my favorites - *The Age of Inheritance: The Activation of the 13 Chakras* and *The Intelligence Code*. Her classes and writings help us to think "out of the box" and expand our awareness and consciousness considerably. I have personally had a number of her amazing healings from her, but one healing in particular stands out from all the rest. While we were visiting in Colorado this summer, a malfunctioning folding stool we used to get into our RV broke into a dozen pieces and threw me backwards on the back of my head, back and sacrum. The pain was excruciating and I literally saw stars and colors. We had to cut our vacation short and drove back to Phoenix where I got X-rays and treatment for a displaced coccyx (tailbone) and various injuries. Even with medical treatment the pain was intense and on-going for days. I tried everything but the pain continued. Sherry called and asked me if I would like her to do a distance healing on me while I slept. The next morning, I woke up pain free for the first time in weeks. I have continued to be pain free. Sherry was able to do her "magic" not only at a distance but also while I slept. Besides being a really great healing channel, Sherry has one of the most warm and delightful personalities of anyone you will ever meet. You feel better just being around her - and when she does a specific healing treatment, the results are nothing short of miraculous.

"She writes with the same charisma and spirit that she has in person. Her books are on-going teaching tools to use all your life. Can't wait to read the next book she writes."

Rev. Anne Puryear, Vice-President, The Logos Center
Author of *Stephen Lives!* and *Messages from God*

"I met Sherry Anshara on a 105-degree afternoon in May of 2009.

"Being a New England girl, the scorching heat of Scottsdale, Arizona almost dropped me to my knees on that walk from my hotel to her classroom. However, it was to be one of the very best days of my life. And, it was also my birthday.

"During that first class, I sat close to the door just in case I melted down into a dissociative PTSD episode and required a quick exit. I also feared if I were to speak up, all my trauma tales would fall out of my mouth and I would regret it.

"None of that happened. In fact, that first experience with Sherry was so powerful in my healing journey, five months later, I flew back across the country to take the continuing class session. I have been back twice since and continue to follow the Anshara Method in my daily life intentions.

"Understanding that the power of healing lies within self-love and validation was life changing. I had been living in the limiting beliefs of my past stories and the fear of my future expectations based on those stories. Staying stuck kept me in that vulnerable victim vibration. And the Anshara Method taught me that I was the one choosing to stay there. Or not.

"The birthday gift I gave myself on that scorching hot day in 2009 seemed to be a purification of sorts. Now, gone are the old patterns of dis-empowering myself. I have healed my truth and detoxed all that was not serving me in my life journey.

"I am grateful beyond words for Sherry and the Anshara Method. As Sherry says, it's molecule rattling. And that it is...in the most wondrous of ways."

Nancy Shappell
Author of - *A Voice in the Tide: How I Spoke My Truth in the Undertow of Denial and Self-Blame*

"At the core of human existence is soul, a pure, unchangeable energy. Layers of personality characteristics, attitudes, lessons learned, emotions and experiences wrap the soul with many threads. The Anshara Method allows a person to understand the ways your threads join to other humans and beliefs to become bands of energy. Seeing the energies of threads and bands allows for deep understanding of self, beliefs and humanity as a whole. This I believe, for I have experienced how the Anshara Method worked for me."

Mary L. Holden
editor, writer, and co-founder of new72media

"I had hit rock bottom. My husband had walked out on me and my 2-year-old son after 9 years together and having spent the last 12+ months trying for another baby. My stomach was black from all of the IVF shots and my hormones were all over the place. As I sat sobbing in front of my fertility doctor explaining why we had to stop treatments, he asked me what my beliefs where and what I was open to spiritually, and very gently suggested that I meet with a woman by the name of Sherry Anshara.

"I called Sherry and left a voicemail as soon as I left his office, and soon afterward, I received a call from the most cheerful voice and secured the first available appointment. I'm not going to repeat what we covered in our session, but I will tell you that I walked into her office a sobbing, blubbering mess, and I walked out feeling like the weight of the world had been lifted from my shoulders and viewed my divorce in an entirely different way. I was so emotionally sound and resolved with it, I actually had people tell me that they were "concerned" because I wasn't responding to the trauma of divorce "appropriately". This is what Sherry calls a "belief system", aka "B.S.".

"Nearly a year after my first meeting with Sherry, I started to date a man and recommend that he see Sherry as well. He had also hit rock bottom. Had lost his business and all of his financial resources was used by a woman to gain U.S. citizenship, and had spent years working on business deals that never seemed to cross the finish line and had been reduced from All-American baseball player and multi-millionaire working with the Chinese government to driving for Uber. During this time, he and I had invented a product but couldn't seem to get it off the ground with any investment. Once he started seeing Sherry regularly, things in his life started to change for the better. In fact, the very night after he and I had attended Sherry's weekend seminar, he was driving for Uber and picked up a man from the airport. They drove for over 45 minutes, and all the while my boyfriend told the man about the product we invented. Less than two months later, this man became our first investor – and not only was he our first investor, he assisted us in closing our first round of funding in ten days! To celebrate, we were invited to his and his wife's home where we met all of the other first round investors face to face. To our utter shock and amazement, through the course of lighthearted conversation, we learned that EVERY. PERSON. IN. THAT. ROOM. knew of Sherry and none of us were aware of it until that very moment. Most would think to cue the Twilight Zone theme song right then, but this wasn't a coincidence. This meeting was created and manifested by all involved.

"My boyfriend and I are now married, and our product has been picked up by one of the largest retailers in the world and many others within the past six months of business. My husband was also able to secure a high-profile position with another company and is the sole provider for our family while I grow our business. We are living proof that the Anshara Method WORKS. We are so grateful for Sherry's assistance; she is a tremendous part of our lives, and we love her dearly!"

Donna McReynolds-Sanchez
Co-Founder and Co-Inventor of CUP-O Protein

"Seeing is believing! In my decades of nursing practice in behavioral health I have never witnessed the immediate results I observed with the Anshara Method. It is an incredible mind and body experience yielding a release of mental, emotional and physical barriers. The result is astonishing!"

Victoria Booth, MSN RN

"Sherry Anshara is one of the most loving, kind and spiritual people that I had the pleasure and honor of meeting. I value and appreciate her unique healing and intuitive abilities to support people in their emotional, physical and spiritual healing. Sherry created a holistic intervention approach that unlocks old emotional and psychological trauma and belief systems that interfere with one's health, happiness and well-being. Her Anshara Method transforms human potential for self-healing and promotes living a productive and fulfilling life. As a healthcare professional, I always search for the most effective methods of preventing and healing dis-ease. I attended Sherry's 3-day workshop several years ago and felt a shift in my views and self-healing abilities. I am so grateful that I met this amazingly talented person, Sherry Anshara. Thank you for all you do!"

Inna Olshansky, OTD, OTR/L

"In Sherry's classes, we begin to know our Self. And in doing so, we begin to fall in love with our Self."

Myrna Solano

"Everybody, as soon as they're born, requires to see Sherry Anshara!"

Andrea Roman

"You are my life preserver Sherry. You brought me out of the depths of depression and into the light. All I have to do is think of you and all that you taught me comes to surface. I am so thankful to have you as my dear friend."

Carole Riddell

"Sherry Anshara always states that these five words mean the same thing... Emotional, Mental, Physical, Spiritual and Financial... because what is the cost to you to not be healthy in all these areas... Everyone likes to buttonhole Sherry Anshara that she does "Healing Work"... she does not... what she does is assist, support and guide you to remove the limited Belief Systems, the B.S. that may be limiting you in any of these areas…

"Sherry, this is wonderful! Reading your book "The Age of Inheritance" again, the book that you gift to everyone in the Intuitive Powers course… Seeing where the Duality Belief Systems, the B.S. of Judgment, Lack & Take Away, are holding Business owners and Businesses down. Abundance while still in Duality is temporary due to the abundance of lack which says you do not deserve it! Self-fulfilling, people prove and validate they really didn't deserve the 'good thing.' Wow, this is heavy. All the Law of Attraction, Abundance, and Wealth programs that are out there are mostly head-games, or programming the computer/brain and subconscious. It's really an illusion, yes, also a TRAP to KEEP the people down, to not succeed or 'get too big for your britches.' So, you can't be Empowered. If you were, you would not require a "Master" to tell you…so you unconsciously tell Your Self…"see I (computer/brain) told you it wouldn't work!!" This is depressing for the whole human race. I feel like crying as I see how I and most everyone has been sucked up into this master/slave program…all the opportunities missed. Continuing year after year NEVER to SEE your own TRUTH! Sherry Anshara teaches you how to use the tools of Energy in and for your Business…and by the way, personal and professional are the same!"

Marlene Allen

"A few years ago, I had the privilege of reading *The Age of Inheritance: The Activation of the 13 Chakras*, which is the first incarnation of this book, *Take Back Your Power: You Becoming You*. The first book was a game changer for me as I was beginning a wondrous journey of awakening. The information I gained from it provided a platform upon which I built a new life filled with profound changes. In this newest iteration, this book promises the reader an even more power-packed download of how to stand confidently in your power and truly become who you were always meant to be. It will change your life."

Tom Hamblin

"I cannot begin to describe the profound impact that working with Sherry has had on my life. The multi-verse had 'dropped' information about Sherry in my path several times before I came to see her. After 'traditional' medicine failed to find answers for an acute medical crisis, I chose to take the hints that the multi-verse provided and see Sherry. After the first one-hour treatment, the results and improvement were visibly and dramatically noticeable.

"I have continued to see Sherry in private sessions and in classes over the last two and a half years and gotten to the core of the duality programs I had been running that had been keeping me chronically ill for many years. And the results have been measurable. For example, as I found my voice to speak my truth, lab tests have shown a steady improvement in my thyroid levels and I am almost completely weaned off thyroid medication. As I became the non-emotional observer, I stopped giving away my power to others and my need for pain medication, to manage chronic pain, is almost non-existent. Even in the face of adversity, I have learned to respond from my truth. I walk my walk. I talk my talk. With Sherry's assistance, I have taken back my power."

Tanya Hall

"I have been blessed and grateful to know Sherry Anshara for 12 years. She is an inspiration to not only me, but everyone that meets with her and witnesses the positive changes that occur with Sherry's "energy" treatment. She has you tap into your body and I have, personally, had the honor to be involved with Sherry's weekend seminars. They are "life-changing" for so many people. I always recommend Sherry to whoever is experiencing any type of difficulty in their life because Sherry can "assist" anyone with any issue. She has empowered so many to take back their lives…

"The Anshara Method is the perfect name for Sherry… Because, after all, it is her "method"… There is no one else like Sherry… She is a blessing to so many people and she has changed lives with her "method"…"

Candy Kaiser

"As we live on this planet it's challenging being You! We are all born with intuition and that inner knowingness. However, with societal programs and belief systems our gifts are put to sleep. Thanks to Sherry's method that assists you to wake your gifts up and teach you how to use them on daily basis, you can be your Authentic Self and live a fulfilled life in every way.

"Thank you, Sherry, for being here and bringing the Truth to life."

Julia Ismailova

"I am so thankful for Sherry and all she has assisted me and my brother with. With her, I have taken back the control of my life, my health, and my future. I have left limitations and harmful belief systems in the past. In just 12 short hours, I was able to fly across the country to attend one of Sherry's classes. This is something I previously thought I would never be able to do because of a diagnosis of Crohn's Disease. However, I shed these limiting belief systems and now life is new and so exciting! I am having deeper connections and better relationships with family members, friends, and even people I have just met! Seeing this happen in my brother as well after a short 4 hours with Sherry is amazing! To live in heartness and allness and connectedness is something everyone deserves. The experiences and opportunities created from this are truly spiritual. To me, this is what life is about...to be living in the present moment for the experiences that you create. Sherry gave me the information and tools to do that and I will never be able to thank her enough!"

With gratitude and love, Thomas Smith
(millennial)

"What I would like for you to know is that your article [*Selfish, Selfless, or Centered in Self?*] reminded me of a time in my life when I literally felt like I was invisible, where I could move through a crowd of people and see everyone else but felt that no one was seeing me. It was as if everyone else mattered except me. I felt like I was a spectator in life, not a participant. I felt like everyone else's needs and opinions were more important than my own, and to that end I spent most of my life giving to others and not to myself. I had depleted myself to the point of virtual "invisibility".

"Utilizing your tools helped me to "awaken" from the individual and cultural "programming" that had been dominating my belief systems and influencing my life actions. With a renewed "self-awareness", I was able to see myself in the overall scheme of life/truth of the universe rather than through the illusion of life that I had been living. I felt like the movie character Neo who chose to swallow the red pill and was then disconnected from The Matrix and awakened to true reality. Self-awareness/elevated consciousness helped me to better understand life and my purpose in it, that I am a co-creator of it and that I DO matter (everyone does). These were ABSOLUTELY LIFE-CHANGING REVELATIONS to me! And, of course, I never felt invisible again."

Gary Fuller

GLOSSARY

Agreements: Agreements are conscious partnerships. Cancel all the Contracts! They are inflexible and are basically trauma-dramas (he said, she said, they said, somebody said…but no one is *listening*). Instead, make agreeable Agreements that you can change. They are flexible, supportive, practical, productive, and honoring. With clear, conscious Agreements, you can even agree to disagree without the Duality Programs of Judgment, Lack, and Take-Away. Agreements do not have expectations like contracts do. You give your Self the freedom to be you without the confinements of the Duality boxes, and you support your Profiles (your family, friends, frenemies, neighbors, co-workers, acquaintances, strangers, etc.) to be free. The key is to not be attached to the outcome of how you thinky-thinky they are supposed to act or be. And the best part is…there is *listening* involved without judgment.

Allness: Allness honors uniqueness. Without judging Oneness, which makes everyone the same, Allness allows you to recognize and acknowledge your uniqueness and the uniqueness of all life in this Universe and the Multi-verses and *feel* the CONNECTION to ALL LIFE without the Duality burden of sameness.

Bands of Duality: These are the physical energy bands of Belief Systems you are emitting from your body. They are infused with the Third Dimensional Fear Programs of Judgment, Lack, and Take-Away from the beginning of your continuum here on Earth.

The perception is that they are invisible or do not exist. As you expand your resonance of Consciousness, you can *see* the bands, and you can *feel* them as you release these physical bands from your body.

Belief Systems: These are the ideas, concepts, and core beliefs acquired, consciously or unconsciously, throughout your time continuum. Creating your life from Duality's Belief Systems is NOT creating your life consciously. It is actualizing your life through someone else's or some group's opinion. Duality's Fear-based Belief Systems "support" you to be limited by hindering your unlimited Creative Power.

Cellular Memorization: This is the composite of the memorized information in your cells via the conditioning of ideas, Belief Systems, concepts, etc. in this current lifetime.

Cellular Memory: This is the composite of information stored in your cells from all of your experiences in your time continuum.

Cellular Sound: Every experience you have ever experienced throughout your current lifetime and your continuum is accompanied by all the expressions of sound around you and within you. These sounds are stored in your cells as Cellular Sound.

This is a sound planet, a sound Universe, and a sound Multi-verse. Your body is a Multi-Dimensional Being of sound. You are impacted and influenced by the sound of words (Wordology Is Your Biology), music, tones, vibrations, frequencies, and resonances. Your body not only hears sound, it *feels* sound, even when you are not fully aware of the sound. Even silence has a sound; you *feel* it.

7 Chakras: "Chakra" is a Sanskrit word which means "circle". The 7 Chakra System is comprised of circles, or vortices, of information and Consciousness embedded within each individual Chakra (Crown, Third Eye, Throat, Heart, Solar Plexus, Creative/Sexual/Generative, and Base Chakras) within the human body.

Each circle encompasses both the Consciousness as well as the physicality of each area of the body. For example, the Heart Chakra incorporates the physical heart, lungs, trachea, bronchi, esophagus, chest cavity, bones, spinal column, breast/chest, arms, hands, muscles, blood vessels, etc. When the Consciousness of the Heart Chakra is under emotional duress, so is the entire physicality of all that comprises the Heart Chakra. Your emotions are as physical as the physicality of your body.

All of the Chakras are connected to each other. Disconnection in the Consciousness of your Chakras causes both physical and emotional struggles for the body.

13 Chakras: The 13 Chakras is the New Paradigm of Ascension/Transcension. This is the Involved Conscious Evolution of the human body and the human condition out of the limited, repeatable, 3D Duality Belief Systems. The unlimited expansion of Consciousness within the body is achieved through the knowledge of the 13 Chakras with the focus and objective to create, implement, manifest, and actualize your life through your Truth. This is your Newness and Heartness journey of freedom, beauty, connection, Total Acceptance, and Unconditional Love. This is achievable within your Self in this lifetime.

Childish Adult Ego (CAE): Your Childish Adult Ego lives through your Script until you are willing to let go of the Belief System Programs and create your life consciously. Your Childish Adult Ego is the master of manipulation and control. He/She is stuck in the past, struggles to be validated, and wanty-needys to be "right".

Wherever your Childish Adult Ego is stuck in the past at the various ages of the traumas and the dramas is the place or places from where your CAE is running your life, regardless of your current age or time frame.

This planet is run by Childish Adult Egos demanding to be "right". It is long overdue for everyone's CAE to grow up and move beyond Duality and the Third Dimension on this planet.

Choice/Choose: As a Non-Emotional Observer and a Conscious Creator, you are In Charge of Your Life. No matter what the scenario or condition, you comprehend without doubt that you have choices and options. You can even change what you choose. As the observer, you realize with *real eyes* that you are not bound by the old Duality Programming.

Completion: Completion is both the newness of Non-Duality and the finale of Duality. In the Clear Consciousness of completion, you can be finished with Self-Judgment, Judgment of others, and Lack in all forms. You *see* that there is no sane reason to be caught up in the Take-Away Dualistic Karma, Lessons, and Re-incarnation Programs any longer. You are DONE with that B.S.!

Consciousness: Consciousness is awareness. However, you can be aware without being fully conscious. There are various degrees or different spaces of Consciousness. The more conscious you are, the deeper the level of comprehension you have about a situation, an issue, a person...and your Self.

Contract: Contracts are the carefully crafted outlines, physically and metaphorically written in Duality, which are supposed to teach you your Lessons, Karma, and Re-incarnation agendas. Through your contracts, the objective is to "ascend" your Self above your emotional and physical attachments to your past(s). In Duality, your contracts are the binds or handcuffs that keep you stuck in the re-cycle bins of your left computer/brain's Duality Fear Programs of Self-Judgment, Lack, and Take-Away. The scenes, clothes, times, and gender may change, but your Role, your Behaviors, and your emotional attachments to your Duality Profiles keep you stuck in the re-do loops of infinity.

Control: Control is a dysfunctional Duality Program which is based on force. It is based on forcing your Self or someone else to comply within the framework of a limited Belief System which does NOT support life to be lived freely and creatively. Control has no flexibility. Control takes away your personal Power.

Decision: You settle for less by "selecting" an option that was created *outside* of you by someone else. Because of the Fear Programs ingrained in you, you *think* you do NOT have options or choices to empower your Self. You bought into the limiting Belief Systems, the B.S. Programs that run your life, instead of consciously actualizing your *real* desires.

Detachment: Detachment is the perspective of being NEO, the Non-Emotional Observer, who *sees* the facts of the situations, events, and experiences clearly. Being NEO is empowering and freeing.

Detachment entails emotionally and physically *detaching* from your Childish Adult Ego's ideas of control and manipulation and no longer being attached to how people and things are supposed to be according to Duality's Self-Judging and Judgment-of-Others Programs.

Dimensions: Within the concept of Consciousness or Belief Systems, dimensions are levels, spaces, or places of realities and existences. The Earth is the Third Dimension, which is based on Belief Systems of Duality – good vs. evil, light vs. dark, and the never-ending time continuum of right and wrong.

Disconnected Attachments: In dysfunctional relationships, both personal and professional, disconnected attachments are the non-effective emotional hooks which keep you stuck in the past, affecting your current time frame! Disconnected attachments are timeless in Duality's Programs of Judgment, Lack, and Take-Away. You are stuck in the past(s) attached to the dysfunctional Profiles of the people in your life, caught up in your repeated dysfunctional Behaviors through the Roles you are assigned. You are disconnected from your Self and your Inner Truth and you are attached to *wanty-needy* the "outside" validation or invalidation of you. You are attached to giving away your Power.

Duality: Duality is a resonance of fear in all its forms.

Energy: Energy is a by-product of either clear Consciousness or limited Duality Belief Systems. Energy is the form of creation. Energy is emitted from within every living Being, i.e., humans, animals, fish, plants, insects, rocks…EVERYTHING emits energy. The importance is *how* the energy is emitted from either the Duality of Destruction *or* the Non-Duality of Life.

When energy is flowing within your body through every cell and system and physical part of you, you are in physical, mental, emotional, financial, and spiritual health. When energy is "blocked" at the Cellular Level, you may feel "stuck" in a behavior, situation, or circumstance, etc.

By clearing your Consciousness at the Cellular Level, you release blocked energies to restore your health. Once blocked energies are released, you have the capacity to consciously direct your energies to support your requirements and desires.

Heartness: Your Heart is the most expanded resonance field in your body when you are consciously creating and living in the moment. Heartness is the Total Acceptance and Unconditional Love essence within you. Heartness is timeless beyond Duality.

In Charge: In Charge is your ability as the Non-Emotional Observer to *see* life through the facts and not the emotional conditions that suppress your freedom and your creativity. When you are In Charge of Your Life, you have all the facts, you can make clear choices instead of emotional decisions, and your life flows fearlessly. You have a clear, deep sense of your own personal Power to be who you are.

Non-Emotional Observer (NEO): As the Non-Emotional Observer, you can observe from a viewpoint of the facts and NOT from emotional attachments to previous experiences or repetitive experiences. As NEO, you support your Self to *see* not only how you are participating in a situation but also the participations of the other individual(s) who are in your life. As NEO, you can begin to clearly *see* the aspects or components of your own Behaviors, the repeated, dysfunctional Profiles you attract into your life, and the repeated Roles you have played out in your situations, conditions, and experiences. As the Non-Emotional Observer, you free your Self from being controlled and manipulated, and you stop controlling and manipulating your Self back into repeated patterns that do not serve you. You are in your Power.

Perfect Child Within (PCW): The Perfect Child Within is your natural, inherent Christed Consciousness of unlimitedness. Your Perfect Child Within is the activator of your 13 Chakras.

Potentiality: This is your unlimited capacity to create newness in your life without the Fear Programs of Judgment, Lack, and Take-Away influencing your choices. In the space of your unlimited potential – your Quantum Field – you have the capacity to Be In Charge of Your Life and *clearly* create and manifest on an ongoing basis.

Profiles: A Profile is not one person. It is a label for an aspect of people that you have been conditioned or programmed to accept in your life. Profiles are the subjective labels you place on "them" (and on your Self) when you put "them" in boxes with unrealistic emotional expectations of how the relationships are supposed to be.

Here is an example of a Victim Profile. If you are programmed to be a Victim, then you must dysfunctionally attract a Victimizer Profile to you. It does not matter about gender. It is the resonance of the Profile that you have been programmed to project.

Programming: Programming is related to ongoing exposure, repetition, training, and encoding in Duality. Consciously or unconsciously, your Belief Systems are "programmed" into your Consciousness.

Quantum Field: The Quantum Field is the space of clarity within the human body that is not connected to the Programs of Duality. This is the space and place from which you have the capacity to be the Conscious Creator of your life. In the Quantum Field, there is no resonance of fear to affect or infect your creativity and actualization of your desires. This is the place to begin creating your "Heaven on Earth", whatever that means to you and your Heart.

Real/Realness: Without illusions or delusions, Realness is the Truth of your Clear Consciousness.

Reality/Realities: Realities are Duality's versions of the illusions or delusions.

Resonance: Frequency and vibration are by-products of Resonance. Your Resonance is the key to your Power. Your Resonance is either based on a Duality Belief System of lack and limitation *or* based on your Clear Consciousness as the powerful Conscious Creator of your experiences. So, the difference when you are resonating consciously and clearly is that you are sending out a clear frequency and vibration...and no dysfunction! You resonate with powerful, unlimited creativity. You resonate with your Truth. You do NOT resonate to giving your Power away.

Victimhood results when your Resonance is based on a Duality Belief System. You resonate to being a victim, and so your frequency and vibration go out and you attract a victimizer.

As the Non-Emotional Observer (NEO), you can have UNLIMITED Resonances. So why bring a Resonance of some experience from your Past which no longer resonates with you into the Present Moment? Sure, perhaps you can *see* the magnificence of your creativity in your trauma-dramas or not, but when you bring it into this Moment by making it your "story"...what are you doing? Are you setting your Self up for another re-run? Are you making it more important than the Truth inside of YOU? If you choose to "live" in the Past, it doesn't matter what the calendar date is. You are in that Resonance of the Past.

In your "story", you have a choice to create magnificence in your life with purpose on purpose *or* you can make a Belief System "decision" based on the trauma-drama that you keep re-creating, explaining, and complaining about... So, what are you willing to do?

When you resonate to Duality Belief Systems, you resonate to forceful dysfunctions called Karma, Lessons, and Reincarnation...the do-over programming. The density of the Duality Resonance makes you sick.

The point is...get the point of the lesson, learn it and don't repeat it. Just move on! What does not resonate is not compatible. As your Resonance evolves, it makes a tremendous difference in your words, in your communications, in your interactions, in your experiences, and in your life! It also makes a difference to the people around you. Be the Resonance difference that matters...or not.

Roles: These are labels assigned to you from the beginning of you in your current and past lives, whether you resonate to them or not. Most of the time, you are placed in labeled "boxes" which prevent you from being the Truth of you. You get caught up in these Roles, trying, trying, and trying to *fit in*. Beyond the confines of Duality Reality, you can let go of these assigned Roles which do not fit you.

Spirals: Utilizing Spirals through your clear Non-Duality intentions from your Heart through Heartness, you create multiple opportunities to create, implement, manifest, and actualize your intentions. Through Spirals, you can send out an unlimited number of intentions, propelling your Heart-based/Heartness intentions through your Clear Conscious Energy Field to be actualized in the perfect timing in this lifetime. In using the Spiral, be clear and specific with your intentions and stay out of the outcome so that the options and opportunities can show up in your life.

Still Point: It is the origination point for your intentions. Still Point is the place to initiate your clear, focused, and directed intentions using the Spiral to activate the movement which puts your intentions into motion.

Thinky-Thinky: Thinky-thinky is NOT based on facts. It's based on conjecture and perceptions which are the receptions and deceptions of your conceptions based on emotional stories from the past.

Thinky-thinky prevents you from being in the current moment and it prevents you from being connected to and grounded in your body. When you are stuck in your head/computer brain, your brain has no idea what time it is. You cannot have clear thoughts.

As you stay in your left computer/brain, you get stuck in your brain's neuro-nets in a non-productive experience, situation, or event that happened 98% of the time the past. The other 2% of the thinky-thinky turmoil occurs when you are projecting into a future that has not yet occurred.

The results of thinky-thinky include: not being able to go to sleep at night, not connected to your body, and out-of-body situations of being completely ungrounded.

Third Dimension: It is a dimension of limited Consciousness, embedded with the Fear Programs of Judgment, Lack, and Take-Away that recycle the conditions of Karma, Lessons, and dysfunctional Re-incarnation.

Wanty-Needy: The resonance of wanty-needy is the dysfunctional behavior of craving, wishing, and hoping to be loved. The wanty-needy resonance is powerless. It keeps you looking outside of your Self for love. To release this low-based, wanty-needy resonance, the first step is loving your Self unconditionally and totally accepting that you are lovable regardless of anyone else's opinion. Replace the wanty-needy resonance with REQUIRE. "Require" is an action word. It has a resonance of empowerment. Wanty-needy has no empowerment to offer. Wanty-needy is the resonance of a victim.

Wordology Is Your Biology: The words you use represent your Consciousness. They provide you with information that you can use to observe your current space of Consciousness. By using words that support your desires, you support your creativity into actuality.

In the English language, there are more non-supportive words than supportive ones. These non-supportive words resonate to keep you stuck in the fear-based Third Dimension Duality Reality.

Your Script: Before you enter this life on Earth, you carefully craft your Script. You write in all of those individuals, situations, and conditions – known as your journey – to find your Self. You write in your challenges, select your relationships, and create your trauma-dramas, all for the purpose of awakening your Consciousness from your Cellular Level and moving beyond the limitations of your Duality Programming.

In your Script, you create many opportunities to extricate your Self from the continuous dysfunctional loop of the Fear Programs. By expanding your Consciousness, you clearly *see* the opportunities to move beyond the oppressive, suppressive Duality Reality.

Zero Point: When you get to the origination point of an emotional, physical, and mental issue, you have the choice in this particular moment – Zero Point – to resolve the problem and release it from your Cellular Level of Consciousness. Or, you may decide to keep the limited, fear-based Belief System and continue to manifest the painful symptoms in your life. It's up to you!

ABOUT THE AUTHOR

Through an amazing awakening, which includes 4 Near-Death Experiences, Sherry Anshara has become known as "The Consciousness Expert". Even though she has assisted thousands upon thousands of individuals to heal their bodies, their relationships, and their lives, Sherry Anshara is still one of the best kept secrets on this planet.

Her mission, her passion, her commitment, and her legacy are all about sharing with you the practical know-how she gained by healing her own broken neck, broken back, smashed head, and her life to become her fearless, conscious Self!

> "From my own clear realness, I create MY LIFE ON PURPOSE WITH PURPOSES every day! My bliss is to show you how to live your realness as real for you. There is no greater joy for me than to witness my students and clients connect to their Selves and to their bodies, and to watch them release the grip of their dysfunctional past so it no longer has to affect, effect, or infect their relationships, personal and professional, or their health as they create the lives they require, desire, and deserve…with no Duality limitations, with no Belief Systems…no B.S.! In these moments, for the first time, they experience the freedom to be who they are… unlimited and unrestricted!" – *Sherry Anshara*

The great news is that you don't have to waste another minute of your life searching for your answers. Through her groundbreaking work with Cellular Memory, Sherry Anshara created the Anshara Method of Accelerated Healing & Abundance.

In the Anshara Method courses and private sessions, you learn how to get to the root causes of your symptoms and issues quickly, and you begin to resolve and dissolve them. These shortcuts show you the way out of unwanted limitations, restrictions, negative thought patterns, and toxic behavior, which have been imprinted in your body since conception, so you can be truly happy and successful in all aspects of your life. You learn how to TAKE BACK YOUR POWER and BE the UNLIMITED YOU!

Sherry Anshara is the Founder of the Anshara Center in Scottsdale, Arizona. She is also a world-renowned Medical Intuitive, internationally best-selling Author, Professional Speaker, Radio and Television Personality, and an Involved Conscious Evolutionary Revolutionary.

Here are ways you can experience the Anshara Method with Sherry Anshara:

- Individual Private Session Packages
  - In Person
  - Via Skype, Zoom, or phone
- Anshara Method Courses
  - In-Person Courses
  - Online Courses
  - Certified Anshara Method Facilitator Training
  - Certified Anshara Method Train the Trainer Training

Sherry Anshara is available for speaking engagements. For more information, visit www.SherryAnshara.com or call the Anshara Center at (480) 609-0874.

Books written by Sherry Anshara:

- The Age of Inheritance: The Activation of the 13 Chakras
- And the Point Is…? Beyond Duality
- Glossary of QuantumPathic® Terms: How to Understand the Quantum Energy of Human Life
- The Intelligence Code: How the QuantumPathic® Energy Method Transformed 14 Lives
- Depression Doesn't Have to Leave You Depressed (e-book)
- Getting Your Answers in 10 Minutes or Less (e-book)

Meditation CD's by Sherry Anshara:

- Awakening the Divine Being Within Yourself
- Beyond the Seven Chakra System
- Clear Conscious Meditation
- Expanding Your Awareness
- Opening Your Heart Chakra and Speaking Your Truth
- Total Relaxation Meditation

The Anshara Center
6701 E. Clinton St., Scottsdale, AZ 85254
(480) 609-0874

 ## The Anshara Method
of Accelerated Healing & Abundance

Sign up for the free **Anshara Newsletter** at:
www.SherryAnshara.com

*Join the conversation...*Facebook Live
www.facebook.com/SherryAnshara

www.linkedin.com/in/SherryAnshara

Twitter: @TheAnshara

The Past was one second ago...

Your Future is one second from now...

TAKE BACK YOUR POWER

Made in the USA
Monee, IL
29 January 2021